D1468409

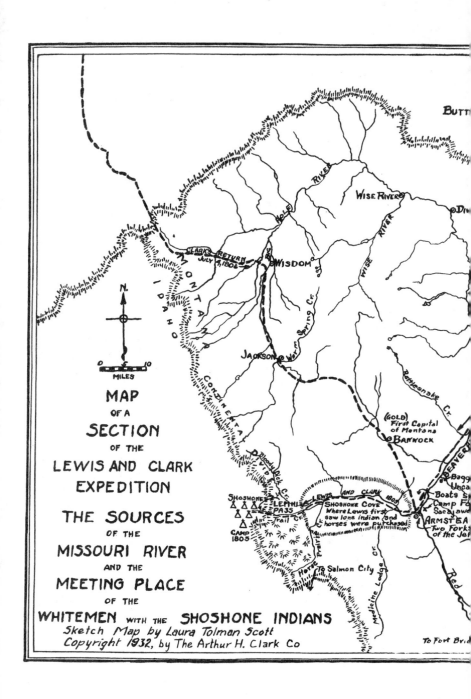

MAP

OF A

SECTION

OF THE

LEWIS AND CLARK EXPEDITION

THE SOURCES

OF THE

MISSOURI RIVER

AND THE

MEETING PLACE

OF THE

WHITEMEN WITH THE SHOSHONE INDIANS

Sketch Map by Laura Tolman Scott
Copyright 1932, by The Arthur H. Clark Co

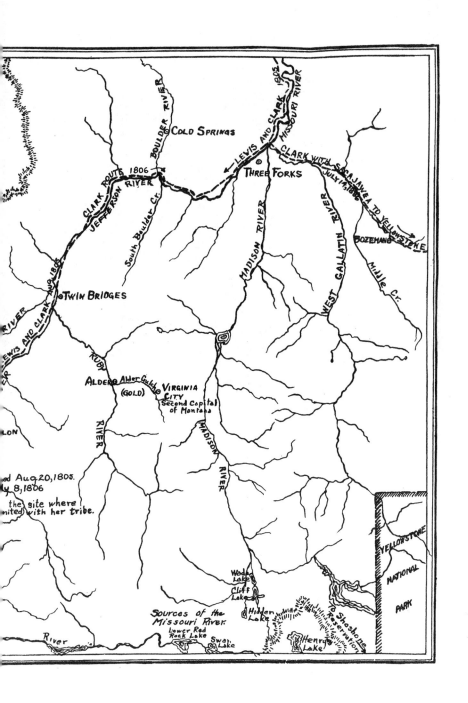

REUNION OF SACAJAWEA AND HER SHOSHONE PEOPLE

Historic moment on August 17, 1805, when, by Shoshone sign language, the Indian interpreter for Lewis and Clark is saying, "I am Sacajawea," and the women of her tribe are responding, "Sacajawea, the boat woman." Clark and Charbonneau are in the foreground. Painting conceived by John E. Rees, historian, and T. R. Dunlap, artist; never before reproduced.

SACAJAWEA

Guide and Interpreter of Lewis and Clark

Grace Raymond Hebard

DOVER PUBLICATIONS, INC.
Mineola, New York

Published in Canada by General Publishing Company, Ltd., 895 Don Mills Road, 400-2 Park Centre, Toronto, Ontario M3C 1W3.
Published in the United Kingdom by David & Charles, Brunel House, Forde Close, Newton Abbot, Devon TQ12 4PU.

Bibliographical Note

This Dover edition, first published in 2002, is an unabridged reprint of the work published as *Sacajawea: A guide and interpreter of the Lewis and Clark expedition, with an account of the travels of Toussaint Charbonneau, and of Jean Baptiste, the expedition papoose* by the Arthur H. Clark Company, Glendale, California, in 1957. The book was originally published in 1932.

Library of Congress Cataloging-in-Publication Data

Hebard, Grace Raymond, 1861–1936.
　　Sacajawea : guide and interpreter of Lewis and Clark / Grace Raymond Hebard.
　　　　p. cm.
　　Originally published: Glendale, Calif. : Arthur H. Clark Co., 1932.
　　Includes bibliographical references and index.
　　ISBN 0-486-42149-X (pbk.)
　　　1. Sacagawea, 1786–1884. 2. Shoshoni women—West (U.S.)—Biography. 3. Shoshoni Indians—West (U.S.)—Biography. 4. West (U.S.)—Discovery and exploration. 5. West (U.S.)—Description and travel. 6. Sacagawea, 1786–1884—Family. 7. Charbonneau, Toussaint, ca. 1758–ca. 1839. 8. Charbonneau, Jean-Baptiste, 1805–1885. 9. Lewis and Clark Expedition (1804–1806) I. Title.

F592.7 .S123 2002
978.004'9745'0092—dc21
[B]

　　　　　　　　　　　　　　　　　　　　　　　　　　　　　2001047910

Manufactured in the United States of America
Dover Publications, Inc., 31 East 2nd Street, Mineola, N.Y. 11501

To my sister

ALICE MARVIN HEBARD

A companion on the trails

Contents

Illustrations

Foreword to the 1957 Edition

In issuing the second printing of this book, the publisher takes cognizance of the fact that there are some who disagree with some of the facts on which Dr. Hebard's work is based. Since death terminated her work in October of 1936, her side of the interpretation of documentary sources must rest with the words printed here.

The basic point questioned is the date of the death of Sacajawea. There are contemporary documents showing that one of the wives of Charbonneau died at Fort Manuel in 1812, and there are able and conscientious supporters of the belief that the wife was Sacajawea. Dr. Hebard held an opposite opinion, contending that Sacajawea died in 1884. That Dr. Hebard spent many years in her research on the book goes without question, and that she was an able and intellectually honest historian has been stated by many qualified observers. That she is no longer living to furnish further basis for her contention, or to revise it, is a matter of regret. With the impossibility of further work by her, it is the belief of the publisher that her work is worthy of further consideration in another printing. Time, further research, or archaeological discovery will have to be the test of her work.

For a discussion of the "death in 1812" opinion, the reader is referred to the *Wi-iyohi,* monthly bulletin of the South Dakota Historical Society, issues of September 1, 1956, and February 1, 1957, as well as the documents cited in those issues.

THE ARTHUR H. CLARK COMPANY

Preface

The St. Louis exposition of 1904 created a widespread interest in the historic background of the Louisiana purchase, whose centennial it officially commemorated, and brought new significance to that great epic of western exploration, the Lewis and Clark expedition. Among the many by-products of this interest was the search for a typical model for a statue to be erected at the outer gates of the exposition. This search led to a study of the life and services of Sacajawea, the guide of the Lewis and Clark expedition, and to an interest in the career of that remarkable woman, which has continued unabated for nearly thirty years. This volume is the product of that interest. For three decades, with the aid of trained assistants, the author has prosecuted her search for authentic historical material which would enable her to rescue Sacajawea from the semi-oblivion into which her name had fallen, and give to her her legitimate place in the history of the great northwest.

In this volume the author has also sought to unravel the tangled skein of Sacajawea's family life; to trace the career of her son, Baptiste, the papoose of the Lewis and Clark expedition, and of her adopted son, Bazil, one of the signers of the treaty of 1868 at Fort Bridger; to portray as accurately as possible her personal traits and characteristics; to trace her wanderings far and wide through the west; and especially to record the significant services she rendered not only as guide to Lewis and

Clark but also for many years and on many occasions as counsellor to her own people and to the whites.

In this long study much significant information heretofore unknown has been brought to light; many facts misinterpreted or seen in false perspective have been given their proper setting; new light has been thrown on numerous controversial issues; and much that was confused has been cleared of uncertainty and presented in its true setting.

Among some of the specific contributions of the volume are the verification of Baptiste's journey to Europe with Prince Paul of Würtemberg; the proof that Baptiste and Toussaint, whose common father was old Charbonneau, were born of different mothers; the explanation of the real motives which led Sacajawea to leave Charbonneau; the true interpretation of the word Sacajawea, commonly but erroneously given as "Bird Woman"; the account of Sacajawea's "lost years" among the Comanches and of her return to her own people, the Shoshones; and the story of her long life thereafter among them on the reservation.

In the Thwaites edition of the Lewis and Clark *Journals,* published in 1904, a letter written in 1806 by Captain William Clark to Charbonneau appeared for the first time. A great deal of confusion was created by Clark's use in this letter of certain names and expressions such as "your famn Janey," "Pomp," "your dancing boy, Baptiste," etc. From the material appearing later in these pages it will be shown that "Janey" was Sacajawea, the "famn" of Charbonneau; and that the "dancing boy, Baptiste," was the child of Sacajawea and Charbonneau, born in 1805 at the Mandan villages and spoken of as the papoose of the expedition. He was also called "Pomp" according to the Indian custom of so designating the oldest child. Read in this way, the letter enables us to understand Captain Clark's expenditures for the education of Baptiste Charbonneau in St. Louis a few years later. The facts bearing on this matter are brought out in detail in later chapters.

Verification has also been found, in the work of Dr. Charles A. Eastman and in the researches of Mr. and Mrs. W. H. Clift among the Comanches on behalf of the author, for the statements of Andrew Bazil, the grandson of Sacajawea, regarding his grandmother's life among the Comanches. But most unexpected of all was the corroboration of the testimony of Sacajawea's descendants that Baptiste had visited a land to the east beyond the "Big Waters" and there learned to speak a number of languages. When the Indians on the reservation told of the big houses on the water and of people on the other side who wore wooden shoes, "Wo-be-namp-tiko," the author naturally recorded their statements with some wonder and skepticism. She could not openly question them, however, or show her astonishment; for the interview would then have ended immediately, because the Indians spoke as to a friend without "forked tongues," and any question of their truthfulness would have constituted an unpardonable offense. The startling verification of Baptiste's education in Germany, revealed by a study of the Stuttgart archives, confirmed unmistakably the trustworthiness and value of Indian testimony.

The researches in the Stuttgart archives were carried out by a trained archivist, Herr Friedrich Bauser, who brought to light the writings of Prince Paul of Würtemberg, with their account of the prince's travels in the

United States and their mention of the Indian boy, Baptiste. Prince Paul's request for permission to make the inland voyage in 1823, and Captain Clark's reply were discovered in the Missouri archives; and the quaint drawings of the prince's artist are given to the world again in this volume.

The material in the volume has been carefully examined for errors by numerous authorities familiar with the field and, while mistakes may have been made in the details of the narrative, the work rests upon authentic and carefully verified sources. Much of the information and a large part of the testimony upon which the narrative is based have never appeared before in print, and all of the maps and illustrations are here printed for the first time.

The printed sources upon which in part the volume is based will be discussed in subsequent pages. Some explanation should be given here, however, as to the Indian testimony which constitutes so large a part of the contents of the volume. Although the Indians have no written history, their memories are trained to a remarkable degree to retain tribal history; and Indian verbal testimony is, therefore, as much to be relied upon as the writings of any other race. In seeking information from Indian sources, care was taken to see that during an interview all other Indians were excluded except the Indian being examined and the necessary witnesses thereto. In all such interviews, a government interpreter was nearly always employed, and the questions and answers were recorded by a trained stenographer. In order to insure absolute accuracy, two Shoshone witnesses, who also understood English, certified that the questions in English had been accurately rendered in

Shoshone, and that the answers were as accurately translated into English by the interpreter.

After the material secured at these interviews had been typewritten, the Indian interviewed and the Indian witnesses signed the document by "thumb print." Other witnesses signed by name. No hearsay evidence was accepted, and every effort was made to prevent collusion. Thus, on one occasion, three Indians living long distances apart were interviewed on the same morning to prevent any chance of consultation between them.

As to the other authorities whose statements have been used in the preparation of the volume, their names are sufficiently well known to establish the value of their testimony. Among these may be listed the Reverend John Roberts, spiritual leader of the Shoshones for nearly a half century; Mrs. James Irwin; Mr. Fincelius G. Burnett, agricultural adviser on the reservation since 1871; John C. Burnet; and James I. Patten, teacher and missionary.[1]

To those who have assisted through their collaboration and research, the author desires to express her appreciation, and also to that large number of historical writers who have made this publication possible. Especially do I desire to express my gratitude to the Indians on the Shoshone reservation, many of whom are descendants of Sacajawea and some of whom knew her per-

---

[1] In 1905 Mr. Patten informed the author that years before he had prepared several descendants of Sacajawea for baptism by Bishop George Maxwell Randall of Colorado and Wyoming. A personal examination of the baptismal records in Denver shows that on August 19, 1873, Bishop Randall baptised four of the grandchildren of Bazil and Baptiste, the sons of Sacajawea, and that their sponsors were S. M. Irwin and James I. Patten. United States government officials have also furnished verification of the fact that Mrs. James Irwin (nee Sarah Mathilde Trumble) taught English to Sacajawea and in turn learned Shoshone from her. Mr. and Mrs. Irwin were married on the reservation, and their bodies now lie buried on the cemetery hill nearby.

sonally, for the information they have placed at my disposal. I desire also to express my gratitude to the Reverend John Roberts, missionary-clergyman of the Protestant Episcopal church to the Indians in Wyoming; to Mr. Lawrence J. Burpee, Canada; Mr. Fincelius G. Burnett; the Reverend James I. Patten; Mr. John C. Burnet; Mrs. A. D. Lane; James E. Compton, interpreter; and the stenographers who gave willingly and abundantly of their time and skill; to those in the Indian field service, H. E. Wadsworth, Chester E. Faris, and R. Paul Haas; to Mrs. Eva Emery Dye; to the state librarians, historians, and historical societies of Wyoming, North Dakota, South Dakota, Montana, Utah, Idaho, Colorado, Oregon, Washington, Kansas, Wisconsin, Missouri, and Oklahoma; to the University of Wyoming librarians who have for thirty years furnished needed information for this and other publications; to Mrs. Calvin Page, artist; to the historical department of the Church of Jesus Christ of the Latter Day Saints at Salt Lake city; to the Jesuits of Missouri, through Father Charles Van Tourehout, St. Genevieve archives of St. Louis university; to the Episcopalians of Wyoming and Colorado, to which denomination the Shoshones have been assigned; to the Comanche Indians of the Oklahoma country, a very few of whom remember the Shoshone woman; to United States Senators F. E. Warren, Joseph M. Carey, John B. Kendrick, and Robert D. Carey; to Representatives Charles E. Winter and Vincent Carter; to Brigadier-general Walter S. Schuyler and Colonel Richard H. Wilson; to William A. Carter Jr., E. A. Carter, John E. Rees, and James K. Moore Jr.; to Miss Stella M. Drumm, librarian of the Missouri historical society; Mrs. Daniel R. Russell, daughter of W. C. Kennerly; William E. Connelley of Kansas and Le Roy Hafen of Colorado; to Mrs. Laura T. Scott, Miss Jean Bishop, and Fred Lockley; to Chancellor M. A. Brannon; to Friedrich Bauser of Germany, Professor Louis C. Butscher, Mrs. L. M. Wells, Albert W. Johnson, Earle R. Forrest, and Milo M. Quaife; to the publishers for written consent to reprint from their publications; to the several U.S. departments at Washington, D.C., particularly to the commissioner of Indian affairs; to Mr. W. H. Clift and his wife, Edith Connelley Clift (daughter of the Honorable William E. Connelley), who together conducted the research among the Comanches of Oklahoma; to Mr. Willard O. Walters of the Henry E. Huntington library and art gallery, California; to William M. Camp, J. Neilson Barry, Olin D. Wheeler, Agnes C. Laut, Reuben Gold Thwaites, General William Clark Kennerly, Alfred J. Mokler, J. Cecil Alter, George Bird Grinnell, E. N. Roberts, Charles Alexander Eastman; and, finally, to Dr. June E. Downey of the University of Wyoming for a life-time friendship and faith in this work, and to Professor Wilson O. Clough of the University of Wyoming for constructive criticism on the manuscript.

Of her own work,

. . . the author has this apology: he has done as well and as much as he could, that whatever was worthy of mention might have it. . . And now he hath done, he hath not pulled up the ladder after him; others may go on as they please with a completer composure.[2]

GRACE RAYMOND HEBARD

University of Wyoming
June 21, 1932

---

[2] Cotton Mather, *Decennium Luctuosum*, 182-183.

An Appreciation

The romance of this history has stirred me as, day by day, like fragments fitting into a puzzle-picture, it has grown in the busy brain of the writer of this book into a semblance of the life of the famous Indian woman who is the subject of her sketch.

Today, as I pause on the threshold of her workroom, I find her meditating upon letters by airplane from Germany, written by a diligent archivist in Würtemberg who spends long days tumbling over the wealth of manuscript and letters of a princely visitor to far western prairies. Or, I find her smoothing with loving fingers a thin frayed paper sent her by the same archivist—a paper containing a sketch of the prince by his personal artist, showing him in lordly high hat with suave pet dog beside him, sitting in a small horse-drawn cart, while around him swarm Indians of the plains. Tomorrow, she has received from her interpreter the prince's journal, story of that Indian attack, with its lively intimations of cool courage and deliberation of an explorer, single-handed but fertile-minded, who changes an attack into a reception. Here she opens the journal of a French priest and reads to me the story of his encounter on Nebraskan plains with a German traveler, accompanied only by his artist, who, oblivious of Indians and other perils, pursues his leisurely way. Much the priest marvelled.

French priest and German prince—their paths cross

once on a wide, wide prairie in an unexplored continent. A century later an historian, reading two journals, matches their words with a thrill of wonder. The priest too noted the quaint hat and the pet dog, representations of which appear in the sketch recently uncovered in the Stuttgart archives.

The heart of the plot is a little Indian boy whom the prince took with him to Germany, for this little Indian boy is Baptiste, a son of the famous woman guide, Sacajawea, and it is the adventures of the little son that give one more clue by means of which to reconstruct the life of the mother during the lost years after she left the Lewis and Clark expedition.

French priest, German prince, Indian boy – they are not the only members of the cast in this historic drama. A saintly missionary on an Indian reservation stands beside a grave, and from this grave the trail of exploration leads back to incidents in the lifetime of the Shoshone woman. A gay young lad hangs on the outskirts of a council of the plains, too busy in his preoccupation with boyish pleasures to listen to the speeches of Indian chieftains and white statesmen, or to note the presence in the council of the wise woman. Indian ancients on reservations in Wyoming and Montana and Oklahoma tell over their memories, like beads on a rosary, lingering over those that concern the life history of their famous kinswoman. An old, old book sequestered in a Los Angeles library, one annotated in fine German script, yields its secrets.

Hunting in the crannies of time for the lost years of an Indian woman's life – it has indeed been a task of love on the part of the historian, Grace Raymond Hebard.

JUNE E. DOWNEY

Introduction

Introduction

Before discussing the contributions of Sacajawea to the Lewis and Clark expedition, it is desirable to describe briefly the sources upon which our knowledge of this "national epic of exploration" rests, and to say something of the capacity and training of the two leaders, Meriwether Lewis and William Clark, for the great task entrusted to them.

Lewis was born in Virginia in 1774. His early education and training developed in him unusual powers of observation and gave him a knowledge and an understanding of nature which proved of great value to him as the leader of the expedition. He also served for three years prior to the expedition as private secretary to President Jefferson, and was thus a man of unusual educational and cultural attainments. Captain William Clark, in his turn, had seen service under General Scott and "Mad Anthony" Wayne as an engineer in the construction of roads and forts. This experience gave him more than ordinary skill in topography and in the drafting of maps.

The two men thus supplemented each other, and together supplied all the qualifications essential for the success of so great an undertaking. Each had confidence in and affection for the other, an attitude clearly expressed by Lewis when he wrote to Clark:

I could neither hope, wish, or expect from a union with any man on earth more perfect support or further aid in the discharge of the several duties in the mission than that which I am confident I shall derive from being associated with yourself.

Detailed written instructions were given to the commanders of the expedition by President Jefferson concerning the keeping of journals and the collecting and recording of scientific data. Both Lewis and Clark followed these instructions with remarkable faithfulness and painstaking care, so that neither the trying conditions of exploration in unknown country, the threat of Indian attack, or weariness and fatigue could prevent them from recording the experiences they encountered day by day, and of noting down significant scientific data.

The journal which Captain Clark kept is more complete than that of Captain Lewis. It contains a daily record for all but ten days of the entire journey, and even the events of this brief period are covered in a single entry. In Lewis's journal, on the other hand, the records of four hundred forty-one days of the expedition are lacking. It is possible indeed that the original journals showed no such omissions and that some day these long missing portions will be found.[3] At least there is no known reason, such as prolonged sickness, to account for the great gap in his journal. Often the record of Lewis closely parallels that of Clark, and vice versa, for the two sometimes copied even verbatim from each other. Generally, however, each described an event in his own way, using his own characteristic phraseology.[4] In ad-

[3] Thwaites writes: "Whether the missing Lewis entries are still in existence or not is unknown to the present writer. There appears to be no doubt that he regularly kept his diary. It is possible that the missing notes, in whole or in part, were with him when he met his death in Tennessee, and were either accidentally or purposely destroyed by others." *Original journals of Lewis and Clark,* vol. V, p. xxxv.

[4] Clark carried with him a writing desk until the expedition was well into

dition to the journals kept by Lewis and Clark, the leaders of the expedition also urged individual members of the party to keep journals or diaries for themselves. Apparently three of the twenty-three privates and four sergeants complied with these instructions.[5]

The three privates who recorded their experiences were Joseph Whitehouse; Robert Fraser, a former dancing master from Vermont; and George Shannon, the youngest member of the expedition. Whitehouse's journal covers only the period from May 14, 1804, to November 6, 1805. Whitehouse is said to have given the manuscript of his diary to his confessor on his death bed, and the latter in turn sold it in 1894 to a private collector, from whom it was purchased by the publisher of Reuben Gold Thwaites's *Early western travels*. Thwaites considered the journal authentic and of definite historical value, although some of the entries are not in Whitehouse's own handwriting. Among other contributions of value to this volume, Whitehouse definitely establishes the fact that Charbonneau, the interpreter for Lewis and Clark, had at least two other wives besides Sacajawea.[6] The whereabouts of the journals of the other two privates are unknown.

Of the journals kept by the four sergeants, that of

the mountains, where a horse carrying the desk slipped down the mountain side and destroyed it. Inside one of the cabins at Clatsop, after the expedition reached the coast, the stump of a large fir tree was allowed to stand, and on this improvised table Clark drew his map of the rivers and mountains over which the expedition had passed, or retranscribed his notes. See Thwaites, *Original journals of Lewis and Clark*, vol. I, 190, etc.

[5] "We have encouraged our men to keep journals and seven of them do," wrote Captain Lewis to President Jefferson from Fort Mandan on April 17, 1805.

[6] This significant fact is brought out in his description of the Christmas festivities at the Mandan villages where he speaks of "three squaws, the interpreter's wives."

Nathaniel Prior, "one of the nine men from Kentucky," afterward ensign and eventually captain in the army, has been lost. Charles Floyd of Kentucky, the only member of the expedition to lose his life while in service, kept a faithful record of the expedition until his death on August 20, 1805. This journal was lost for eighty-five years but was found in its original form in 1895 by Dr. Thwaites and published by him in the original journals of Lewis and Clark. Since Floyd's record ends before the expedition reached the Mandan villages, where Sacajawea first joined the expedition, it finds no further mention in this volume.

Patrick Gass, who was elected sergeant after Floyd's death, was born in Pennsylvania in 1771 of Scotch-Irish parentage and was thus the oldest member of the expedition with the possible exception of Captain Clark. His education was limited to fourteen days in school, but the journal which he kept is one of the chief sources of the expedition, and was first published in 1807, seven years before the journals of Lewis and Clark.[7] Within five years after its first publication in Philadelphia, it was republished three times in the United States and printed also in London and Paris. For our purpose the chief value of Gass's journal lies in the fact that it definitely states that Charbonneau, the interpreter, had more than one wife and also throws light upon a number of other controversial subjects.[8]

_____

[7] Gass, Patrick, *Journal of the voyages and travels of a corps of discovery.* "No American was more keenly appreciative than Astor of the value of the territory comprised in the Louisiana purchase. . . Unwilling to await the formal report of the expedition, he fell upon Patrick Gass's *Journal,* published in 1807, devoured it, realized the profits awaiting him in the untapped fur countries it described, and envisaged an immense expansion of his business."– Smith, Arthur D. Howden, *John Jacob Astor, landlord of New York.*

[8] Gass outlived all the other enlisted members of the expedition, dying at

The journal of John Ordway, another sergeant of the expedition, was lost for more than a century. It too was finally discovered by Dr. Thwaites, who found portions of it in possession of the heirs of Captain William Clark and other portions in the Nicholas Biddle estate where it had been filed with the journals of Lewis and Clark. Ordway's journal gives a complete daily record of the expedition from beginning to end. Whatever gaps occurred, therefore, in the journals of Lewis, Clark, Gass, Floyd, and Whitehouse were thus bridged over by Ordway's careful narrative. Ordway was one of the best educated of the enlisted men, a fact which clearly increases the importance of his diary. He carried his manuscript for safe keeping under his shirt through all the vicissitudes of the expedition, and finally sold it to Lewis and Clark for the sum of ten dollars.[9]

Waugh's mills, Brooke county, West Virginia, on April 2, 1870, at the advanced age of ninety-nine, lacking a few weeks. He reposes in an identified, but unmarked grave in Wellsburg, West Virginia, although he was a soldier in the war of 1812 and fought at Lundy's lane and Fort Erie. It was said of him in 1858, "There is not probably now living a single man who has done so much for the public and received so little."

When Gass was sixty, he married a woman forty years younger. Two of his children lived until 1926, Mrs. Annie Gass Smith who died in Los Angeles, California, and with whom Gass lived in West Virginia until his death; and Mrs. Rachel Gass Brierly, who died in Pennsylvania. Mrs. Brierly had in her posssssion until her death a wooden razor box with an adjustable cover, which was carved for Gass from sycamore or poplar wood by Sacajawea with a knife obtained from the fur-traders or from men of the expedition while they were in winter quarters in 1804-05 in the Mandan stockade. The box is now in the possession of Mrs. Brierly's son. The other daughter had in her keeping the hatchet which her father used in the construction of Fort Mandan and Fort Clatsop.

Writing to Earle R. Forrest of Washington, Pennsylvania, on November 1, 1923, Mrs. Annie Smith said, "Yes, I have heard him [Gass] often speak of Sacajawea, the 'Bird Woman,' a guide for part of the way of the expedition of Lewis and Clark. I do not know what became of her. Father said she went back to her people." Mr. Forrest is authority for the statement that Gass is "pronounced exactly as it is spelled, and not 'Gos.'"

[9] Ordway, John, *Journal,* ed. Milo M. Quaife.

Upon the return of the expedition to St. Louis in September, 1806, Lewis and Clark set about the task of preparing their report for President Jefferson. The original records of the two leaders of the expedition were all retranscribed in red morocco, gilt-edged notebooks which have in part been preserved to the present day. The original notes, however, unfortunately were mostly destroyed. Captain Clark, a draftsman of unusual ability, made for his journal numerous maps of the routes followed by the expedition as well as many rough drawings of birds, rivers, fishes, and the like. These were put into systematized form, and became a valuable asset to the final records of the expedition.

It was the intention of the two leaders to arrange for the publication of their journals immediately after making their report to the president, but unexpected developments made this impossible. Lewis was appointed governor of the new Louisiana territory, and Clark was made superintendent of Indian affairs. These new responsibilities for some years rendered it impossible for the leaders to prepare the final revision of their journals, and to edit them for publication.

In 1809, however, at the earnest request of President Jefferson, Lewis started east in order to undertake the long-delayed task of preparing the journals for the publishers. His death en route at the hands of a murderer left to Captain Clark alone the task of putting the records into proper form for publication.[10] The next year Clark

---

[10] In 1848 the legislature of the state of Tennessee erected a granite monument to the memory of Captain Lewis, and carved upon it President Jefferson's own testimonial to the worth of the man. "His courage was undaunted. His firmness and perseverance yielded to nothing but impossibilities. A rigid disciplinarian, yet tender as a father to those who were committed to his charge; honest, disinterested, liberal, with a sound understanding, and a scrupulous fidelity to truth."

secured the services of Nicholas Biddle to edit the manuscripts, and engaged George Shannon, the youngest
member of the expedition, to act as his assistant.[11] In this
capacity Shannon was able both to interpret the notes
made by the diarists and also to add much valuable material from his own personal experiences as a member of
the expedition and from the vast fund of information
he had gained from conversations with other members
of the company. Clark, on his part, aided the undertaking by frequent correspondence with the editors, and
finally made a special journey to Philadelphia to assist
in the actual assembling and editing of the material.

In the preparation of the Lewis and Clark journals
the editors also had the use of the original copy of
Sergeant Ordway's journal and of the already published
work of Sergeant Gass. Sixteen months were required
to complete the undertaking – from March 25, 1810, to
July 8, 1811. Then when the task was finished it was
difficult to find a publisher for the work. Finally, under
the supervision of Paul Allen, two small volumes were
issued in 1814. This edition, however, omitted the
carefully-prepared, scientific data, including Captain

[11] February, 1810, Captain Clark in a letter to Biddle earnestly sought his
help in the preparation of the volumes on the expedition. "Can't you come to
this place," wrote Clark, "where I have my books and memorandum and
stay a week or two: read over and make yourself thereby acquainted with
everything which may not be explained in the journals? If you will come it
may enable me to give you a more full view of those parts which may not
be thereby explained and enable you to proceed without difficulty. Such parts
as may not be full, I can explain, and add such additional matter as I may
recollect."

In May he sent Shannon to Biddle with a letter of introduction in which he
said, "This will be handed to you by George Shannon, the young man I spoke
to you about, who was with me on the NW expedition; he has agreed to go to
Philadelphia and give such information relative to that tour as may be in his
power. The young gentleman possesses sincere and undisguised heart, he is
highly spoken of by all of his acquaintances, and much respected at the
Lexington university, where he has been for the last two years."

Clark's maps and atlas. These were not published until the Thwaites edition of 1904. The Biddle edition, moreover, comprised less than a fourth of the original manuscripts, which contained over a million and a half words. Such a reduction necessarily involved the omission of much material that was of genuine value. Nevertheless, the volumes have fittingly been ranked by Dr. Thwaites as among the most important and interesting books of American travel. The Biddle edition was later reprinted in England, and also translated and published in the Dutch, German, and French languages.

In evaluating this edition, it must be remembered that it was produced with the aid and under the supervision of the actual members of the expedition; therefore, where corrections were made in the spelling of proper names or revisions effected in the narrative, it must be assumed that these changes reflect the best judgment of both Clark and Shannon. This fact has a direct bearing on several matters about which there has been much dispute. This is especially true of the proper pronunciation and spelling of the name Sacajawea.

It was probable, indeed, that the spelling of unusual words was the peculiar contribution of George Shannon to the Biddle edition. Shannon, who by 1810 had completed part of his college education, seems to have had an unusually keen and discriminating ear for Indian pronunciations. The Indians whom the expedition encountered, of course, had no written language, and the spelling of proper names was therefore wholly a matter of choice on the part of the white man who was seeking to reduce their statements to writing. Shannon's suggestion for the spelling of these Indian proper names was, moreover, approved personally by Captain Clark, who not only collaborated with Biddle and Shannon, as we have seen, but also passed on the entire manuscript before it was published. Consequently, in the matter of the correct pronunciation and spelling of the Indian proper names, the Biddle edition must be accepted as probably the most accurate of all the accounts of the Lewis and Clark expedition.

Following the publication of the original Lewis and Clark journals in the Biddle edition of 1814, no authoritative edition of the narrative of the expedition appears again until 1893. In that year Elliott Coues issued the *History of the expedition under the command of Lewis and Clark* in four volumes. It was the intention of Dr. Coues to follow the Biddle text with scrupulous fidelity in this edition, but after the manuscript had been placed in the hands of the printer, the editor learned of the discovery of the original manuscript of the journals of Lewis and Clark. This new material, however, Coues preferred to use as the basis for copious editorial footnotes rather than to change the original plan of publishing an exact reproduction of the Biddle text of 1814.

In 1904 Dr. Reuben Gold Thwaites, the insatiable student of western exploration, published the definitive edition of the Lewis and Clark expedition in eight volumes under the title, *The original journals of Lewis and Clark, 1804 to 1806.*[12] In this edition the original manuscripts were followed closely, even to the reproduction of curious orthography and varied spelling. The work of the diarists in revising their manuscripts and putting them into final form for publication is also shown in the text by many erasures, interpolations, in-

---

[12] Citations from the original journals appearing in this volume are from the Thwaites edition, unless otherwise indicated.

terlineations, corrections of a later date made in red ink, words in parentheses "dug out with a knife," and entries made of events before the events themselves had actually occurred.[13]

[13] The botanical observations of the expedition have recently been published by Rodney H. True in a monograph entitled, "Some neglected botanical results of the Lewis and Clark expedition." See Bibliography.

With the Lewis and Clark Expedition

Journeyed westward, westward,
Left the fleetest deer behind him,
Left the antelope and bison,
Passed the mountains of the prairie,
Passed the land of Crows and Foxes,
Passed the dwellings of the Blackfeet,
Came unto the Rocky mountains,
To the kingdom of the west-wind. – *Hiawatha*

CHAPTER I

With the Lewis and Clark Expedition

The treaty by which France ceded the Louisiana territory to the United States was signed April 30, 1803, and ratified by congress on October 26 of the same year. It was not until December 20, however, that the formal transfer of the territory, embracing approximately 1,020,571 square miles, actually occurred. The cost of this enormous empire was $15,000,000, or about two and one-half cents an acre.

The American most interested in this transaction, and in many ways most responsible for it, was Thomas Jefferson. As early as 1786 we find him lending his support in Paris to John Ledyard, the "Connecticut Yankee" who dreamed of crossing Asia, sailing to the northwest coast, and making his way overland to the American settlements in the Mississippi valley. Six years later, more than a decade before the confirmation of the Louisiana purchase, Jefferson, then secretary of state, began to discuss the advisability of sending an exploring party to navigate the Missouri river to its source. His object was to open commercial relations with the Indians; secure for our government some of the riches of the region which were being monopolized by traders from Canada; discover, if possible, a waterway to the Pacific; and open a route that would enable us to share in the trade of the orient.

At that time, however, no one had the slightest con-

ception of the vastness of the territory lying beyond the
Missouri, although in 1792 Robert Gray, a ship captain
from Boston, had sailed around the cape to the Pacific
in the ship "Columbia," and cast anchor in the harbor
at the mouth of the river to which he gave the name of
his vessel. From this time on many English and Yankee
ships sailed along the northwest coast gathering furs,
and the region about Vancouver island thus became definitely known. But the territory between the Missouri
and the Pacific was as yet unexplored except as a few adventurous trappers had ascended the Missouri river a
thousand miles or so and set their steel beaver traps along
its tributaries. In 1793 Jefferson engaged the services
of André Michaux, a French botanist, to explore the
territory between the Missouri and the Pacific, instructing him specifically to "seek for and pursue that route
which shall form the shortest and most convenient communication between the higher parts of the Missouri
and the Pacific ocean."[14] Michaux set out upon the
expedition, but before he reached the Mississippi was
recalled by his own government.

Three months, moreover, before the treaty transferring the Louisiana territory to the United States was
actually signed, Jefferson sent a confidential letter to
congress asking for an appropriation of twenty-five
hundred dollars to be used to equip an expedition to
explore the country drained by the Missouri river. It
is interesting to note that an appropriation for even so
small an amount to explore a region that now has taxable
wealth of more than seven billion dollars was difficult
to secure.

In preparing for the expedition that was finally au-

[14] Jefferson, Thomas, *Writings,* ed. Ford, vol. VI, 158-161.

thorized, Jefferson selected the leaders with extraordinary care. As already stated, the chief command was
given to his former private secretary from Virginia,
Captain Meriwether Lewis, and he in turn selected
Captain William Clark, likewise a native of Virginia
but at that time a resident of Kentucky, to be his companion. Preparatory to its final organization, the expedition went into winter quarters at the mouth of the Wood
river about twenty miles above St. Louis. Besides the
two leaders, the party at this time included twenty-seven
men, among whom was Clark's colored body servant,
named York, who proved a rare curiosity to the natives.
Three other men were added to this number before the
expedition started on its westward journey. These included the hunter, Drewyer, or Drouillard as it is
correctly spelled; a head-boatman, Crusatte; and a
water-man named Labiche. Fifteen soldiers, commanded by Warfington, escorted the expedition as a
guard. Twenty of the thirty men comprising the body
of the expedition completed the entire journey. Of these
none was married.

As already stated, the instructions which President
Jefferson issued to the commanders of the expedition
were minute and complete. They were expected to make
careful observations of the country through which they
passed and to keep complete records of these observations. They were also to serve as naturalists, botanists,
geologists, paleontologists, astronomers, engineers, me-
teorologists, minerologists, ornithologists, and ethnolo-
gists. Especially were they charged to be diplomatic and
conciliatory in their dealings with the Indians, for in
this capacity they were the official representatives for
the United States government. As already explained,

because of these instructions the journals kept by Lewis and Clark and the other members of the company became veritable storehouses of valuable information regarding nearly every aspect of the country through which the expedition passed, and of the various Indian tribes of the northwest.

The expedition left its winter quarters at the mouth of Wood river on May 14, 1804. In ascending the Missouri, the party employed three boats, the largest of which was fifty-five feet long, drew three feet of water, and was propelled by one large, square-shaped sail and twenty-two oars. The other two boats were of six and seven oars respectively. Two horses were taken along to assist whenever possible in dragging the boats upstream, and to carry to the boats the game killed by the hunters. The largest boat had a swivel gun, or a small cannon swinging on a pivot, which often did efficient service if in no other way than by its terrifying noise.[15]

Because of the tortuous streams, unknown channels, countless snags, sandbars, and swift currents, the progress of the company was slow and the expedition ordinarily counted itself fortunate to make as much as fifteen miles a day. One hundred sixty-five days were required to reach the Mandan villages, sixteen hundred miles from St. Louis. On the return journey the same distance was covered in thirty-seven days.

[15] "SIR . . . On the evening of the 7th of Apl. 1805 we embarked with our baggage on board 2 large perogues and six small canoes at Fort Mandan on a Voyage of Discovery to the Pacific Ocean. The party consisted of the following persons: my friend and Colleague Capt. Wm. Clark, Interpreters George Drewyer and Touasant Charbono, Sergts. John Ordway, Nathanial Pryor, and Patric Gass, privates John Shields & a Shoshone Woman and child, wife and Infant of Touts Charbono, and York a black man servant to Capt. Clark, making a total with myself of 33 persons." Lewis to Jefferson, Sept. 21, 1806.

Captain Meriwether Lewis and Captain William Clark

There were, of course, no charts or maps for the explorers to follow; the territory was unnamed, uncharted, unexplored. Naturally for an expedition of this magnitude, a vast and varied amount of supplies was necessary. These included food, clothing, camp equipment, firearms and ammunition, and large quantities of articles to be used in bartering with the Indians. It was expected, naturally, that much of the necessary food would be supplied by hunting and fishing from day to day. Powder was carried in small cannisters made of lead. These cannisters not only served as containers for the powder but also were melted up for bullets. Each cannister furnished sufficient bullets to correspond to its original content of powder, so that in this way there was no lost weight.

The supplies were packed in bales, each of which contained a portion of all the articles taken. Thus in case of accident or the loss of a single bale, the entire supply of any one commodity would not be destroyed. Articles to be used as presents to the Indians comprised fourteen additional bales. These consisted of bright-colored beads, tinsel and red cloth, lace coats, brass kettles, fish hooks, looking glasses, small bells, thimbles, handkerchiefs of various colors, flags, medals, knives, tomahawks, articles of dress, and anything else that might please the fancy of bartering Indians. Among the beads, those of a blue color were most popular because they were known as the "chief's beads," and commanded a higher value than those of other colors. Lewis and Clark also took with them three sizes of medals representing varying degrees of honor which were to be given to the chiefs of the tribes with whom they came in contact.

The first stages of the journey which lasted several

months were for the most part uneventful. The weather was generally mild and wild game plentiful. Not infrequently the explorers, making headway against the muddy current of the Missouri, met the crude boats of trappers loaded to the gunwale with hides and pelts, floating down the river to St. Louis – the forerunners of the vast fur-trade soon to be in operation up and down the Missouri river.

On August 3, 1804, Lewis and Clark held their first formal council with the Indians. At this council Lewis told the chiefs about the new government to which they must in the future give their allegiance, and assured them of that government's protection. The chiefs expressed their pleasure at this change of government and sent their greetings to their "Great Father," the president. The place where this council was held was called Council bluffs. The site of this council was on the west bank of the river, in what is now Nebraska, about twenty miles north of the site of the present city of Council bluffs in Iowa.

On October 26 the explorers reached the Mandan villages, near the site of the present city of Bismarck, North Dakota. This site was about five days' journey further up the river from the original Mandan villages discovered by the Vérenderyes in 1738. The expedition members spent the winter of 1805 in these villages, housing themselves in huts and stockades which they constructed under the supervision of Sergeant Patrick Gass, the head-carpenter. The winter was occupied in making boats, mending clothes, jerking meat, and studying the language, habits, and customs of the Indians.

While the expedition was in winter quarters at the Mandan villages, Lewis and Clark secured the services of an interpreter named Toussaint Charbonneau, a French-canadian trapper who had spent his life in the northwest. Charbonneau's career will be described more at length in a later chapter; it is sufficient to note here that his training and experience were such as to fit him to be of great value to the expedition.

Charbonneau brought with him his three Indian wives, one of whom was Sacajawea, the chief figure of this volume.[16] His arrival at the headquarters of the expedition is recorded in nearly all of the journals. Clark, in his entry of November 4, 1804, wrote as follows:

A Mr. Chaubonie [Charbonneau], interpreter from the Gross Ventre nation, came to see us and informed that he came down with several Indians from a hunting expedition up the river to hear what we had told the Indians in council. This man wished to hire as an interpreter.

Similarly Ordway, on November 4, wrote:

A Frenchman's squaw came to our camp who belongs to the Snake nation. She came with our interpreter's wife and brought with them four buffalo robes and gave them to our officers.

An entry of the same date in the Biddle edition reads:

We received a visit of two squaws, prisoners from the Rocky mountains, purchased by Charboneau.

---

[16] After having promised his services to Lewis and Clark, Charbonneau was temporarily released at the request of F. A. Larocque, a fur-trader in the Mandan villages, in order to help locate a Sioux Indian who had killed a Mandan. During his absence from camp on this expedition, which included twenty-five men among whom was Captain Clark, Charbonneau married "a woman of the tribe of 'people of the Snakes' who had been made a prisoner by other Indians." This woman was Sacajawea. The marriage was performed on February 8, 1805, only a few days prior to the birth of Baptiste, and the ceremony was doubtless required by either Lewis or Clark. "Pendant qu'il servait sous Larocque il s'unit, le 8 février 1805, à une femme de la tribu Gens-des-Serpents qui avait été faite prisonniere par d'autres Indians."– *Historical dictionary of the Canadians and the French half-breeds of the west.*

Gass, in speaking of Charbonneau's wives in his entry
of December 25, writes as follows:

At half past two another gun was fired, as a notice to assemble at
the dance, which was continued in a jovial manner till eight at night;
and without the presence of any females except three squaws, wives
to our interpreter, who took no other part than the amusement of
looking on.[17] None of the natives came to the garrison this day; the
commanding officers having requested they should not, which was
strictly attended to. During the remainder of the month we lived in
peace and tranquility in the garrison, and were daily visited by the
natives.

Sacajawea, as stated by Ordway, was a member of the
Snake, or Shoshone tribe of Indians.[18] For this reason
it was felt that she would be a most essential addition to
the company, because it was known that the route of the
expedition lay through the territory occupied by this
tribe. As a child she had been captured by the Minnetarees, Hidatsas, or Gros Ventres of the upper Missouri.
These Hidatsa Indians lived in the vicinity of the junction of the Knife and Missouri rivers in North Dakota.
From these Indians Charbonneau either purchased her
or won her by gambling, and later married her, probably,
as we shall see, at the insistance of Lewis or Clark.

While the expedition was still in winter quarters,
Sacajawea gave birth to a boy. The event is recorded by
four of the diarists of the expedition. Lewis, on February
11, 1805, wrote as follows:

About five o'clock this evening one of the wives of Charboneau was

---

[17] Whitehouse, in his entry of the same date, speaks of "three squaws, the
interpreter's wives."

[18] The official spelling of this word is Shoshoni, Shoshonis, but the form
universally used on the reservation is Shoshone, Shoshones. This spelling is
therefore employed throughout this volume. See also Hodge, Frederick W.,
Handbook of American Indians north of Mexico, vol. II, 1139. "Shoshon,
Sho-sho-nay, Sho-sho-ne, Shoshonee, all equalling Shoshoni."

delivered of a fine boy. It is worthy of remark that this was the first child which this woman has borne.

Gass, on February 12, says:

On the twelfth we arrived at the fort and found that one of our interpreter's wives had, in our absence, made an addition to our number.

Ordway writes on February 11:

An interesting occurence of this day was the birth of a son of the Shoshone woman.

The event is also confirmed by Whitehouse, but is not mentioned in the Biddle narrative.

At five o'clock on the afternoon of April 7, 1805, two expeditions left the Mandans: one returned to St. Louis with letters to President Jefferson and with furs, stuffed and live animals, bones, articles of Indian dress, bows and arrows; the other, with thirty-two members in six canoes, turned its steps toward the uncharted northwest. Charbonneau and Sacajawea, of course, accompanied this latter company as interpreters. Lewis, in speaking of the departure of the expedition, wrote on April 7:

Our party now consists of the following individuals: interpreters George Drewyer and Taussant Charbono; also a black man of the name of York, servant to Captain Clark, an Indian woman, wife to Charbono, with a young child.

Clark, in turn, on the same date mentions

my servant, York; George Drewyer, who acts as hunter and interpreter; Sharbonah and his Indian squaw to act as interpreter and interpretress for the Snake Indians – one Mandan, and Shabonah's infant.

The Biddle narrative, in turn, under the date of April 7 says:

The wife of Charboneau also accompanied us with her young child and we hope may be useful as an interpreter among the Snake Indians. She was, herself, one of that tribe but having been taken in war by the Minetarees by whom she was sold as a slave to Chaboneau, who brought her up and afterwards married her.

During its progress up the Missouri river, the members of the expedition found a great abundance of game such as deer, buffalo, elk, geese, ducks, and prairie chickens. Bear also were very numerous and sometimes dangerous. During this stage of the expedition, Sacajawea made herself useful in many small ways. Lewis, on April 9, says that when the expedition halted for dinner the squaw

busied herself in search for the wild artichokes which the mice [gophers?] collect and deposit in large hordes. This operation she performed by penetrating the earth with a sharp stick about some collection of driftwood. Her labors soon proved successful and she procured a good quantity of these roots.

Clark, on April 18, writes that he left the boat and went on foot across a great bend of the river, accompanied by Charbonneau and Sacajawea with her papoose. Lewis also mentions on April 30 that Clark spent the greater part of the day walking along the shore, accompanied by Charbonneau and Sacajawea.

Not long after this, Sacajawea performed a service of inestimable value to the expedition and one that doubtless greatly raised her in the esteem of its leaders. Clark records this incident, under date of May 14, at some length, as follows:

. . . we proceeded on very well until about six o'clock. A squall of wind struck our sail broadside and turned the perogue nearly over, and in this situation the perogue remained until the sail was cut down, in which time she nearly filled with water. The articles which floated out were nearly all caught by the squaw who was in the rear. This accident had like to have cost us dearly; for in this perogue were embarked our papers, instruments, books, medicine, a great proportion of our merchandise, and, in short, almost every article indispensibly necessary to further the views and insure the success of the enterprise in which we are now launched to the distance of 2,200 miles.

Captain Lewis also pays his tribute to Sacajawea for her coolness and bravery in this emergency, writing as follows:

. . . By four o'clock in the evening our instruments, medicine, merchandise, provisions, were perfectly dried, repacked, and put on board the perogue. The loss we sustained was not so great as we had at first apprehended; our medicine sustained the greatest injury, several articles of which were entirely spoiled, and many considerably injured. The ballance of our losses consisted of some garden seeds, a small quantity of gunpowder, and a few culinary articles which fell overboard and sunk. The Indian woman, to whom I ascribe equal fortitude and resolution with any person on board at the time of the accident, caught and preserved most of the light articles which were washed overboard.

Probably in recognition of this great service which Sacajawea had rendered to the expedition, Lewis records, May 20, that a river was named in her honor. His entry, both because of the spelling of the name and its interpretation, is of definite significance. It reads as follows:

About five miles above the mouth of Shell river, a handsome river of about fifty yards in width discharged itself into the Shell river on the starboard or upper side. This stream we called Sah-ca-ger-we-ah or "Bird Woman's river," after our interpreter, the Snake woman.[19]

At the junction of the Maria's and the Missouri rivers, the expedition cachéd part of its supplies. The common

[19] "With less gallantry, the present generation call it Crooked creek." Editorial note in Ordway's *Journal,* 215, footnote 4; Thwaites, vol. II, 52; Coues, vol. I, 317, also footnote; Biddle, vol. I, 222.

method employed by the mountain men to make such a
caché was as follows: a good dry spot was selected; the
sod was carefully removed and placed to one side, so
that when it was replaced it would not show that it had
been disturbed. After the sod was removed a hole was
dug, and the extra earth that would not be needed to fill
up the hole was carried to the stream and thrown into
the water so that no trace of it might be seen. Then twigs
and branches were placed in the bottom of the hole, and
on these were placed the goods to be cachéd or hidden;
these were then covered with hides and skins to keep out
moisture or water; over all of this was placed enough
of the dirt to fill the hole, leaving space enough for the
sod, which was carefully replaced. Sometimes a fire was
made on the spot to destroy any sign of the work, or horses
were picketed over the caché, or night camps were established. If the greatest care was exercised, even the skilled
eye of the Indian could not detect the hiding-place.

On May 29, soon after leaving this spot, the expedition
reached an abandoned Indian encampment, and from
the fragments of moccasins lying about, Sacajawea concluded that the former occupants, though not of the
Shoshone tribe, belonged to one of the other Rocky
mountain groups. On the thirteenth of June, 1805, the
party reached the Great falls of the Missouri. It was
necessary to portage the supplies and baggage of the
company around these falls, a task which occupied a
month. The men themselves carried much of the baggage
on their backs, but most of the supplies were transported
in a cart, the wheels of which were made of a cottonwood
tree twenty-two inches in diameter. During these opera-
tions the men, whose feet were protected only by moccasins, suffered severely from the prickly pear, or cactus,

through which they had to walk. The thorns of this plant easily pierced the rawhide moccasins and left the feet sore and festering. This, added to the heat, fatigue, and hard work, constituted a fearful strain on the members of the company.

Here, also, Sacajawea fell seriously ill. Both Lewis and Clark record this incident in considerable detail. Lewis, on June 10, writes:

Sahcahgahwea, our Indian woman, is very sick this evening. Captain bled her.

Clark, on the same date, confirms Lewis's statement as follows:

Sahcahgagwea, our Indian woman, very sick. I bled her.

The next day Clark repeated the bleeding, an operation which he said "appeared to be of great service to her." On June 12, Clark wrote:

The interpreter's wife very sick, so much so that I moved her into the back part of our covered part of the perogue, which is cool, her own situation being a very hot one in the bottom of the perogue exposed to the sun.

Clark's entries on the thirteenth and fourteenth record the growing seriousness of Sacajawea's illness. On the sixteenth, Clark records that the poor little Indian woman is

very bad and will take no medicine whatever until her husband, finding her out of her senses, easily prevailed upon her to take medicine. If she dies it will be the fault of her husband.

Lewis, on the same date, speaks at considerable length of the gravity of Sacajawea's illness, of the means employed to bring about a cure, and especially of the great importance he attached to her services in negotiating

with the Indians whom they expected to encounter. His
entry reads as follows:

> About 2 p.m. I reached the camp, found the Indian woman extremely
> ill and much reduced by her indisposition. This gave me some concern,
> as well as for the poor object herself, then with a young child in her
> arms, as from her condition of her being our only dependence for a
> friendly negotiation with the Snake Indians, on whom we depend for
> horses to assist us in our portage from the Missouri to the Columbia
> river.
>
> One of the small canoes was left below this rapid in order to pass
> and repass the river for the purpose of hunting as well as to procure
> the water of the sulpher spring, the virtues of which I now resolved
> to try on the Indian woman.
>
> . . . I caused her to drink the mineral all together. When I first
> came down I found that her pulse was scarcely perceptible, very quick,
> frequently irregular, and attended with strong nervous symptoms;
> that of the twitching of the fingers and the leaders of the arms; now
> the pulse has become regular, much fuller, and a gentle perspiration
> had taken place; the nervous system has also in a great measure abated,
> and she feels herself much freer from pain.

The day following Sacajawea was much better.
Lewis's entry on June 17 records this improvement.

> The Indian woman much better today; I have still continued the
> same course of medicine; she is free from pain, clear of fever, her
> pulse regular, and eats as heartily as I am willing to permit her, of
> broiled buffalo well seasoned with pepper and salt and rich soup of
> the same meat. I think, therefore, that there is every rational hope
> of her recovery.

The next day he wrote:

> The Indian woman is recovering fast. She set up the greater part
> of the day and walked out for the first time since she arrived here.
> She eats heartily and is free from fever or pain.

The day following, however, the patient's ill-advised
diet of raw apples and dried fish came near proving her

undoing. Lewis writes of the incident in the following way:

The Indian woman was much better this morning. She walked out and gathered a considerable quantity of the white apples of which she ate so heartily in this raw state, together with a considerable quantity of dryed fish without my knowledge, that she complained very much and her fever again returned. I rebuked Sharbono severly for suffering her to indulge herself with food, having been previously told what she must only eat.

This was the crisis of Sacajawea's illness. The next day she was free from pain and fever, and celebrated by going fishing. On the twenty-fourth, Lewis records that she was perfectly recovered.[20]

A few days after Sacajawea's recovery, a sudden cloudburst almost swept Sacajawea, her baby, Charbonneau, and Captain Clark, with his negro servant York, to destruction, and if it had not been for Clark's bravery and presence of mind, Sacajawea, Charbonneau, and the baby would almost certainly have been drowned. Lewis, in his entry of June 29, records the near tragedy as follows:

He [Clark] determined himself to pass by the way of the river to camp in order to supply the deficiency of some notes and remarks which he had made as he first ascended the river but which he had unfortunately lost. Accordingly, he left one man at Willow run to guard the baggage, and took with him his black man, York. Sharbono and his Indian woman also accompanied Captain Clark. . . On his arrival at the falls, he perceived a very black cloud rising in the west, which threatened immediate rain; he looked about for a shelter but could find none without being in great danger of being blown into the river should the wind prove as violent as it sometimes is on those occasions in these plains. At length, about a fourth of a mile above

---

[20] Sacajawea's illness is also mentioned in the Ordway, Whitehouse, and Biddle journals.

the falls, he discovered a deep ravine where there were some shelving rocks under which he took shelter near the river with Sharbono and the Indian woman; laying their guns, compass, etc., under a shelving rock on the upper side of the ravine where they were perfectly secure from the rain. The first shower was moderate, accompanied by a violent rain, the effects of which they did but little feel. Soon after, a most violent torrent of rain descended, accompanied with hail. The rain appeared to descend in a body, and instantly collected in the ravine and came down in a rolling current with irresistable force, driving rocks, mud, and everything before it which opposed it's passage. Captain Clark fortunately discovered it a moment before it reached them and, seizing his gun and shot pouch with his left hand, with the right he assisted himself up the steep bluff, shoving occasionally the Indian woman before him who had her child in her arms. Sharbono had the woman by the hand, endeavoring to pull her up the hill, but was so much frightened that he remained frequently motionless, and but for Captain Clark, both himself and his woman and child must have perished. So sudden was the rise of the water that before Captain Clark could reach his gun and begin to ascend the bank, it was up to his waist and wet his watch, and he could scarcely ascend faster than it arose until it had obtained the depth of fifteen feet with a current tremendous to behold. One moment longer and it would have swept them into the river just above the great cataract of 87 feet, where they must have inevitably perished. Sharbono lost his gun, shot pouch, horn, tomahawk, and my wiping rod; Captain Clark his umbrella and compass or circumferenter. They fortunately arrived on the plain safe, where they found the black man, York, in search of them. York had separated from them a little while before the storm in pursuit of some buffalo, and had not seen them enter the ravine. When this gust came on he returned in search of them and not being able to find them for some time was much alarmed. The bier in which the woman carries her child, and all it's clothes were swept away as they lay at her feet, she having time only to grasp her child; the infant was therefore very cold and the woman also, who had just recovered from a severe indisposition, was also wet and cold.

Clark gives substantially the same account, but adds a few significant details. His version reads as follows:

I determined myself to proceed on to the falls and take the river; according we all set out. I took my servant and one man, Charbono our interpreter, and his squaw accompanied. Soon after I arrived at the falls, I perceived a cloud which appeared black and threatened immediate rain. I looked out for a shelter, but could see no place without being in great danger of being blown into the river if the wind should prove as turbulant as it is at some times. About one fourth of a mile above the falls I observed a deep ravine in which was shelving rocks under which we took shelter near the river and placed our guns, the compass, etc., etc. under a shelving rock on the upper side of the creek, in a place which was very secure from rain. The first shower was moderate, accompanied with a violent wind, the effects of which we did not feel. Soon after a torrent of rain and hail fell more violent than ever I saw before; the rain fell like one volley of water falling from the heavens and gave us time only to get out of the way of a torrent of water which was pouring down the hill into the river with immense force, tearing everything before it; taking with it large rocks and mud. I took my gun and shot pouch in my left hand, and with the right scrambled up the hill pushing the interpreter's wife (who had the child in her arms) before me, the interpreter himself making attempts to pull up his wife by the hand, much scared and nearly without motion. We at length reached the top of the hill safe, where I found my servant in search of us, greatly agitated for our welfare. Before I got out of the bottom of the ravine, which was a flat dry rock when I entered it, the water was up to my waist and wet my watch. I scarcely got out before it raised ten feet deep with a torrent which was terrible to behold and by the time I reached the top of the hill, at least fifteen feet of water. I directed the party to return to the camp at the run as fast as possible to get to our lode, where clothes could be got to cover the child, whose clothes were all lost, and the woman, who was but just recovering from a severe indisposition, and was wet and cold. I was fearful of a relapse. I caused her, as also the others of the party, to take a little spirits, which my servant had in a canteen . . . I lost at the river in the torrent the large compass, an elegant fusee, tomahawk, umbrella, shot pouch and horn with powder and ball, moccasins, and the woman lost her child's bier and clothes, bedding, etc.

The same incident is much more briefly recorded by

Gass under date of July 1, and Ordway and Biddle under date of June 29. Biddle, instead of speaking of the basket in which Sacajawea carried her baby as a "bier," calls it a "net."

Near the close of July the expedition began to draw near to the forks of the Missouri river and came into the country of the Shoshone Indians. On July 19 Lewis found several Indian camps of willow brush which had been occupied earlier in the spring. He also found pine trees from which the Indians had stripped the bark for the purpose, as Sacajawea explained, of obtaining the sap and tenderer part of the wood and bark for food. On the twenty-second, Lewis records:

> The Indian woman recognizes the country and assures us that this is the river on which her relations live and that the three forks are at no great distance. This piece of information has cheered the spirits of the party, who now begin to console themselves with the anticipation of shortly seeing the head of the Missouri, yet unknown to the civilized world.

On the twenty-eighth, the same diary contains this entry:

> Our present camp is precisely on the spot that the Snake Indians were encamped at the time the Minnetares of the Knife river first came in sight of them five years since. From hence they retreated about three miles up Jefferson's river and concealed themselves in the woods. The Minnetares pursued, attacked them, killed four men, four women, a number of boys, and made prisoners of all the females and four boys. Sah-cah-gar-we-ah, our Indian woman, was one of the female prisoners taken at that time; though I cannot discover that she shows any emotion of sorrow in recollecting this event, or of joy in being again restored to her native country. If she has enough to eat and a few trinkets to wear, I believe she would be perfectly content anywhere.

The expedition was now at the Three forks of the Missouri, approximately 2,850 miles from home. The three streams, which here came together to make the Missouri, were named the Jefferson, the Madison, and the Gallatin. Here Clark fell sick, and it was not until July 30 that the expedition was able to continue its ascent of the Jefferson river. The same day, according to Clark, "the company passed the place the squaw interpretess was taken." On August 8, the company came to a familiar landmark known as Beaverhead rock, which Lewis described in some detail, at the same time emphasizing the grave necessity of finding Indians who would be able to supply the expedition with horses. His account runs as follows:

The Indian woman recognized the point of high plain to our right, which she informed us was not very distant from the summer retreat of her nation on a river beyond the mountains which runs to the west. This hill she says her nation calls the beaver's head from a conceived resemblance of its figure to the head of that animal. She assures us that we shall either find her people on this river or on the river immediately west of it's source; which, from it's present size, cannot be very distant. As it is now all important with us to meet with these people as soon as possible, I determined to proceed tomorrow with a small party to the source of the principal stream of this river and pass the mountains to the Columbia; and down that river until I found the Indians; in short, it is my resolution to find them or some others, who have horses, if it should cause me a trip of one month, for without horses we shall be obliged to leave a great part of our stores, of which, it appears to me, that we have a stock already sufficiently small for the length of the voyage before us.[21]

On August 14, both Lewis and Clark record that Sacajawea was badly treated by her husband, who was

[21] The same account, with a few variations, is given in the Biddle edition under dates of July 22, 28, 30, and August 8. In this account the Indian woman's name is twice spelled Sacajawea. Gass under date of July 28, Ordway on July 22, and Whitehouse on the same date, all mention Sacajawea's recognition of her own country. This is the last record in Whitehouse of anything relating to Sacajawea.

severely reprimanded by Captain Clark in consequence. The next day, Lewis mentions that Clark and Sacajawea narrowly escaped being bitten by a rattlesnake, a fact which is also confirmed by Clark in his entry of the same date. The day following, Ordway records that Sacajawea found and gathered "a fine persel of servis berrys" and that on the sixteenth, Clark, Charbonneau, and Sacajawea, while walking along the bank, found great quantities of these berries – "the largest and best I ever saw" – and gathering a bucket full gave them out to the party at noon, when they stopped for dinner.

On August 13, when Captain Lewis, with three companions, was proceeding ahead of the main body of the expedition, he saw in the distance an Indian riding on horseback. Although the captain made the sign of friendship customary with the Missouri river and Rocky mountain Indians, of holding his blanket in both hands at the two corners, throwing it above his head and unfolding it when he brought it to the earth as if spreading it out on the ground and inviting them to come and sit on it, he failed to induce the Indian to come to him. Then he ran toward the Indian with a looking-glass and trinkets, calling, "tabba bone, tabba bone" – words that Sacajawea had taught him to use, meaning "white man, white man" – at the same time rolling up his sleeves and opening his shirt to show the white skin of his arms and chest, for his face and hands were browned and tanned to the color of an Indian from the exposure to the wind during months of outdoor life. But despite all his efforts the Indian fled.

The next day, however, Lewis overtook some squaws who conducted him to a camp where he met a chief and about sixty warriors, all well mounted. This chief, named

Cameahwait, Lewis later discovered was the brother of Sacajawea, and after much bartering and bickering, he agreed to furnish horses and a guide to pilot the expedition over the mountains.

While Lewis was carrying on his negotiations with the Shoshone chief, the main body of the expedition under Clark was dragging its boats up the Beaverhead river. On the seventeenth, in a charming valley near the present village of Armstead, where Lewis and Cameahwait had made their camps, Clark and his party came into view. The reunion of Sacajawea with her people which here occurred, her recognition of her brother in the person of Chief Cameahwait, and her meeting with the companion who had been with her when she was taken captive but who had escaped and returned to her people, are graphically given both by Lewis and Clark. Of these events Lewis wrote on August 17 and 19 as follows:

Shortly after, Captain Clark arrived with the interpreter, Charbono, and the Indian woman, who proved to be a sister of the Chief Cameahwait. The meeting of those people was really affecting, particularly between Sah-cah-gar-we-ah and an Indian woman who had been taken prisoner at the same time with her and who had afterwards escaped from Minnetares and rejoined her nation. . . we formed a canopy of one of our large sails, and planted some willow brush in the ground to form a shade for the Indians to set under while we spoke to them, which we thought it best to do this evening. Accordingly, about 4 p.m., we called them together and through the medium of Labuish, Charbono, and Sah-cah-gar-weah, we communicated to them fully the objects which had brought us into this distant part of the country, in which we took care to make them a conspicuous object of our own good wishes and the care of our government.

Lewis also relates the following complication which arose from Sacajawea's unexpected home coming:

The father frequently disposes of his infant daughters in marriage to men who are grown who have sons for whom they think proper to provide wives. The compensation given in such cases usually consists of horses or mules which the father receives at the time of the contract and converts to his own use. . . Sah-car-gar-we-ah had been disposed of before she was taken by the Minnetares. The husband was yet living with this band. He was more than double her age and had two other wives. He claimed her as his wife, but said that as she had had a child by another man, who was Charbono, that he did not want her.

Clark's description of Sacajawea's meeting with her people reads as follows:

I had not proceeded on one mile before I saw at a distance several Indians on horseback coming towards me. The interpreter and squaw, who were before me at some distance, danced for the joyful sight, and she made signs to me that they were her nation. As I approached nearer them, I discovered one of Captain Lewis's party with them dressed in their dress. They met me with great signs of joy. . . The great chief of this nation proved to be the brother of the woman with us, and is a man of influence, sense, and easy and reserved manners, [who] appears to possess a great deal of sincerity.

The description of Sacajawea's return to her tribe in the Biddle edition is significant not only because of the wealth of detail which it adds, but also (especially for the purpose of this narrative), because it records the adoption by Sacajawea of the son of her eldest sister. This is particularly important in tracing the family relations of Sacajawea and in establishing the connection between her and the Indian named Bazil of whom frequent mention is made in subsequent pages of this volume. Biddle's lengthy account herewith follows:

The Indians were all transported with joy, and the chief, in the warmth of his satisfaction, renewed his embrace to Captain Lewis, who was quite as much delighted as the Indians themselves. The report proved most agreeably true. On setting out at seven o'clock, Captain Clark, with Chaboneau and his wife, walked on shore; but they had

INDIAN DRAWING OF THE CUSTER BATTLE, JUNE 25, 1876

Sent to Colonel Walter S. Schuyler by Shoshone Indians to help Washakie locate the hostile savages. The Indians have dark faces, and are wearing hats obtained as plunder. The symbol by which each chief was known is attached to his hat by a cord, e.g., "White Horse," "Big Bear," "Fox," etc.

not gone more than a mile before Captain Clark saw Sacajawea, who was with her husband one hundred yards ahead, begin to dance and show every mark of the most extravagant joy, turning round him and pointing to several Indians, whom he now saw advancing on horseback, sucking her fingers at the same time to indicate that they were of her native tribe. . . We soon drew near to the camp, and just as we approached it a woman made her way through the crowd towards Sacajawea, and recognizing each other, they embraced with the most tender affection. The meeting of these two young women had in it something peculiarly touching, not only in the ardent manner in which their feelings were expressed, but from the real interest of their situation. They had been companions in childhood; in the war with the Minnetarees they had both been taken prisoners in the same battle; they had shared and softened the rigours of their captivity till one of them had escaped from the Minnetarees, with scarce a hope of ever seeing her friend free from the hands of her enemies. While Sacajawea was renewing among the women the friendships of former days, Captain Clark went on, and was received by Captain Lewis and the chief, who, after the first embraces and salutations were over, conducted him to a sort of circular tent or shade of willows. Here he was seated on a white robe, and the chief immediately tied in his hair six small shells resembling pearls, an ornament highly valued by these people, who procured them in the course of trade from the seacoast. The moccasins of the whole party were then taken off, and after much ceremony the smoking began. After this the conference was to be opened, and glad of an opportunity of being able to converse more intelligibly, Sacajawea was sent for; she came into the tent, sat down, and was beginning to interpret, when in the person of Cameahwait she recognized her brother; she instantly jumped up and ran and embraced him, throwing over him her blanket and weeping profusely; the chief himself was moved, though not in the same degree. After some conversation between them she resumed her seat, and attempted to interpret for us, but her new situation seemed to overpower her, and she was frequently interrupted by her tears. After the council was finished the unfortunate woman learned that all her family were dead except two brothers, one of whom was absent, and a son of her eldest sister, a small boy, who was immediately adopted by her.[22]

---

[22] Biddle's is the only journal mentioning Sacajawea's adoption of her

On the seventeenth, Lewis and Clark held a council at which it was agreed that the next day Clark should set out in advance of the main body with eleven men furnished with axes and other tools necessary for making canoes, together with their arms and as much baggage as they could carry. Clark was also to take with him Charbonneau and Sacajawea and leave them at the Shoshone camp so that they might hasten the return of the Indians with their horses to the main camp of the expedition near the forks of the Beaverhead. Clark, however, and his company were to continue to the Columbia, and there construct canoes for the use of the larger party if they found the river navigable.

On the eighteenth, Clark succeeded in purchasing three horses from the Shoshone chief, for which he gave "a chief's coat, some handkerchiefs, a shirt, leggings and a few arrow points." Two of his own coats he gave to two under chiefs "who appeared not well satisfied that the first chief was dressed so much finer than themselves." Charbonneau and Sacajawea, in accordance with the prearranged agreement, were left at the Indian camp to persuade the Indians to bring their horses as soon as possible to the main body of the expedition under Lewis. On August 22 the Indians under Cameahwait met with Lewis near the crest of the Rocky mountains, and for a number of days the latter bargained with them for the purchase of their horses. Lewis, in two entries of August 22 and 24, records these negotiations.

. . . At 11 a.m. Charbono, the Indian woman, Cameahwait, and about fifty men with a number of women and children arrived. They encamped near us. After they had turned out their horses and arranged

nephew. This boy did not accompany the expedition when it left for the coast, but remained with his uncle, Chief Cameahwait.

their camp, I called the chiefs and warriors together and addressed them a second time. . . I gave him a few dryed squashes which we had brought from the Mandans. He had them boiled and declared them to be the best thing he had ever tasted, except sugar, a small lump of which it seems his sister, Sah-cah-gar-wea, had given him.

I had now nine horses and a mule, and two which I had hired made twelve. These I loaded, and the Indian women took the ballance of the baggage. I had given the interpreter some articles with which to purchase a horse for the woman which he had obtained. For each horse I gave an ax, a knife, handkerchief, and a little paint; and for the mules the addition of a knife, a shirt, handkerchief, and a pair of leggings.

Biddle, under entries of the same date, describes this horse-trading episode as follows:

We then produced some battleaxes which we had made at fort Mandan, and a quantity of knives, with both of which they appeared very much pleased; and we were soon able to purchase three horses by giving for each an axe, a knife, a handkerchief, and a little paint. To this we were obliged to add a second knife, a shirt, a handkerchief, and a pair of leggings; and such is the estimation in which those animals are held, that even at this price, which was double that for a horse, the fellow who sold him took upon himself great merit in having given away a mule to us. They now said that they had no more horses for sale, and as we had now nine of our own, two hired horses and a mule, we began loading them as heavily as was prudent, and, placing the rest on the shoulders of the Indian women, left our camp at twelve o'clock. We were all on foot, except Sacajawea, for whom her husband had purchased a horse with some articles which we gave him for that purpose; an Indian, however, had the politeness to offer Captain Lewis one of his horses to ride, which he accepted in order better to direct the march of the party.

As the expedition left this spot, Lewis learned with grave concern that Cameahwait had sent a messenger ahead to summon the remaining Indians on the Lemhi river to join him in the annual buffalo hunt on the Missouri. This hunt, usually undertaken in July, had already been delayed to a late start because of the councils with

Lewis and the negotiations over the horses. Afraid that the Indians would leave him without sufficient horses for the journey over the mountains if they started on this hunt, Lewis prevailed upon Cameahwait to countermand his order until the expedition should reach the Lemhi Indians, whose help was seriously needed. Credit was given to Sacajawea for saving the expedition in this emergency.

Lewis, on August 25, describes the incident as follows:

This morning loaded our horses and set out a little after sunrise. . . sometime after we had halted, Charbono mentioned to me with apparent unconcern that he expected to meet all the Indians from the camp on the Columbia tomorrow on their way to the Missouri. . . he then informed me that the first chief had dispatched some of his young men this morning to this camp requesting the Indians to meet them tomorrow and that he himself and those with him would go on with them down the Missouri, and consequently leave me and my baggage on the mountain or thereabouts. I was out of patience with the folly of Charbono who had not sufficient sagacity to see the consequences which would inevitably flow from such a movement of the Indians, and although he had been in possession of this information since early in the morning when it had been communicated to him by his Indian woman, yet he never mentioned it until the afternoon.

Ordway even more definitely speaks of the inestimable value of the Indian woman's services in this connection.

Whilst at dinner we learned by means of Sacajawea that the young men who left us this morning carried a request from the chief that the village would break up its encampment and meet his party tomorrow, when they would all go down the Missouri into the buffalo country. Alarmed at this new caprice of the Indians, which if not counteracted, threatened to leave ourselves and our baggage on the mountains, or even if we reached the waters of the Columbia, prevent our obtaining horses to go on farther, Captain Lewis immediately called the three chiefs together.

In September, 1805, the party crossed the Bitter Root

mountains amidst snow and drifts and hailed with delight the first westward flowing streams. Here, having branded their horses, they left them in care of a Nez Perce chief. Building themselves canoes, they floated down the Clearwater river to its junction with the Snake river, where Lewistown, Idaho, and Clarkstown, Washington, now stand.[23] On they continued, down the swift-flowing Snake that sped to its junction with the Columbia, a short distance above the present site of Kennewick and Pasco in the state of Washington. Embarked on the broad Columbia, their course was rapid and easy, save for the excitement of shooting an occasional rapid or making a portage. Soon Mt. Hood was seen to the south and Mt. Adams to the north.

East of the mountains game had been very plentiful, furnishing the explorers with an abundance to eat. On the west side of the continental divide, however, they actually suffered for food. Sometimes, indeed, they were reduced to such straits that they were obliged to buy puppies from the Indians from which they made stews that were greatly relished. Horse flesh was also eaten by all the white explorers, but Sacajawea, being a Shoshone, refused to eat the meat either of the horses or the puppies.

On October 28, the explorers were visited by some Indians, one of whom wore a round hat and a sailor's peajacket; another had a British musket; still others possessed a cutlass, a brass teakettle, and bright colored cloths. Lewis and Clark therefore knew that they were near the end of their outward journey, for such articles could only have been obtained from trading vessels along

---

[23] This branding iron was found in 1892 on one of the islands of the Columbia, three and a half miles above the Dalles, and is now an interesting relic in the possession of the Oregon historical society.

the coast. On November 8, the eyes of the weary explorers were rested and their hearts rejoiced by the sight of the goal of so many months of toil and travel – the western sea, the object for which the Vérenderyes had sought so long ago in vain.

One week later Lewis and his party reached the ocean, four thousand one hundred thirty-four miles from home. A few miles from the sea on the south side of the mouth of the Columbia, on a small stream afterward called Lewis and Clark river, they built Fort Clatsop. Here establishing their winter quarters, they stayed until March 23, 1806.[24]

After their long journey across the continent, the men were almost naked. Clothes had to be made for immediate wear and for the return journey. During the winter the men made over four hundred pairs of moccasins and clothes of all kinds from the skins of elk, deer, beaver, and sea otter. Many gallons of salt were also made by evaporating sea water, and numerous packs of jerked venison were prepared for the return journey.

The blubber of a whale, discovered on the beach, was also made into oil for the use of the expedition. In describing these matters on January 5, 1806, Lewis writes:

Willard and Wiser returned . . . they informed us . . . they could find a convenient place for making salt; that they had at length

---

[24] On the long journey from the Mandan villages to the Pacific, as already indicated, Sacajawea had been an aid to the expedition in many ways. Even her very presence was an evidence to the Indians that the party came on an errand of peace instead of war. Thus, on October 13, Clark records that the presence of Sacajawea "reconciles all the Indians as to our friendly intentions," and on the nineteenth he writes: "As soon as they saw the squaw wife of the interpreter, they pointed to her and informed those who continued yet in the same position I first found them. They immediately all came out and appeared to assume new life. The sight of this Indian woman, wife to one of our interpreters, confirmed those people of our friendly intentions, as no woman ever accompanies a war party of Indians in this quarter."

established themselves on the coast about fifteen miles southwest from this, near the lodge of some Killamuck families; that the Indians were very friendly and had given them a considerable quantity of the blubber of the whale which perished on the coast some distance southeast of them. Part of this blubber they brought with them. It was white and not unlike the fat of pork, though the texture was more spongy and somewhat coarser. I had a part of it cooked and found it very pallitable and tender; it resembled the beaver or the dog in flavor.[25]

On the same date Clark also writes:

The Indians were very friendly and had given them a considerable quantity of the blubber of the whale which perished on the coast some distance southeast of them. It was white and not unlike the fat of pork, though the texture was more spongy and somewhat coarser.

Sacajawea, hearing of the "large fish," begged to be allowed to go to the beach, seventeen miles distant by the shortest route, or thirty-five miles of easier travel. As the Indian woman had not yet visited the ocean, she was permitted to take the journey. Lewis's entry of January 6 reads:

Captain Clark set out after an early breakfast, with the party in two canoes as had been concerted last evening; Charbono and his Indian woman were also of the party; the Indian woman was very importunate to be permitted to go, and was therefore indulged.[26]

Sacajawea never forgot this experience, and long years afterward in her home on the reservation in Wyoming she used to describe this visit to the sea and the enormous "fish" lying on the sand.

While in winter quarters at Fort Clatsop, Lewis and Clark were visited by many Indians with whom they carried on a limited trade and from whom they received much interesting information. The daily events at this

---

[25] Also Gass, Dec. 26-28, 1805; and Ordway, Jan. 5, 1806.
[26] See also Gass, Jan. 7, 1806.

camp, the site of which Sacajawea was largely instrumental in selecting, judging from Clark's entry of November 24, are pictured in the following extracts from the various diaries. On November 20, Clark wrote:

Found many of the Chin-nooks with Captain Lewis, of whom there was two chiefs, Com-com-mo-ly and Chil-lar-la-wil, to whom we gave medals and to one a flag. One of the Indians had on a robe made of two sea otter skins. The fur of them were more beautiful than any fur I had ever seen. Both Captain Lewis and myself endeavored to purchase the robe with different articles. At length we procured it for a belt of blue beads which the squaw-wife of our interpreter, Shabono, wore around her waist. We gave the squaw a coat of blue cloth for the belt of blue beads we gave for the sea otter skins purchased from an Indian.[27]

On November 30 Clark wrote:

The squaw gave me a piece of bread made of flour she had reserved for her child and kept until this time, which has unfortunately got wet and a little sour. This bread I eat with great satisfaction, it being the only mouthful I had tasted for several months past.

His entry of December 3, 1805, reads:

The squaw broke the two shank bones of the elk after the marrow was taken out, boiled them, and extracted a pint of grease or tallow from them . . . after eating the marrow out of two shank bones of an elk, the squaw chopped the bones fine, boiled them, extracted a pint of grease, which is superior to the tallow of the animal.

Again, on December 25, Clark writes:

I received a present of Captain Lewis of a fleece hosiery, shirt, drawers and socks; a pair of moccasins of Whitehouse; a small Indian basket of Gutherich; two dozen white weazil's tails of the Indian woman; and some black root of the Indians before their departure.

On March 23, 1806, after presenting Chief Coboway

---

[27] See also Gass, Nov. 21; Ordway, Nov. 21; Biddle, Nov. 20. Comcomly was a one-eyed chief who later figured in the story of the Astorians.

with Fort Clatsop and the equipment, Lewis and Clark pushed their boats from the shore and the home journey began.[28] On April sixteenth, Captain Clark, in company with Charbonneau, Sacajawea, and nine men, undertook to trade with the Indians for horses, employing a large part of the remaining stock of merchandise for that purpose. On the route to the Walla Wallas, some difficulty was encountered over the theft of a robe belonging to Captain Clark, but on April 28 Lewis records that they found a Shoshone woman

prisoner among these people by means of whom and Sahcahgarweah we found the means of conversing with the Wallahwallahs. We conversed with them for several hours and fully satisfied all their enquiries with respect to ourselves and the objects of our pursuit. They were much pleased.

Clark, in turn, makes a similar statement.

We found a Sho-sho-ne woman, prisoner among those people by means of whom and Sah-cah-gah-weah, Shabono's wife, we found means of conversing with the Wallahwallars.[29]

On the return journey Sacajawea proved to be of as much value to the expedition as she had been on the journey to the Pacific. Thus, on May 11, 1806, Clark wrote of her services as an interpreter to the Chopunnisk Indians:

The one-eyed chief, Yoom-park-kar-tim, arrived, and we gave him

[28] Lewis and Clark greatly hoped that a vessel would arrive from the United States by way of Cape Horn or from China, but none came while they were on the coast. When they began the return journey, therefore, the explorers posted at the fort a notice telling of their trip, the names of the members of the expedition, and a map of the route they had taken. Subsequently this was given by the natives to a Captain Hill who was in command of a ship that arrived at the mouth of the Columbia. Captain Hill took the document to China, and later brought it to the United States.

[29] See also Ordway, Apr. 28, 1806; Biddle, same date.

a medal of the small size and spoke to the Indians through a Snake boy, Shabono, and his wife. We informed them who we were, where we came from and our intentions towards them, which pleased them very much . . . we drew a map of the country with a coal on the mat in their way, and by the assistance of the Snake boy and our interpreters were enabled to make ourselves understood by them although it had to pass through French, Minnetare, Shoshone, and Chopunnish languages.

In the Biddle edition the same incident is described in a little more detail, as follows, under date of May 11:

It was not without difficulty, nor until after nearly half the day was spent, that we were able to convey all this information to the Chopunnish, much of which might have been lost or distorted in its circuitous route through a variety of languages; for in the first place we spoke in English to one of our men, who translated it into French to Chaboneau; he interpreted it to his wife in the Minnetaree language, and she then put it into Shoshonee, and the young Shoshonee prisoner explained it to the Chopunnish in their own dialect.

At times the expedition found it difficult to secure supplies from the Indians because the merchandise, so necessary for trade, was almost exhausted. When the company left the coast it had on hand for exchange only

six blue robes, one of scarlet, five made out of the old United States flag that had floated over many a council; a few old clothes; Clark's uniform, coat, and hat; and a few little trinkets that might be tied in a handkerchief.

At the Clearwater river the leaders of the expedition had to render medical service to the Indians in order to obtain necessary supplies. Eye water was at a premium, and cures for rheumatism in great demand, and by the relief thus afforded to the suffering Indians, Lewis and Clark won their good will.

Finally, however, the medicine chest was exhausted; brass buttons had departed from the soldiers' uniforms;

needles, thread, fishhooks, files, and awls had been exchanged for food; and now these "made-to-order" doc-
tors had to resort to every device to obtain from the
natives the commonest commodities. In the eyes of the
Indians they were wonderful "medicine men." One can
fancy how mystified the red men were over a watch, with
its even ticking inside the case; the magnet, with its
power to make a piece of steel move without touching
it; phosphorus, invisible in the daytime but ghastly at
night; the spyglass, bringing objects at a distance within
reach of the hand; the burning glass, stealing fire from
heaven; and the air-gun, with its terrifying noise. No
wonder the Indians thought the white men were more
than human beings, and that the exhibition of these
mysteries brought to the party the much-needed food
and supplies. Sacajawea also acquainted the members
of the expedition with the virtues of fennel roots, and
gathered large quantities of this food for use in the passage of the Rocky mountains.[30]

After crossing the Rocky mountains, the expedition

[30] The following entries in the various diaries refer to Sacajawea's industry
in the gathering of these roots. "Our sick men are much better today. Sahcar-
garweah gathered a quantity of the roots of a species of fennel, which we
found very agreeable food. The flavor of this root is not unlike annis seed."
[Lewis, May 16]

"Shabono's squaw gathered a quantity of fennel roots which we find a very
palatable and nourishing food. The onion we also find in abundance and boil
it with our meat." [Clark, May 16]

"Our Indian woman was busy engaged today in laying in a store of fennel
roots for the Rocky Mountains. These are called by the Shoshones *year-pah*."
[Lewis, May 18]

"The squaw wife to Shabono busied herself gathering the roots of the fennel,
called by the Snake Indians *year-pah*, for the purpose of drying to eat on the
Rocky mountains. Those roots are very palatable either fresh, roasted, boiled,
or dried, and are generally between the size of a quill and that of a man's
finger, and about the length of the latter." [Clark, May 18]

On May 25, Gass records that Sacajawea's child, Baptiste, had been very
sick, but was recovering. The Biddle edition records the same fact on May 23.

was divided into four parties to carry out further explorations. These parties were instructed to unite at the
mouth of the Yellowstone. One of these companies, under
command of Captain Clark, included Sacajawea and
Charbonneau. Clark was under instructions to proceed
to the Yellowstone river and descend this river in canoes
to its junction with the Missouri. Here he would await
the arrival of Captain Lewis and the rest of the expedition. Describing this incident on July 3, Clark wrote:

Took my leave of Captain Lewis and his Indians. Set out with nineteen men, interpreter Shabono and his wife and child (as an interpreter and interpretess) for the Crow Indians and the latter for the
Shoshoni with fifty horses.

Three days later Sacajawea pointed out the gap in
the mountains now known as Bozeman pass, and described the surrounding country in some detail to Captain Clark. Clark mentions this in his journal in the
following paragraph:

The Indian woman, wife to Shabono, informed me that she had
been in this plain frequently and knew it well; that the creek which
we descended was a branch of Wisdom river, and when we ascended
the higher part of the plain we would discover a gap in the mountains
in our direction to the canoes; and when we arrived at that gap we
would see a high point of a mountain covered with snow in our direction to the canoes.

Ordway also mentions the incident in an entry of the
same date, and in the Biddle edition under date of July
6 appears the following:

In the afternoon we passed along the hillside north of the creek,
till in the course of six miles we entered an extensive level plain. Here
the tracks of the Indians scattered so much that we could no longer
pursue it, but Sacajaweah recognized the plain immediately. She had
travelled often during her childhood, and informed us that it was

the great resort of the Shoshonees, who came for the purpose of gathering quamash and cows, and of taking beaver, with which the plain abounded. . . Surrounded on all sides by high points of mountains covered with snow, among which was the gap pointed out by the squaw, bearing s. 56 E.

The next day the Biddle narrative mentions the fact that the party was now nearing the spot where a caché had been made the preceding August, and the record of the eighth reads:

We proceeded down the west branch of Jefferson river, and at the distance of nine miles reached its forks, where we had deposited our merchandise in the month of August. . . We found everything safe, though some of the goods were a little damp and one of the canoes had a hole.

On the ninth, Clark records that Sacajawea brought him a plant the root of which was eaten by the Indians.

This root resembled a carrot in form and size and something of its colour, but a paler yellow than that of our carrot.

On July thirteenth, Clark started in the direction of Bozeman pass, taking with him Charbonneau, Sacajawea and her papoose, and his negro servant, York. On that date he wrote:

I observe several leading roads with appear to pass to a gap of the mountain in the E.N.E. direction about 18 or 20 miles distant. The Indian woman, who has been of great service to me as a pilot through this country, recommends a gap in the mountains more south which I shall cross.

On August 3, the company started its descent of the Yellowstone, an event which Clark describes as follows:

I descended in two small canoes lashed together in which I had the following persons: John Shields, George Gibson, William Bratten, W. Labeech, Toust. Shabono, his wife and child, and my man York.

The Rochejhone, or Yellowstone river is large and navigable with but few obstructions quite into the Rocky mountains.

The Biddle edition, under entry of the next day, speaks of the great annoyance caused by the mosquitoes during this stage of the expedition.

Captain Clark therefore determined to go on to some spot which would be free from mosquitoes . . . he proceeded down the river to the second point and encamped on a sandbar; but here the mosquitoes seemed to be even more numerous than above. The face of the Indian child is considerably puffed up and swollen with the bites of these animals, nor could the men procure scarcely any sleep during the night.

On August 9 Clark wrote that Sacajawea brought him a

large and well-flavored gooseberry of a rich crimson colour, and a deep purple berry of the large cherry of the current species and which is common on this river as low as the Mandans, the engagés call it the Indian current.

Captain Lewis, dissatisfied with his previous exploration up the Maria's river, after his separation from Clark took with him Drewyer, the interpreter and hunter, and the two Field brothers, and traveled northeast to what is now Great falls, Montana, and then northwest, trying to find the source of the Maria's river. Here he had an unpleasant encounter with the Blackfeet, the most treacherous of all the Indians. In camp early one morning a Blackfoot stole Field's rifle, whereupon Field stabbed the thief to the heart and recovered his rifle; but in the heat of the struggle the Indians were discovered trying to drive away the horses. Without horses, Lewis and his men would have been helpless, miles from their party and in a strange country, surrounded by hostile Indians. In this emergency it was necessary to act vigorously and immediately. Lewis therefore at once opened fire, killing one of the Indians, and in exchange received a shot which fortunately only passed through his hair. His men then seized the horses of the Indians and fled for the Missouri. The party rode sixty miles without stopping, covering over one hundred twenty miles in twenty-four hours, until they reached the junction of the Maria's and the Missouri rivers. Here Captain Lewis found another detachment of the expedition.

Opening the cachés which they had made here the preceding year, the explorers found much of their buried goods spoiled by water, but fortunately the iron boat was in good condition. Turning the horses loose here on the prairies, the company sailed down the Missouri and met Clark, Charbonneau, Sacajawea, and the rest of the party at the mouth of the Yellowstone. Two days after this reunion, the entire expedition arrived at the Mandan villages where they found that during their absence their fort had been destroyed by fire.[31]

Charbonneau and Sacajawea remained at the Mandan villages when the expedition continued on its way to St. Louis.[32] The parting is described by Clark, Gass,

---

[31] While hunting one day Lewis was mistaken for an elk by a companion, and was shot in the hip. The wound, though not dangerous, incapacitated him for a time, thus throwing upon Clark responsibility for command of the expedition.

[32] The Gass account mentions the fact that John Colter, a member of the expedition, elected to remain with the Indians rather than to return with his companions. Colter has the distinction of being the discoverer of Yellowstone park. Gass also records the fact that "Chief Big-White concluded to go down with us, and we agreed to stay until 12 o'clock to-morrow; that he might have an opportunity to get ready for his voyage and mission. The commanding officers gave discharges to the man [John Colter] who agreed to return with the hunters up the river, and the interpreter, who intends settling among these Indians, and to whom they gave the blacksmith's tools supposing they might be useful to the nation. They also gave a small piece of ordnance to the Grossventres, which they appeared very fond of."

and Biddle. The entries describing this incident from all of these journals are reprinted here because of the significant tribute they pay to Sacajawea and also because of the mention they make of Clark's offer to take Sacajawea's nineteen-months-old boy, Baptiste, to civilization with him. Of this incident Clark wrote as follows:

Settled with Touisant Chabono for his services as an interpreter the price of a horse and lodge purchased of him for public service, in all amounting to five hundred dollars, thirty-three and one third cents . . . we also took our leave of T. Chabono, his Snake Indian wife and their child, who had accompanied us on our route to the Pacific ocean in the capacity of interpreter and interpretess. T. Chabono wished much to accompany us in the said capacity. . . I offered to take his little son, a beautiful, promising child who is nineteen months old, to which they both himself and his wife were willing, provided the child had been weened. They observed that in one year the boy would be sufficiently old to leave his mother, and he would then take him to me if I would be so friendly as to raise the child for him in such a manner as I thought proper, to which I agreed, etc.

The Biddle edition, under date of August 16, contains the following entry:

The principal chiefs of the Minnetarees came down to bid us farewell, as none of them could be prevailed on to go with us. This circumstance induced our interpreter, Chaboneau, with his wife and child, to remain here, as he could be no longer useful; and notwithstanding our offers of taking him with us to the United States, he said that he had there no acquaintance and no chance of making a livelihood, and preferred remaining among the Indians. This man has been very serviceable to us, and his wife particularly useful among the Shoshonees. Indeed, she has borne with a patience truly admirable the fatigues of so long a route incumbered with the charge of an infant, who is even now only nineteen months old. We therefore paid him his wages, amounting to five hundred dollars and thirty-three cents, including the price of a horse and a lodge [a leather tent] purchased of him.

After leaving the Mandan villages, Clark, on August 20, wrote at great length to Charbonneau showing his very deep interest in the interpreter and his family, and expressing an earnest desire to adopt Sacajawea's child, Baptiste. Clark's reference in this letter to "your little son" and "my boy Pomp" are of especial significance. Because of its importance, this letter, already referred to in the preface to this volume, is here reprinted in full. The text of it is as follows:

CHARBONO:

SIR: Your present situation with the Indians gives me some concern – I wish now I had advised you to come on with me to the Illinois where it most probably would be in my power to put you on some way to do something for yourself. . . You have been a long time with me and have conducted yourself in such a manner as to gain my friendship; your woman, who accompanied you that long dangerous and fatiguing route to the Pacific ocean and back, deserved a greater reward for her attention and services on that route than we had in our power to give her at the Mandans. As to your little son (my boy Pomp) you well know my fondness for him and my anxiety to take and raise him as my own child. I once more tell you if you will bring your son Baptiste to me, I will educate him and treat him as my own child – I do not forget the promise which I made to you and shall now repeat them that you may be certain – Charbono, if you wish to live with the white people, and will come to me, I will give you a piece of land and furnish you with horses cows and hogs – If you wish to visit your friends in Montreall, I will let you have a horse, and your family shall be taken care of until your return – if you wish to return as an interpreter for the Menetarras when the troops come up to form the establishment, you will be with me ready and I will procure you the place – or if you wish to return to trade with the Indians and will leave your little son Pomp with me, I will assist you with merchandise for that purpose, and become myself concerned with you in trade on a small scale, that is to say not exceeding a perogue load at one time. If you are disposed to accept either of my offers to you, and will bring down your son, your famn Janey had best come along with you to take care of the boy until I get him – let me advise you to keep your bill of exchange and what furs and pelteries you have in possession, and get as much more as you can, and get as many robes, and big horn and cabbra skins as you can collect in the course of this winter. And take them down to St. Louis as early as possible. Enquire of the governor of that place for a letter which I shall leave with the governor. I shall inform you what you had best do with your furs pelteries and robes, etc. when you get to St. Louis write a letter to me by the post and let me know your situation – If you do not intend to go down either this fall or in the spring, write a letter to me by the first opportunity and inform me what you intend to do that I may know if I may expect you or not. If you ever intend to come down this fall or the next spring will be the best time – this fall would be best if you could get down before the winter. I shall be found either in St. Louis or in Clarksville at the falls of the Ohio.

Wishing you and your family great success, and with anxious expectations of seeing my little dancing boy, Baptiste, I shall remain your friend.

WILLIAM CLARK

Keep this letter and let not more than one or two persons see it, and when you write to me seal your letter. I think you best not determine which of my offers to accept until you see me. Come prepared to accept of either which you may choose after you get down.

Mr. Teousant Charbono, Menetarras Villages [33]

With the departure of the expedition from the Mandan villages and the separation of Lewis and Clark from the interpreter Charbonneau, his wife Sacajawea, and "my boy Pomp," the history of these three comes to an end so far as the journals of Lewis, Clark, Gass, Ordway, and Whitehouse are concerned. Henceforth we must look to other sources for the further story of the Charbonneau family, which the later chapters of this book contain.

[33] Captain Clark's letter to Charbonneau of Aug. 20, 1806, was discovered in the possession of Mrs. Julia Clark Vorhees and Miss Ellen Vorhees. It was published in the *Century Magazine,* October, 1904. It was also published in the Thwaites edition of the Lewis and Clark journals, vol. III, 247.

Charbonneau, the Interpreter

Perhaps the most picturesque and unique figure of the expedition was Toussaint Charboneau, the French-canadian interpreter, whom the explorers found at Fort Mandan. . . It has been rather the fashion of later-day writers and critics to sneer at and decry the old interpreter. No one can read Maximilian without feeling that Charboneau was, after all, a man of fairly commendable traits considering his environments, notwithstanding that he struck his wife, in comparison with whom he was, as Coues states, a minus function.—OLIN D. WHEELER

CHAPTER II
Charbonneau, the Interpreter

In the letter from Clark to Charbonneau, quoted in the last chapter, the American commander proposed that Charbonneau come to St. Louis to live, and promised to aid him in securing land and property. Clark's interest, however, was apparently far stronger in Sacajawea and her son, Baptiste, than in Charbonneau. In the letter he wrote,

As to your little son, my boy Pomp, you well know my fondness for him and my anxiety to take and raise him as my own child. I once more tell you if you will bring your son Baptiste to me I will educate him and treat him as my own child.

The same letter also urges Charbonneau to bring "your famn Janey," or Sacajawea, to St. Louis to take care of the little dancing boy, Baptiste.

In this invitation Clark showed true diplomatic skill. In order to bring Sacajawea and Baptiste to St. Louis it was necessary to win Charbonneau's good will and to avoid arousing his antagonism. This Clark did so successfully that within a few years we find Charbonneau, Sacajawea, and Baptiste living in St. Louis, which was then the great emporium of the fur-trade.[34]

A number of the names used by Captain Clark in his

[34] Captain Clark was always easily singled out when on the expedition by his hair, politely called auburn. St. Louis was therefore known to the Indians as "Red Hair's Town."

letter to Charbonneau require brief interpretation. His expression "my boy Pomp" and "your boy Pomp" apply, of course, to the same child – the infant born to Sacajawea at the Mandan villages. He is also referred to in the letter as "your son Baptiste," and "my little dancing boy Baptiste." Pomp is a name often given to the oldest boy in a Shoshone family, and means "head" or "the leader." It is bestowed upon the oldest son, and thus becomes a title of primogeniture, and the bearer of it is recognized as one having authority.

Two of the landmarks on the expedition were named for this little boy, Sacajawea's son. Both names apparently were given on the same day. One was a small stream flowing into the Yellowstone, called Baptiste creek. The other was the great rock overlooking the Yellowstone, just north of the present site of Billings, Montana. This was designated on Captain Clark's map of 1814 as Pomp's tower, but it is now called Pompey's pillar. On one of the sides of this rock Captain Clark records that he marked his "name and the day of the month and year, Wm. Clark, July 25, 1806."

Prior to the publication of Captain Clark's letter to Charbonneau, Dr. Elliott Coues stated that the Baptiste creek, referred to in the preceding paragraph, was named for Baptiste Lepage who was engaged by Lewis and Clark at the Mandan villages on November 3, 1804, to accompany the expedition. Lepage was a Frenchcanadian and a friend of Charbonneau, but since the discovery of Clark's letter, it is evident that the name was given in honor of Sacajawea's son, Baptiste.[35] The

[35] Olin D. Wheeler also records that Baptiste creek was named for Lepage; but he, too, was apparently unaware of Clark's letter to Charbonneau. See Wheeler, Olin D., *Trail of Lewis and Clark,* vol. I, 133, vol. II, 352.

little dancing boy was evidently exceedingly popular
with the members of the expedition, and as soon as he
could stand alone, with his chubby hands holding fast
to Sacajawea's fingers, he made his tiny moccasined feet
move to the rhythm of the violin; and when he could
balance himself and stand unsupported he danced with
the men about the campfire – danced just as small Indian
children dance today on the Shoshone reservation where
Sacajawea, in her later years, watched her grandchildren dance to the rhythm of modern Indian instruments.

Charbonneau with his two Shoshone wives and his
two sons reached St. Louis in August, 1806. Leaving
his family here, the interpreter accepted an offer to trap
for a fur company on the rivers of the southwest – perhaps branches of the Red or Arkansas – in territory
inhabited by various Indian tribes including especially
that branch of the Shoshones known as the Comanches.[36] Four years later we find Charbonneau once more
in St. Louis. Here, on October 30, 1810, he purchased
from Captain Clark, who was then Indian agent for the
Louisiana territory, a tract of land on the Missouri river
in Saint Ferdinand township. Within a few months,
however, Charbonneau disposed of this land to Captain
Clark for the sum of one hundred dollars. The transaction is recorded in the records of the court for March
26, 1811. "This instrument," writes Miss Drumm, "in-
dicates that Charbonneau bought this land with a view

---

[36] The Siouan stock is divided into several branches, among which are the
Mandan, Gros Ventres or Minnetaree or Hidatsa, the Kaw or Kansa, Osage,
Comanche (Shoshonean family). All of these tribes are associated with the
history of Charbonneau and the members of his family, the wanderings of
which extended over the present states of Idaho, Montana, Oregon, Wash-
ington, North and South Dakota, Nebraska, Missouri, Kansas, Louisiana,
Oklahoma, Texas, New Mexico, Arizona, California and Wyoming. Coues,
Elliott, *op. cit.*, vol. I, 98; Chittenden, *The American fur-trade*, vol. II, 872.

to settling down to civilized life but, becoming weary of it, transferred his property to Clark and returned to the Mandans."

An entry in the Auguste Chouteau manuscript to the effect that Charbonneau on March 20 purchased from Chouteau fifty pounds of biscuit or hard tack, doubtless to be used on an expedition into the wilderness, evidently confirms Miss Drumm's conclusion that Charbonneau was leaving St. Louis for an extended period. From other sources we learn that in April, 1811, Charbonneau entered the service of Henry M. Brackenridge, the explorer, on his expedition up the Missouri. Brackenridge sailed from St. Louis on April 2, taking with him Charbonneau and one of the latter's wives known as the "Otter Woman." This woman, a Shoshone, was somewhat older than Sacajawea, with whom she was on friendly terms, and was the mother of one of Charbonneau's other sons, Toussaint, a lad a few years older than his half-brother, Baptiste. Toussaint in later years was also frequently called "Tessou."

When Charbonneau started on the expedition with Brackenridge, he left Sacajawea, Baptiste, and Toussaint in the care of Captain Clark at St. Louis. Captain Clark acted as guardian for the two boys, though not in a legal capacity. The entry in Brackenridge's journal, which speaks of the departure of the expedition, reads as follows:

We have on board a Frenchman named Charbonet, with his wife, an Indian woman of the Snake nation, both of whom accompanied Lewis and Clark to the Pacific, and were of great service. The woman, a good creature, of a mild and gentle disposition, was greatly attached to the whites, whose manners and airs she tries to imitate; but she had become sickly and longed to revisit her native country; her hus-

PRINCE PAUL'S APPLICATION TO GENERAL WILLIAM CLARK

Facsimile of letter to General William Clark requesting passport to ascend the Missouri river, May 5, 1823.

band also, who had spend many years amongst the Indians, was become weary of civilized life.[37]

In this account Brackenridge seems to identify the woman who accompanied his expedition with Sacajawea, but investigation shows this to be incorrect. Charbonneau at this time had at least three wives; two Shoshone and one Mandan, and the woman mentioned by Brackenridge was not Sacajawea but his other Shoshone wife, the mother of Toussaint. Baptiste was still too young to be left in St. Louis without his mother's care, since he was only six years old, and Sacajawea remained to care for her son and also to have oversight of the other boy, Toussaint. Further confirmation of this fact will be found in a later chapter.

It is desirable here to trace briefly the career of Charbonneau from this time on until his death.[38] As already stated in an earlier chapter, Charbonneau was born in Canada, of French parentage, about the year 1758. In 1793 he is first mentioned as an engagé of the Northwest Fur company, serving as a trader at Pine fort on the Assiniboine. Two years later he moved into the Missouri valley, where he became established among the Minnetaree or Gros Ventres on the Knife river at their central village, Mentaharter.

In 1796 Charbonneau went to live in the Mandan villages, where he was the only white man in the territory. Since at that time there were no trade relations with St. Louis, he was obliged to purchase his supplies from

37 Brackenridge, Henry M., "Journal of voyage up the River Missouri," in Thwaites, *Early western travels,* vol. VI. See also the W. M. Boggs manuscript, in *Colorado Magazine,* vol. VII, 67.

38 Scarcely any two writers spell Charbonneau's name the same. The following variations appear in the various journals: Chaboneau, Chabonneau, Chabono, Charbonneau, Charboneuau, Chaubonie, Charbonet, Sharbono, Sharbonot, Charbono, Shabounar.

the English traders further north. Some time prior to the Lewis and Clark expedition, he entered the employ of the American Fur company, and in 1803 and 1804 had charge of Fort Pembina with Alexander Henry. In addition to serving as guide for Lewis and Clark, he also served with Major S. H. Long and with various later expeditions to the Rocky mountains.

In many respects, Charbonneau's character apparently left something to be desired. In sudden emergency or danger he was likely to prove himself an arrant coward, as was evidenced by his conduct in the sudden flood which nearly swept Captain Clark and his party to destruction. He also at times shamefully abused his wife, Sacajawea, his conduct eventually forcing her to leave him; and at times his trustworthiness seems to have been seriously open to question. Shortly before the departure of Lewis and Clark from the Mandan villages in the spring of 1805, for example, Charbonneau apparently sought to break his engagement with the explorers to enter the service of the Northwest company. This would have left the American expedition without an interpreter, and would have deprived it also of the services of Sacajawea. Clark wrote on March 12, 1805:

Charbonneau sent a Frenchman to our party [to say] that he was sorry for the foolish part he had acted and if we pleased he would accompany us agreeably to the terms we had proposed and do everything we wished him to do, etc., etc. . . . He agreed to our terms and we agreed he might go on with us.

Larocque of the Northwest company, on the other hand, defends Charbonneau in this transaction. In his journal of 1804 and 1805 he wrote:

Spoke to Charbonneau about helping as interpreter in the trade to the

Big-Bellies,[39] he told me that, being engaged to the Americans, he could not come without leave from Captain Lewis, and desired me to speak to him, which I did, with the result that Lewis gave consent.[40]

As we have already seen, when Lewis and Clark returned to the Mandans from their expedition to the Pacific, they left Charbonneau and Sacajawea with these Indians while they continued their journey to St. Louis. As already stated in Clark's letter, quoted in the previous chapter, for his nineteen months of service to the expedition, Charbonneau received the sum of five hundred dollars and thirty-three cents, including the price of a horse and a lodge, or leather tent, purchased from him. The value of the service that he rendered the explorers has been the subject of some dispute. Both Lewis and Clark, it is true, commend him as a useful servant, and Clark afterward offered to aid him if he wished to return to civilization; but this offer, as we have seen, may have been inspired in part by Clark's affection for the little boy, Baptiste.[41]

Apparently Charbonneau discharged his duties as interpreter in good faith, though his knowledge of the Indian languages was probably not as adequate as he pretended. Among Charbonneau's most caustic critics is Dr. Elliott Coues, who makes numerous references to the unfortunate interpreter's clumsiness and boorish manners. Says Coues:

In the light of the narrative he appears to have been a poor specimen,

[39] Gros Ventres.

[40] Wheeler, *ibid.*, 132.

[41] At least on two occasions, as we have seen, Charbonneau appears in a much less favorable light during the expedition than his wife, Sacajawea. The first of these was when the boat upset on the Missouri and only Sacajawea's presence of mind and coolness saved the papers and other articles of such great value. The second was the occasion when Clark had to save Sacajawea and her child from being swept away by the sudden cloud-burst.

consisting chiefly of a tongue to wag in a mouth to fill: and had he possessed the comprehensive saintliness of his baptismal name he would have been a minus function in comparison with his wife, Sacajawea, who contributed a full man's share to the success of the expedition besides taking care of her baby.

Dr. Coues also speaks scathingly of Charbonneau's attempt to desert the expedition just before its start from the Mandan towns, saying: "It is a wonder he was not frozen out of the garrison."

Coues writes further of Charbonneau and Sacajawea:

It could have hardly occurred to any one in 1806, that Charbonneau's wife earned her wages too. What Charbonneau's services were, except on rare occasions when his wife interpreted to him, does not appear in the history to naked eyes. This individual remained among the Indians for many years. He was found by Maximilian in 1832-34; and he 'candidly confessed' to the Prince of Wied that after a residence of thirty-seven years among the Minnetarees, he 'could never learn to pronounce their language correctly.' He must therefore have been a fool as well as the coward and wife-beater that we know he was. But his linguistic accomplishments were equal to abuse of Sacajawea in more than one dialect, and interpreters received good pay in those days.

Among his contemporaries, Charbonneau also had critics almost as sarcastic as Dr. Coues. Luttig, in his journal, spoke in derision of him, accusing him of exaggeration and cowardice, and saying that he gave wild accounts of the dangers from the Indians to excite fear among the engagés.[42]

Again, when in 1834 James Kipp of the Columbia Fur company took Charbonneau into his service,

[42] With Charbonneau at the time of the trip with Brackenridge was also Jesseaume, interpreter for Lewis and Clark during the winter at the Mandan villages. Luttig's comment is that both Charbonneau and Jesseaume "ought to be hung;" and Alexander Henry characterized Jesseaume as "that old sneaking cheat whose character is more despicable than the worst among the natives."

William Laidlaw, also of the Columbia company and in charge of Fort Pierre, wrote his disapproval, saying:

I am much surprised at your taking Charbonneau into favor, after showing so much ingratitude upon all occasions. The knave, what does he say for himself?

Evidently, judging from these quotations, the old interpreter's reputation was not unblemished, and certainly Sacajawea's fondness for the white captains was due in part to the kindness and protection they gave her from this "loutish, brutal fellow." [43] Despite all these limitations, however, Charbonneau on the whole apparently discharged his duties as interpreter faithfully enough. But his knowledge of the Indian tongue was not nearly so great as he pretended, and as a consequence he made at times some serious blunders. One of the most unfortunate of these was in causing the wrong interpretation to be given to the name Sacajawea, which in reality means the "Canoe Launcher" instead of the "Bird Woman." The error apparently arose in the following manner: when interrogated as to the meaning of the name of his Indian woman, Charbonneau attempted in his clumsy and self-important way to explain its meaning by Indian signs, which were understood to refer to the flight of a bird. He made signs of flying by motions of his hands and arms, working them at the level of his shoulders, which thus given were naturally interpreted as "Bird Woman." The proper signs for the Shoshone name, Sacajawea, however, should have been made with the arms and hands near the waist line to indicate the motion of one who propels a canoe or boat—thus giving

---

[43] In 1926 in a personal interview with the author on the Shoshone reservation, Mr. F. G. Burnett spoke at some length of the kindness and protection Lewis and Clark had afforded Sacajawea, and said that the latter had many times commented on the thoughtfulness of the explorers toward her.

to the word its true meaning, the "Boat or Canoe Launcher." [44]

During his thirty-seven years among the Mandans, Charbonneau himself acquired various names. These included "The Chief of the Little Village," "The Man who possesses many Gourds," "The Great Horse Came from Afar," "The Bear of the Forest."

In addition to the frequent mention he received in the various journals of the Lewis and Clark expedition, Charbonneau's name appears frequently in the writings of other explorers and travelers. Among these are Henry

[44] During the past thirty years the author has made extensive researches as to the meaning of the name Sacajawea, and feels that the above translation, "boat woman," is correct. "Bird Woman," the other translation, was never a name. It was a sub-title given to Sacajawea at one time to identify her as the Indian woman taken captive by the Crows or "Bird people," and possessed and owned by this tribe. It was solely a means of tribal identification, and not a translation of the name Sacajawea. See Hodge, F. W., *Handbook of the American Indians north of Mexico*, vol. II, 367. In this decision Mrs. Laura Tolman (Mrs. J. W.) Scott and Prof. John E. Rees, who have made equally extensive researches, concur.

Mrs. Laura Tolman Scott, a trained and enthusiastic student, has lived in the Beaverhead valley for half a century. She is recognized as the authority on the detailed movements of the Lewis and Clark expedition from Three forks, Montana, to the Lemhi valley west of the Rocky mountains in Idaho. She has cooperated with both Professor Rees and the author on this problem, and has been consulted from time to time by most of the writers on the history of this region.

Prof. John E. Rees is probably one of the best-trained students in Indian nomenclature. As a trader for seventeen years among the Shoshones, he has studied the Indian languages of the northwest and has become thoroughly proficient therein. For more than forty years he has dwelt among various tribes, and was a co-research worker with Dr. Elliott Coues in the Beaverhead and Lemhi valleys where the Shoshone, Snake, or Lemhi Indians made their home at the period of the Lewis and Clark expedition.

Many other authors and students, as well as Indian agents, missionaries, and government translators and interpreters concur in this translation. The Rev. John Roberts, O. D. Wheeler, the Rev. James I. Patten, F. G. Burnett, Dr. James Irwin, H. E. Wadsworth, and Dr. Elliott Coues spell the name Sacajawea, meaning "boat-pusher," "boat woman," "canoe-puller." It is always pronounced by these research workers as "Sac-a-jár-we-a."

Brackenridge and John Bradbury in 1811; John Luttig in 1812; Prince Paul of Würtemberg in 1823; General Henry Atkinson, 1825; General Stephen W. Kearny, also in 1825; Maximilian, Prince of Wied, 1833; Charles Larpenteur, 1838; and "every fur-trader and trapper of the early days in the upper Missouri regions." From these references, it is possible to reconstruct with some degree of accuracy the outline of Chabonneau's career after he left St. Louis in 1811.

As we have seen, Charbonneau accompanied Henry Brackenridge on his expedition up the Missouri in 1811. In July, 1816, he was engaged by Julius DeMun for Auguste P. Chouteau and company, to go from St. Louis on a trading voyage up and down the Arkansas and Platte rivers. The engagement was for one year. Three years later his name appears on the pay-roll of Captain Clark, the superintendent of Indian affairs, for "salary as interpreter, $200, from July 17–December 31, 1819."

General Henry Atkinson in 1825 makes several references to Charbonneau, one of which was to the effect that at the time "Shabono" with his wife and her brother were at the Mandan villages. Major Stephen Kearny, in his journal of August 11, 1825, mentions Charbonneau creek, named for "a Frenchman who accompanied Lewis and Clark across the mountains," and whom he saw living at the Mandans, plying his trade as a trader among these Indians.

On the records of the United States agent, John F. A. Sanford, on the upper Missouri, is to be found under date of February 29, 1828, a notation of wages paid to "Tassant Charboneau," interpreter for the Mandan and Gros Ventre Indians. In the books of the Mandan sub-agency, covering a period of six years, it is recorded that payments were made to Toussaint Charbonneau, interpreter, which equalled the sum of $2,437.32 from November 30, 1828, to September 30, 1834. Charbonneau served at this fort as interpreter between the agents and the Mandans, Gros Ventre, Minnetaree and Crow Indians.

The letter-books at Fort Clark, under date of May 30, 1830, contain the accounts of purchases made in the name of "His Royal Highness," Prince Paul of Würtemberg. These include goods to be delivered to James Kipp, who in turn "is to send the purchase to Charbonneau at the Gros Ventres village." On May 5 the same royal explorer bought additional goods, including powder and tobacco for Charbonneau. Two weeks later he visited Fort Union, where he made further purchases which were to be given to the "interpreter, Charbonneau." [45]

In 1833 Kipp, while among the Mandans, carried on a conversation "by the help of the old interpreter, Charbonneau, who had lived thirty-seven years in the villages of the Mandans." [46] This item and date establish rather definitely the length of Charbonneau's residence among the Mandans. And the fact that even after this long period he could not "correctly pronounce" Indian names, may help to explain in part why the orthography and pronunciation of the word "Sacajawea," which he attempted to give to Lewis and Clark, appeared with

[45] We are informed by Captain R. Holmes, of the u.s. army, who met "old Charbonneau" in 1830 at a gathering of white men in the mountains, that the interpreter never carried arms, but used only his knife for a weapon.

[46] James Kipp, a Canadian, located on the upper Missouri in 1818 and became an agent for the Columbia Fur company. Later he entered the service of the American Fur company, and for many years was chief factor at Fort Clark. In 1845 he was placed in charge of Fort Union. See Thwaites, *op. cit.*, vol. XXII, also *Travels of Maximilian*, vol. I, 345.

CLARK REQUESTS A PASSPORT FOR PRINCE PAUL

Communication from General William Clark, superintendent of Indian affairs at St. Louis, to Honorable John H. Eaton, secretary of war, December 23, 1829, requesting a passport to permit Prince Paul of Würtemberg to go up the Missouri to the sub-agency of Mr. Sanford and from there extend his journey to the Columbia river.

many variations in the journals of the expedition. Maximilian, Prince of Wied, also spoke of the inability of Charbonneau to pronounce Mandan words correctly.

He generally lives at Awatichai, the second village of the Manitaries, and excepting some journeys, has always remained at this spot; hence, he is well acquainted with the Manitaries and their language, though as he candidly confessed he could never learn to pronounce it.

In 1833 the famous royal traveler, above referred to, secured from the American Fur company the privilege of passing the winter at Fort Clark, where he built for himself a small house within the stockade and later engaged the services of Toussaint Charbonneau, "former interpreter of Lewis and Clark."

In April, 1833, Prince Maximilian received from Captain William Clark, then superintendent of Indian affairs at St. Louis, a passport to travel up the Missouri to the Indian territory. With Maximilian, when he reached the Mandans, was "old Charbonneau," whom he frequently mentions from this time on in his journal.

In June, 1833, a short time after the arrival of the party at the Mandans, when the Indians tried to force him to trade his compass for a horse, Maximilian wrote:

It was only by the assistance of old Charbonneau that I escaped a disagreeable and, perhaps, violent scene.

Again, on this same day, he says:

Charbonneau acted as interpreter in the Manitari language.[47]

47 Other references to Charbonneau in the prince's journal are as follows: "The Missouri is joined by the Knife river, on which the three villages of the Manitaries are built. The largest is called Elah-Sa, the middle one Awatichey where Charbonneau, the interpreter, lives." "Received from Charbonneau many particulars respecting these villages in which he has lived for thirty-seven years."

In November, when Maximilian returned from a trip into the north, he wrote: "Back to the center of the territory of the Manitaries from up the

Charbonneau told Maximilian many of the incidents
which had occurred during his thirty-seven years of
residence in the Minnetaree and Mandan villages. He
stated that he had reached the Mandans, who at one
time dwelt near the Heart river "at the end of the last
century," at a time when the Indians used the shoulder-
blade of a buffalo for plowing, and flint for arrowheads.
He said also that the "father's brother is called father
and the mother's sister, mother; and that cousins were
called brothers and sisters." [48]

Prince Maximilian speaks, for the most part, in favorable terms of Charbonneau, saying that he was in-
debted to the old French-canadian for many valuable
accounts concerning the manners, morals, and habits
of the different Indian tribes with which the interpreter
was acquainted. On the other hand, speaking of a document or treaty which was shown him, he said:

This document was written on long paper in English and Manitari
language. Most of the Indian names, which were doubtless given by
Charbonneau, were incorrectly written.

In October, 1834, old Charbonneau, then well advanced in years, went with one of his squaws in quest of
a runaway wife. The incident is recorded in Chardon's

Missouri. We recognized old Charbonneau and landed at once." Sublette and
Campbell, the fur-traders, had recently started a trading-post in the Manitari
villages. Here Charbonneau, who had recently "quitted" the American Fur
company, was engaged by the Indian agent as interpreter. During this visit
Charbonneau took Maximilian to look for a petrified trunk of a tree which
the interpreter had discovered. Maximilian also frequently mentions that
Charbonneau took him to see Indian scalp and buffalo dances.

[48] This is often found as a custom among the Indians, and has a bearing
on the history of Sacajawea, as will appear, in connection with her being
known as "Bazil's mother" on the Shoshone reservation. Bazil was, in reality,
the small nephew whom Sacajawea had adopted when she found her people
on the Lewis and Clark expedition.

"Fort Clark Journal" under date of October 22, as follows:

Charboneau and his lady started for the Gros Ventres on a visit (or to tell the truth) in quest of one of his runaway wives – for I must inform you he had two lively ones. Poor old man.[49]

Another entry of September 10, 1837, reads:

Charbonneau arrived last night from the Gros Ventres – all well in that quarter, the disease [a steamer had recently arrived with small-pox aboard] had not yet broke out among them, except his squaw, who died four days ago.

On October 27, 1838, when four score years of age, Charbonneau made his last venture into matrimony. Chardon records:

Old Charbonneau, an old man of 80, took to himself a young wife, a young Assinneboine of 14, a prisoner that was taken in the fight of this summer, and bought by me of the Rees, the young men of the Fort, and two Rees, gave to the old man a splendid Charivaree the drums, pans, kittles, etc., beating; guns fireing, etc. the old gentlemen gave a feast to the men, and a glass of grog. The two Indians who had never seen the like before, were under the apprehension that we were for killing of them, and sneaked off.[50]

[49] In the letter from Fort Clark, dated June 10, 1836, David D. Mitchell wrote Major W. N. Fulkerson, Indian agent for the Mandans, giving an account of the murder by a Sioux of William E. Premeau, who was taking several loads of merchandise to the Mandan and Assiniboine Indians. In the description of the fight, Mitchell relates the danger through which Charbonneau passed when "after telling their melancholy tale, one of the young Sioux deliberately fired at a Gros Ventre boy in the interpreter's room. Old Charbona made a narrow escape, two balls having passed through his hat."

[50] Chardon, Francis A., "Fort Clark Journal." Chardon lived for many years among the Osage Indians, and later entered the American Fur company's employ.

The first night after the marriage, according to Chardon, Charbonneau offered to place his bride at the disposal of the camp. See F. G. Burnett's letter in Appendix B, which suggests that the beating of Sacajawea referred to in Chapter II and the consequent reprimand of Charbonneau by Clark was caused by a similar proposal. A Shoshone woman would not have submitted to such a disgrace. See Lewis and Clark *Journal* under date of Aug. 14, 1805.

In most accounts the story of Toussaint Charbonneau ends about this time. But in the spring of 1838 Charles Larpenteur and his party of fur-traders met Charbonneau on the Missouri and were greatly rejoiced to learn through him that they were then only seventy miles from Fort Clark. Charbonneau further told Larpenteur that he had been forty years among the Missouri Indians and that when he came the river was so small that he could straddle it. Larpenteur's statement that Charbonneau at this time was wearing pants and a red flannel shirt would indicate that the old man had never wholly adopted Indian garb.[51]

A more recent historical research, moreover, has brought to light one further reference to Charbonneau.[52] In August, 1839, the old man appeared at the office of the superintendent of Indian affairs in St. Louis, having made the journey from the Mandan villages, a distance of 1600 miles. Here the old interpreter, penniless and laboring under the infirmities of eighty winters, asked for the payment of salary due him for services long since rendered and as long since forgotten. "This man," states Joshua Pilcher, who was then superintendent, "has been a faithful servant to the government, though in a humble capacity. . . For the last fifteen years he has been employed as the government interpreter at the Mandan." Whatsoever sum was due Charbonneau was paid him on August 26, 1839. This is the last official reference to Toussaint Charbonneau, interpreter for the Lewis and Clark expedition.

The exact date of the death of Charbonneau has not been ascertained, and even his burial place is unknown.[53]

---

[51] Larpenteur, Charles, *Forty years a fur-trader,* ed. Elliott Coues, 141.

[52] Luttig, John C., *Journal of a fur-trading expedition,* ed. Drumm, 139.

[53] Andrew Bazil, son of Sacajawea's adopted son, Bazil, stated that Char-

Vague rumors still persist among the Shoshone Indians of the Wind river reservation, that Charbonneau married a Ute woman and eventually died and was buried among the Ute Indians in Utah. But there are no Charbonneaus on the Ute reservation, and no one can be found there who claims relationship with the old interpreter.[54]

bonneau was buried somewhere on the Shoshone reservation, but where he did not know.

[54] Careful investigation both at the Fort Hall school and reservation and at the Uintah and Ouray agencies in Utah, and interrogation of those who might have information on the subject have failed to disclose any descendants of Charbonneau among the Utah Indians. A faint possibility, however, still remains that a family of Shavanaughs in Utah, who scorn the idea that there is any white blood in them, and claim that they have also "always been full-blooded Indian as far as memory runneth" may be the offspring of the old interpreter.

Toussaint and Baptiste

No man, even the most polished and civilized, who has once savored the sweet liberty of the plains and mountains, ever went back to the monotony of the settlements without regrets and everlasting determination to return.—STANLEY VESTAL

CHAPTER III

Toussaint and Baptiste

In the preceding chapter, mention was made of the fact that in April, 1811, Henry M. Brackenridge ascended the Missouri river, taking with him Charbonneau and one of the latter's Indian wives. At that time at the headquarters of the great fur-trader, Manuel Lisa, on the upper Missouri, John C. Luttig was acting in the capacity of clerk, having come into the employ of the Missouri Fur company three years before.[55] On December 20, 1812, Luttig made the following entry in his journal:

> This evening the wife of Charbonneau, a Snake squaw, died of a putrid fever. She was the best woman in the fort, aged about twenty-five years. She left a fine infant child.[56]

This child, named Lizette, was born in August, and was thus about four months old at the time of her mother's death. It is evident, moreover, that this Indian mother was the "Otter Woman," referred to by Brackenridge, and that she had only the one child with her at the time of her death. Had it been otherwise the fact would certainly have been noted in Luttig's journal.

A number of Indian tribes were then hostile to American traders, and, as a consequence, Charbonneau left his

---

[55] Chittenden, H. M., *The American fur-trade of the far west,* 3 vols.

[56] Luttig, John C., *Journal,* ed. Drumm. This wife has been designated by Dr. Charles A. Eastman as the "Otter Woman," a name generally used by authors writing of the death of one of Charbonneau's wives.

motherless child with some of the Indian women at Lisa's headquarters when he accompanied the expeditions of the fur-traders.[57] From one of these expeditions Charbonneau failed to return to the Mandan country and Luttig, therefore, supposing that he was dead, took Charbonneau's baby, Lizette, to St. Louis in the fall of 1813 to have a guardian appointed for her. Her brother, Toussaint, as we have already seen in a preceding chapter, was then already in St. Louis. When Luttig reached St. Louis, Clark was temporarily absent from the city. As a consequence, the court named Luttig temporary guardian of the two children, but when Clark returned to St. Louis, he relieved Luttig of this responsibility. The court record reads as follows:

The court appoints John A. Luttig [this name is crossed out and that of William Clark substituted] guardian to the infant children of Tousant Charbonneau deceased, to wit: Tousant Charbonneau, a boy about the age of ten years; and Lizette Charbonneau, a girl about one year old. The said infant children not being possessed of any property within the knowledge of the court, the said guardian is not required to give bond.[58]

At this time Sacajawea and her son Baptiste were also in St. Louis living under Clark's protection. Clark, however, did not assume the legal guardianship of Baptiste because the boy was still living with his mother and a guardianship was hence unnecessary. Sacajawea, indeed, had never left or abandoned her son to the care of anyone since his birth in the Mandan country eight and one half years before. It is also certain that Sacaja-

---

[57] These tribes include the Arikaras, Cheyennes, Gros Ventre, Crows, and Arapahos. "The British Northwest company, having a number of trading houses within a short distance of the Missouri, are enabled to embroil our people with the savages who are constantly urged to cut them off." Missouri Gazette, June 5, 1813.

[58] Luttig, op. cit., 133.

wea had not returned with Charbonneau to the Mandans in 1811. This conclusion is amply confirmed by the report of Dr. Charles A. Eastman to the office of Indian affairs in 1925:

The court record shows that Baptiste, the child of Sacajawea, was conspicuously absent. This means that Baptiste had been retained in St. Louis when Charbonneau and his other Snake wife had gone back to the Indian country as stated by Brackenridge. Baptiste was too young to be separated from his mother, and my knowledge of the Indian mother's traits and habits is such that she could not have permitted to be separated from her child at that age, especially those times. It would have been impossible for Clark to retain Baptiste without his mother, but as he determined either to adopt or educate the boy, the youngest member of the expedition across the continent, he had to provide for the Bird Woman in order to keep Baptiste in St. Louis so that he may see to his education. As he could not trust Tousant Charbonneau to take the child back up the Missouri, therefore he retains him, and that is why Baptiste was not mentioned in the Orphans Court when Luttig applied for guardian.

And again:

The evidence given by Wolfe, Chief of the Hidatsa, and Mrs. Weidemann shows that Charbonneau did have two Shoshone wives and a Mandan wife besides. They clearly stated that Charbonneau took both of his Shoshone wives with him when he visited St. Louis some time in 1807 to 1808, and it is evident that he had returned with but one Shoshone wife, who died on December 20, 1812.[59]

It is thus evident that, in 1811, Sacajawea and Baptiste were living in St. Louis under the protection of Captain Clark, and that Baptiste's half-brother and sister, Toussaint and Lizette, for whom Captain Clark was acting as legal guardian, were in 1813 also living in the same city.

In the fulfillment of his promise to Charbonneau, Clark assumed responsibility for the education of Bap-

---

[59] Dr. Charles A. Eastman's report to the department of Indian affairs, Washington, D.C., 1925.

tiste, and apparently undertook the same responsibility for his ward, Toussaint. Various entries in Clark's abstract of expenditures when serving as superintendent of Indian affairs throw significant light upon the education of these two boys.[60] One account stood in the name of Reverend J. E. Welch, a Baptist minister who boarded and taught Indian and half-breed boys. He was paid for tutoring J. B. [Jean Baptiste] Charbonneau. Another account for expenses incurred for Toussaint Charbonneau was paid to Reverend Francis Neil, a Catholic priest, who conducted a boys' school in St. Louis, which later became the present St. Louis university. Both of these accounts were made out to Captain Clark, and in them Baptiste and Toussaint were spoken of as "half-Indian boys."

From July 1 to December 31, 1819, Charbonneau senior, the father of the boys, received $200 as compensation for serving as interpreter for Captain Clark. On January 22, 1820, Mr. Welch was paid an additional sum for "two quarters tuition for J. B. Charbonneau, a half-Indian boy, and for fire-wood and ink for the same individual." On March 31, an additional sum was paid for three months' boarding, lodging, and washing, to L. T. Honore for "J. B. Charbonneau;" again on April 1, a payment was made to J. and G. H. Kennerly for school supplies and clothing for "Charbonneau, a half-Indian."

Among other items appearing in this "Abstract of Expenditures" for Charbonneau are shoes, books, writing paper and quills, Scott's *Lessons,* a dictionary, a hat, one ciphering book, a Roman history, a slate and pencils, and the sum of 62 cents in cash. On April eleventh of

---

[60] American State Papers, St. Louis, 1820, 29. See Appendix A.

the same year [1820], Mr. Welch was again paid certain sums for tuition, and for fuel and ink for "J. B. Charboneau, half-Indian boy." The teaching of these "half-Indian boys" was carried on in French, the language of their father and the language then taught in the schools of St. Louis.

In this official record of expenses the entries all appear as having been paid to "T. Charboneau," or "Charboneau." Charbonneau in turn paid his sons' teachers. Since these various items for tuition, board, and lodging are all for "half-Indian boys," it is ridiculous to suppose that they represent sums paid for the education of old Charbonneau himself as some have unthinkingly suggested. Charbonneau not only gloried in the fact that he was a full-blooded white man, but at the time was over sixty years of age. It would be preposterous to suppose that he attended school at Captain Clark's expense and was there listed as a "half-Indian boy."

Further confirmation of the fact that both Toussaint and Baptiste were educated in St. Louis by Captain Clark is derived from a more recent source. In 1902, Mrs. Eva Emery Dye had a personal interview in St. Louis with Captain William Clark Kennerly, a nephew by marriage of Captain Clark. Captain Kennerly stated in this interview that he knew Charbonneau's boy, Baptiste, when the boy was in school in St. Louis.[61]

In December, 1906, and the two months following, the author of this volume received a series of letters,

---

[61] Kennerly was with Jefferson Kennerly Clark, youngest son of Clark, in 1843, at Fort Laramie. They accompanied Sir William Drummond Stewart on a hunting trip for buffalo and other game. At the fort were many lodges of Sioux Indians, and the warriors hailed young Jefferson with delight as "Red Hair" on account of his resemblance to his father, the color of their hair being identical and of a striking hue.

mentioned elsewhere, written by Captain Kennerly from his home in St. Louis, in which he affirmed that he had known Sacajawea and Charbonneau in St. Louis and had seen them frequently in that city. He added that he had also known their child, Baptiste, who was then being educated by Captain Clark. Later he met Baptiste at Fort Laramie in 1843, when the Indian was acting as guide and hunter for overland expeditions, and at the time was serving as "a cart driver" for Sir William Drummond Stewart.[62]

In the Boggs manuscript, which describes men and conditions at Fort Bent, mention is made both of Baptiste Charbonneau and of Toussaint, who was at Fort Bent in 1844-45. Boggs wrote:

Another half-breed at the Fort was "Tessou." His father was French and his mother an Indian, but the writer was not informed of what tribe. "Tessou" was in some way related to Charbenau. Both of them were very high strung, but Tessou was quick and passionate. He fired a rifle across the court of the Fort at the head of a large negro blacksmith, only missing his skull about a quarter of an inch, because the negro had been in a party that chivaried Tessou the evening before, and being a dangerous man, Captain Vrain gave him an outfit and sent him away from the Fort.[63]

With this entry, the brief history of Toussaint Charbonneau comes to a close. So far at least, no later record of him has been found.

[62] Certain other sources, which do not refer to Baptiste, make some mention of Toussaint Charbonneau. Thus, in the *American State Papers,* an item for twelve dollars appears under date of May 17, 1820, for a quarter tuition for Toussaint Charbonneau, "a half-Indian," the sum being the amount due Father Neil for instructing the half-Indian boy. This sum was paid by Captain Clark, U.S. agent of Indian affairs.

[63] Manuscript prepared by W. M. Boggs at the request of Harry L. Lubers, Denver, and presented to the state historical society of Colorado. Published and edited by LeRoy R. Hafen, historian and curator of the department of history in the *Colorado Magazine,* March, 1930, vol. VII, no. 2, 66-67.

The story of Baptiste, however, contains still further material of varied and peculiar interest. It is with this story that the remainder of this chapter is concerned. A number of authors writing of the early history of the fur-trade and the fur-traders of the far west make frequent references to Charbonneau, whom they usually speak of as "a half-breed." Some of them refer to his residence and education in Europe, and to the fact that he was familiar with several languages, including English, Shoshone, German, French, and Spanish. That "this classically" educated Indian boy was Jean Baptiste Charbonneau, the first child of Sacajawea, there is now no shadow of a doubt. The documentary evidence of Baptiste's travels abroad with a member of the royal family of Germany, however, remained unknown in many of its essential historical facts until very recently, and is here published for the first time.

Among the interesting personages who came to the United States to travel through the far west in the days of the fur-traders, was Prince Paul of Würtemberg. A brief summary of the prince's experiences and early travels in the west is given in the following account from Chittenden.

In 1823 an individual referred to in the Chouteau correspondence as Prince Paul of Würtemberg, went up the river and passed the winter. He returned to New Orleans in the summer of 1824. In 1829 he again went up and was found among the Mandans April 22, 1830, by Joshua Pilcher, who was then returning from his tour of the Hudson's Bay company posts. The purpose of his journey, as stated in the correspondence, was the pursuit of knowledge. He left Fort Tecumseh in August, 1830, and was in St. Louis in October of that year. In reference to this last visit, a local paper, under date of January 29, 1830, had the following: "Paul William of Würtemberg, nephew of the king of England, arrived at New Orleans the 1st inst., from

Europe. About six years ago he spent some time exploring the upper regions of the Missouri, but business requiring his return to Europe, he has revisited the American hemisphere and will, in the prosecution of his former plan, cross the Rocky mountains and visit the continent of the Pacific. He is in his 33rd year." He does not seem to have crossed the continent at this time, for he was back in St. Louis in the fall of 1830. There is no record of his making any other trip up the Missouri.[64]

In this last statement Chittenden plainly is in error, as we shall presently discover.

As already indicated, Prince Paul made his first journey to the United States in 1823, sailing in that year from Hamburg to New Orleans. He was granted permission by the secretary of state, John Quincy Adams, to enter and travel through the United States, and the federal authorities of the west were instructed to provide him with every means in their power to further and safeguard his movements and to furnish him military escort when it should be deemed necessary. On May 5, 1823, Prince Paul requested "General" Clark of St. Louis to furnish him a passport to travel up the Missouri river, stating that the sole object of his contemplated expedition was for his own instruction. This request was granted by the secretary of war on June 10, 1823.

On this expedition the prince of Würtemberg made the acquaintance of Jean Baptiste Charbonneau, and of his mother, Sacajawea, as well as of Charbonneau himself, whose services he used as an interpreter. The meeting with Jean Baptiste was near the mouth of the Kaw river on June 21, 1823. In his journal published in 1835

[64] Smet, P. J. de, *Life, letters, and travels, 1801-1873*, ed. Chittenden and Richardson, vol. II, 685. Prince Paul was only distantly related to William II, king of England. He was, however, the nephew of King Friedrich of Würtemberg and also of Paul I of Russia, and consequently a cousin of Nicholas I and Alexander I. His full name was Paul Charles Friedrich Augustus. He died in November, 1860, at the age of 63.

FACSIMILE OF MANUSCRIPT OF PRINCE PAUL OF WÜRTEMBERG
Written August 10, 1850, at the ranch of Colonel Sutter, Fort Sutter, California.
Manuscript discovered, 1930, at Stuttgart, Germany.

the prince describes this meeting, and the fact of Baptiste's return with him to Europe.[65] On June 21, 1823, he wrote:

The settlements of the fur-traders, two spacious dwelling houses, are found a short half-mile farther on the right bank of the Missouri, and I rode thither in order to visit their respective owners, the Messrs. Curtiss and Wood. But I failed to find them, though I did the wife of the latter, a Creole, and daughter of the aged Chauvin with whom I had spent a night not far from St. Charles. The entire population of the settlement consisted of but a few persons, Creoles and half-breeds, whose occupation is the trading with Kansas Indians, confined mostly to the chase and the cultivation of the soil. Here I found also a youth of sixteen, whose mother was of the tribe of Sho-sho-ne, or Snake Indians, and who had accompanied the Messrs. Lewis and Clarke to the Pacific ocean in the years 1804 to 1806 as interpretess.

This Indian woman was married to the French interpreter of the expedition, Toussaint Charbonneau by name. Charbonneau rendered me service also, some time later in this same capacity, and Baptiste, his son (the youth of sixteen) of whom I made mention above, joined me on my return and followed me to Europe and has remained with me ever since.[66]

On December 3, Prince Paul sailed from St. Louis to New Orleans on the steamboat "Cincinnati," and on the twenty-fourth of that month he and Baptiste embarked on the brig "Smyrne" for the Atlantic seaboard on the first leg of their long journey to Europe.

In 1828, Prince Paul wrote an account of his western

---

[65] Paul Wilhelm, Friedrich, Herzog von Würtemberg, *Erste reise nach dem nördlichen Amerika in den jahren 1822 bis 1824,* Stuttgart und Tübingen, J. G. Cotta'schen Buchhandlung, 1835, 259, 348, 379.

[66] Other entries in the prince's diary referring to Charbonneau are as follows: "October 9, 1823: On the ninth I reached the boat 'The Kansas,' where I stopped for several hours and took on the son of Toussaint Charbonneau who was to accompany me to Europe."

"October 24-25, 1823: Decided to go to St. Louis, as I found no suitable opportunity to continue my trip to New Orleans. I therefore improved my time in visiting the Messieurs Chouteau on their country estates and was treated there with most lavish hospitality."

travels under the title *Trip to North America in the years 1822, 1823, and 1824*. Only one copy of this book apparently was ever printed. This is now preserved in the Henry E. Huntington library and art gallery in San Marino, California, and at the request of the author, Mr. Willard O. Walters of the library permitted Professor Louis C. Butscher of the University of Wyoming to examine this volume. The volume, which was probably printed merely for the author's inspection, contains "hundreds of marginal manuscript notes" written in German script by the author.

Prince Paul, although educated and trained for a military career, was more interested in science, literature, and philosophy, than in war. Consequently, he resigned his military position and devoted himself to the study of botany and zoology under the direction of Gay-Lussac, Cuvier, Jussien, and Hay. He came to the United States again in 1829, unattended except by "a hardy hunter and master of woodcraft." At St. Louis the royal traveler again petitioned Captain Clark for a passport to visit the Indian lodges in the north, and this courtesy, at Captain Clark's request, was granted by John Eaton, secretary of war.[67]

This journey carried Prince Paul as far as the Mandan villages, the former home of Charbonneau and Sacajawea. The prince kept a complete journal of this journey (as he did of all the others), which he carefully prepared for publication; but despite diligent search, the manuscript has never been found. This is most unfortunate

[67] Through the research of Mrs. Edith Connelley Clift and her father, Mr. William E. Connelley, the letters containing the request of the prince for a passport, and the letter of Captain Clark to Secretary Eaton were discovered. The writing of Prince Paul is in English, showing a fine style of penmanship and perfect diction.

from the standpoint of the present volume, since it would undoubtedly throw great light upon Baptiste's stay in Europe, including as it did in addition to a record of the expedition, the history of the life of Prince Paul from the time he left America in December, 1823, until he returned to this country in 1829.

Despite the fact that both on his earlier and later visits the prince was shown every courtesy by the officials of the American government, there was serious question in official quarters as to the real motives which lay behind his "search for knowledge," and whether this did not conceal a plan of establishing a German colony somewhere in North America, or of seeking to develop an extensive foreign fur-trade by establishing new companies in the fur territory. Neither of these purposes, however, was in any way revealed by the prince's activities.[68]

A final reference is made by Prince Paul in his account of his travels in North America to the young half-breed Baptiste, who had been an inmate of his family for six years and for whom he had come to have a very genuine affection. This reference occurs in the account of his fourth journey, made nearly twenty years after his second expedition up the Missouri.[69] This began in

[68] On Apr. 30, 1830, in the records of Fort Clark on the Missouri, appears a bill for certain goods charged to the account of "His Royal Highness, Paul, Prince of Wurtemburg." The prince signed the account, asking that the goods be delivered to James Kipp. Endorsed on the back of this order appear the following instructions: "The following delivered after the prince's departure by his request to Duseau, from Charbonneau at Gros Ventres village." Among other purchases of Prince Paul when at Fort Union on May 19, 1830, appears the item: "2 Madress Hkfs to Charbonneau – $5.00." On Mar. 13 and Aug. 22, 1830, at Fort Clark, he purchased $471.25 worth of merchandise. Appearing in this account is the item, "4 pounds tobacco, $12.00. Delivered for Charbonneau."

[69] Prince Paul paid five visits in all to the United States. He made his first

1849, and carried him through west Texas, across Mexico to Acapulco, thence by steamer to San Pedro in California, and up the Pacific coast to Sutter's fort near Sacramento. In his journal he records in considerable detail his life and experiences while a guest of the hospitable Swiss land baron.[70] In the course of the de-

expedition to the west in 1822; a second in 1829; and a third from 1839 to 1841. He traveled again extensively from 1849 to 1856, and made his final tour in 1857 and 1858.

[70] "This farm is one of the first cultivated agricultural homesteads in the country, and since Mr. Sutter knew how to make friends of the neighboring Hock Indians through humane treatment, he never suffered from lack of laborers. As is well known, the first gold was discovered near the site of a big sawmill belonging to Mr. Sutter and located on the south fork of the American river, a short distance above Brightown – which gave the main impulse for the settlement of that country.

"Mr. Sutter had made an attempt to employ his Indians in the placer mining of gold, but reverted, however, very soon to wheat-growing, the culture of which has grown at this time to be its main product. The wheat harvest had been finished some time before, and this was threshed out on a hard clay floor, just as I have seen it done in Algiers, Italy, and South America, with ponies driven over the thickly-scattered sheaves by the Indians. They had not as yet introduced the wonderful American threshing machines into California. The garden, in which aside from the maize there were growing melons and vegetables, and also attempts made with grapes and other products, consisted of a considerable flat area of cultivated ground in which a great many trees, hoary with age, waved their majestic tops with the breeze.

"The entire afternoon and evening I derived immense amusement from watching the wild, unbridled milling of the horses urged on by the Indians with ceaseless yells and flaying of great, long, rawhide whips. They were mounted on small but incredibly tough ponies that were themselves as savage as their riders. The latter wore their tribal costumes.

"It is not alone men of the Hock nation who are in the employ of Mr. Sutter as farm laborers, but also redmen of tribes such as the Juba, the Kosoni, the Willi, and the Kulu – even a few Sho-sho-nis, or Snake Indians, who joined him on one of his return trips from the eastern states, and followed him from their mountains to the western sea. One of these Snakes was a fine young lad, quite intelligent, who reminded me strangely and with a certain sadness of B. Charbonneau, who had followed me in 1823 to Europe, and whose mother was of the tribe of the Sho-sho-nis."

These fragments from the travel diary of Duke Paul William of Würtemberg were transcribed for the author by Friedrich Bauser of Stuttgart, Germany, archivist, from the Würtemberg state library, roll IX, 521-23 inclusive.

FACSIMILE OF ORIGINAL DeSMET MANUSCRIPT

The communication is addressed to "Very Dear Father Provincial, St. Louis University, October 26, 1851." It notes the meeting of DeSmet with Prince Paul and his artist, Möllhausen.

scription, part of which is devoted to an account of the Indians in Sutter's employ, occurs this sentence:

> One of these Snakes was a fine young lad, quite intelligent, who reminded me strangely and with a certain sadness of B. Charbonneau, who had followed me in 1825 to Europe, and whose mother was of the tribe of the Sho-sho-nis.

From Sutter's fort the Prince of Würtemberg returned to New Orleans early in the spring of 1851 by way of the Isthmus of Panama, and continued on to St. Louis. This, instead of the rough border town of 5,000 inhabitants he had visited in 1823, he now found to be a city of 80,000 people. From St. Louis the prince traveled up the Missouri river and thence to the west, following the Platte and North Platte, by way of the old "covered wagon" road or Oregon trail. In his journal he mentions Independence rock, Devil's gate, South pass, the Great Salt lake, and the Mormon colony in Salt Lake city. It was on this journey that he likewise fell in with Father DeSmet, near Ash hollow on the Platte river. An extended account of this chance meeting in the wilderness between these two interesting men, the one a great missionary of the cross, the other an adventurous member of one of Europe's ruling families, is given in the following extract from Father DeSmet's journal.

> Quite late in the afternoon of the 23rd of September, 1851, I bade farewell to the Creoles, Canadians, and half-bloods. I exhorted them to live well and to pray to God, and to hope that he would soon send them spiritual succor for their temporal and external happiness and that of their children. I shook hands for the last time with the great chiefs and with a large number of the Indians, and addressed them

The translation is by Professor Louis G. Butscher of the University of Wyoming.

some encouraging words and promised to plead their cause with the great chiefs of the black-gowns, and make known the desire, good intentions, and hopes they had expressed to me, while they would daily, in all sincerity of heart, implore the "Master of Life" to send them zealous priests to instruct them in the way of salvation, which Jesus Christ, his only son, came to trace to his own children on earth.

I directed my course toward "the springs," situated about 14 miles distant, in the vicinity of Robidoux's trading-house, for Colonel Mitchell had named this as the rendezvous for all those who proposed going directly to the United States. On the 24th, before sunrise, we set out in good and numerous company. I visited, in my way, two trading-houses in order to baptize five half-blood children. In the course of the day we passed the famous Chimney rock, so often described by travelers. I had already seen it, in 1840 and 1841, in my first visit to the Rocky mountains, and mentioned it in my letters. I found it considerably diminished in height.

We cast around a last look upon the singular productions of nature, the castle and tower, which are near the chimney, and resemble the ruins of lordly residences scattered over several acres, presenting a very elevated and broken surface amid a level plain.

Arrived on the Platte, at the place known as Ash hollow, we turned our steps toward the South fork, fifteen miles away, over a beautiful rolling country of great elevation. Here we met Prince Paul accompanied only by a Prussian officer, on their way to enjoy a hunt in the Wind river mountains. We exchanged our little news, and received with pleasure the interesting information which the prince gave us. His excellency must be indeed courageous, to undertake at his age so long a journey in such a wilderness, with but one man as suite, and in a wretched little open wagon, which carried the prince and his officer as well as their whole baggage and provisions. Later I learned that the prince intends to choose a location suited to agriculture, for the purpose of founding a German colony.

We live in an age when wonders multiply; we cannot say what, in the way of colonization, may not come to pass in a short time, after witnessing the success of the Mormons, who in less than five years have changed the face of a frightful desert and live there in great abundance. Yet I am free to maintain that if the prince has really formed the plan ascribed to him which I scarcely credit, I pity from the bottom of my heart those who first embark in the expedition. The enemies whom they would have to meet are still too powerful: Crows, Blackfeet, Sioux, Cheyennes, Arapahos, and Snakes are the most feared and warlike of the desert. A colony established in such a neighborhood, and against the will of the numerous warlike tribes in the vicinity of those mountains, would run great dangers and meet heavy obstacles. The influence of religion alone can prepare these parts for such a transformation. The threats and promises of colonists, their guns and sabres, would never effect what can be accomplished by the peaceful sign of the black-gown and the sight of the humanizing sign of the cross.[71]

Prince Paul was accompanied on this journey by his artist named Möllhausen. For part of the way, at least, the two traveled "in a wretched little open wagon" which was also described as "an apparently crazy open vehicle." A month after their meeting with DeSmet, the prince and his companion narrowly escaped massacre at the hands of a marauding band of savages. The account of this experience, though it has no bearing upon the history of Sacajawea or Baptiste, is nevertheless appropriately recorded in this volume. The prince's account reads as follows:[72]

On October 26, 1851, there was clear sunshine and N.N.W. wind early in the day.

After I had traveled about five miles I recognized among some grazing buffalo two forms which I knew at once to be Indians. They were close to the road we were traveling. Soon I saw their blankets, and observed that they were Indian warriors with cavalry swords and otherwise armed to the teeth. They were leading a great, wolflike hound between them, and approached our outfit shouting "Schayenne." They seemed to be quite friendly, but at the same time they inspired me with suspicion, and they were more like Cayuwas or Kowas than anything else, evil, thieving Indians who are fond of killing off the white people and of robbing them.[73]

---

[71] Smet, *Life, letters, and travels,* ed. Chittenden and Richardson, vol. II, 685.

[72] The manuscript containing the account of this attack was found in a "black trunk" in Stuttgart, Germany, by Herr Bauser.

[73] They had only a short time before massacred part of a troop of U.S. soldiers,

As we observed that their war party was approaching, all afoot and well armed with cavalry sabers, carbines, rifles, bows, and tomahawks, there seemed to be nothing for us to do but wait quietly and tranquilly what was to ensue. In such extremes the sole means of salvation lies in sheer courage and equanimity in order to pull oneself out of a serious situation such as that of being confronted by a troup of wild people on the warpath.

This body consisted of fourteen or fifteen savages, mostly young bucks completely armed, well dressed, and imposing looking. At first they pretended to be friendly. They wanted to look at my arms, and demanded foodstuffs and whiskey, both of which I willingly acceded to, inasmuch as I had mostly bacon in my grub-box, a viand which the Indians of the west despise.

Now they were growing even more importunate. They grabbed my double-barreled shot-gun, a short, fine hunting knife, and an old but very fine traveling pistol of the make of Fecht, which I had carried with me for years during my travels. When they once had these arms in their possession they became quite insolent. They now tore my Mexican serape and my cap from me bodily, and then, at a signal from the leader, some of them took their firearms, cocked them, while others drew their bows. Then one of them, an evil-looking ruffian, struck one of my horses with his tomahawk. Gradually advancing, the warriors, half a dozen or more, pushed their rifles against my breast and head. One young buck pointed his arrow within a hand's breadth of my right eye, and all gave to me and to Mr. Möllhausen, who was himself subjected to the same terror and who conducted himself with the utmost sangfroid, to understand that we were to suffer death, and that they would add our scalps to those that dangled, fresh and gory, from their belts. They declared themselves the mortal enemies of the Gankise.[74] I smiled at these threats, showed before them the greatest calmness, and remarked that I was a Washi.[75] Quite cooly I showed my ten fingers raised above my head, and said, "squaw,"[76] then pointed to myself

and were wearing their arms and some of their clothing.

[74] Gankise or Ankise-hu, a corrupted term for Yankee, was used by many tribes of the western prairies for American hunters and settlers.

[75] Washi, Indian term for French Creoles and Canadians, both of which were in high favor with the Indian of western plains in contrast to the Angloamericans, who were cordially hated.

[76] Squaw, meaning "cowardly men."

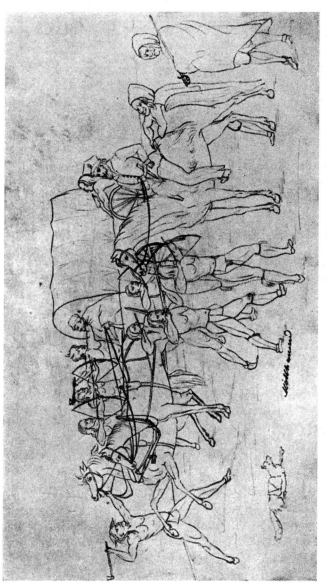

An Encounter with the Kiowas

Sketch by Möllhausen of the attack on Prince Paul, October 26, 1851, by the Kiowas on the Platte in Nebraska. Prince Paul wears the royal hat, and Möllhausen is driving the covered wagon. The original drawing, located in Stuttgart, Germany, has never been reproduced before.

and Mr. Möllhausen and exclaimed "men," which should convey to them my opinion that ten to fifteen Gankise, or Ankise-hu, a corrupted term for Yankee used by many Indians, if they wanted to attack two unarmed men, were cowards, and if we two were Washi, they betrayed friends; also, that two brave white men did not propose to be intimidated by any number of warriors.

This had an immediate and most startling effect. All weapons were lowered, all booty taken from us was, even to the smallest object, put back to the place from which it had been snatched, quietly and in an orderly manner. The chief, who seemed to be the most reasonable of all, restored to me with profound respect both cap and serape. Only a young buck, who had taken my cherished pistol, had vanished. So then the leader came forward again and placed a fine six-chambered revolver on my wagon, pointing in the distance to where a slain buffalo lay, and in the crowd, with repeated protestations of friendship, dispersed and soon vanished from view. But in the mêlée Mr. Möllhausen has lost his diary, which contained a great number of fine sketches.[77]

The rest of the day passed serenely, and I made camp some fifteen miles farther on, with a violent, cool wind blowing from the southeast. The night was beautiful. We were a mile away from the river.[78]

The expedition of 1839-1841, by Prince Paul and the two subsequent to that date, are described in a single manuscript volume of great interest and historic value, which was discovered by Herr Friedrich Bauser in Stuttgart in 1929. In the archives of the state library at Stuttgart, Herr Bauser also discovered a pencil sketch of the Indian surprise attack of the Kiowas on the Platte river, which pictures the Indians in the act of torturing Prince Paul and his artist companion. In October, 1930, the same investigator discovered another picture labeled "The Race of the Cheyenne Maidens." In the summer

---

[77] Mr. Möllhausen or Moellhausen, who later, through his long and perilous travels to the west coast, became famous as a talented sketch artist and painter.

[78] Extract from manuscript of Prince Paul, "Third Expedition, 1849-57." Transcribed for the author by Herr Friedrich Bauser, and translated by Professor L. C. Butscher.

of 1927 the Reverend Henry Hartig of Minnesota, upon
a visit to Stuttgart, his birth place, saw in that city an
oil painting in one of the "aulas" of a school building
entitled "Prince Paul and his Indian boy." Although
diligent search was made for this painting by Herr
Bauser, he was unsuccessful in locating it, but one is
certainly justified in accepting Hartig's statement that
he saw such a painting.[79]

Although there is altogether too scant mention of
Baptiste's six years in Europe in Prince Paul's manuscripts, and though nothing further touching on this
strange interlude in the young half-breed's life may ever
be found, the evidence from these long-forgotten records
furnishes strange and unexpected verification of statements made to the author of this volume, and carefully
preserved on the Shoshone reservation. When Baptiste's
daughter and his nephew declared that Baptiste had
been educated in the land to the east beyond the big
waters, and told of the big houses on the water and of
the people with wooden shoes (Wo-be-namp-Tiko, or
Wooden-Shoe-White-Man, as Baptiste was called), it
was difficult to believe that their statements were more
than some misunderstood legend. But only a few years
later the discovery of the prince's manuscripts served at
once to support the simple verbal testimony, and to make
more certain the true identity both of Baptiste and
Sacajawea.

---

[79] Apparently Prince Paul planned to publish all of his journals, and pre-
sumably selected his son, Maximilian, to carry out this task. The prince died,
however, while he was still engaged in the task of editing his journals, and
his heir placed the manuscripts in the custody of the royal library. Until 1929,
these records of the prince's travels in North America remained undisturbed
in the vaults of this massive old building. Here they were discovered and
examined for the first time since the prince's death by Herr Friedrich Bauser,
already referred to.

Baptiste's career from the time of his return to the United States with Prince Paul, until he went to live with his mother's people, the Shoshones, in the Bridger valley on the Wind river reservation in 1852, can be traced with some degree of accuracy in the frequent references made to him in the journals of western fur-traders and explorers during this period.

In the narrative of W. A. Ferris, one of the employees of the American Fur company from 1830 to 1835, who trapped much of the territory explored by Lewis and Clark, Baptiste is mentioned in connection with one of his adventures.

We spent the following morning in the charitable office conveying water to our enfeebled companions who lingered behind, and the poor beasts that had also been left by the way, and succeeded in getting them all to camp, except the person and animals of Charbonneau, one of our men, who could no where be found. . . This was the infant who, together with his mother, was saved from a sudden flood near the Falls of Missouri, by Captain Lewis – *vide* Lewis, in Lewis and Clark's expedition. [It was Clark, however, rather than Lewis who saved the lives of Sacajawea and Baptiste.] [80]

In the same year Fitzpatrick, known as "Broken Hand," Sublette, and the "Blanket Chief," James Bridger, went to the Big Horn country with two hundred men, crossed the Yellowstone, and followed that river to its junction with the Missouri. From here the fur-men ascended the Missouri to the Three forks, and then trapped up the Jefferson. This is the country, it will be remembered, where Sacajawea in August, 1805, found her people, the Shoshones, and adopted her sister's son, Bazil. Later the three members of the Rocky Mountain Fur company turned eastward "in time to reach the

---

[80] Ferris, Warren Angus, "Life in the Rocky mountains, 1830-1835," in *Wonderland*, 1901, 129.

valley of the Powder river before winter set in." The Powder river valley, in what is now Wyoming, was a favorite winter ground, and it was here that the three fur-traders, with their hunters, exchanged furs, fights, beads, and bullets. During the winter, Joseph Meek was sent with an express from this encampment to St. Louis. On his way to the Platte, however, Meek "fell in with an express on its way to St. Louis, to whom he delivered his dispatch, returning at once to the Powder river camp. On this journey he was accompanied only by a Frenchman, Cabeneau." [81]

In the writings of Nathaniel Wyeth, frequent mention is made of a Charbonneau, whom we may presume to have been Baptiste, during the years 1832 to 1833. Thus Wyeth records that Charbonneau, a half-breed, was with Jim Bridger in August, 1832. On May 19 of the next year, he speaks of a half-breed, "Charloi," who was one of four hunters going to trap beaver in the Blackfoot country. Three of these hunters, among whom was a Churboye, returned on June 21. On August 1 of that year, Wyeth writes:

Mr. Bridger sent four men to this river to look for us, viz: Mr. Smith, Thompson, Charbonneau, a half-breed.

Following an attack by Indians, Wyeth later wrote:

The Indians got seven horses; all there were. Charbonneau pursued them on foot and got his gun wet crossing a little stream and only snapped twice. [82]

It may be remarked in passing that a vast amount of territory was covered on this hunt, which extended up Clark fork to the source of the Salmon, covered the

---

[81] Victor, Francis Fuller, *The river of the west*, 96.
[82] Wyeth, Capt. N. J., "Correspondence and journals," ed. F. G. Young, in *Sources of the history of Oregon*, vol. I, 196, 202, 207.

upper regions of the Green and the Popo Agie, came
down the Snake within sight of the Grand Teton, to
the source of the Wind river, and thence passed down
the Big Horn to the Yellowstone.[83]

In 1839 we find "Charbonard," the half-breed son of
Sacajawea, graceful, urbane, fluent, reciting his victories
over the Indians to the fur-men of Kit Carson's company.[84] A somewhat extended reference is also made to
Baptiste by Willard Smith in his journal of 1839 to
1840. Smith mentions a Mr. Shabenare who went down
the Platte river two thousand miles from the mountains
in sixty days, carrying peltries to the market in St.
Louis.[85] The same writer also speaks of the half-breeds
who had been employed by Mr. Thompson, in command of a trading post on the western side of the mountains. "One of these," he says, "was the son of Captain
Clark, the great western traveler and companion of
Lewis. He had received an education in Europe during
seven years." On December 17, Smith's hunters were
on the Green river where it crossed the boundary between Utah and Wyoming. Moving westward, they came
to "about twenty lodges of Indians of the Snake tribe.

[83] In Francis A. Chardon's "Fort Clark Journals" for July 4, 1836, there is
this entry: "The agent went to the Gros Ventres to make them presents, sent
with him Manto and Bazil rigged off with cart and bull." The brothers Baptiste
and Bazil may at times have followed the same occupation – that of "cart
drivers." "The fur companies transported on two-wheeled carts, each drawn
by two mules and loaded with 800 or 900 pounds," says F. A. Wislizenus in
Journey to the Rocky mountains, 1839, Missouri historical society, 1912, 28-29.

[84] Vestal, Stanley, *Kit Carson,* 169.

[85] The quarterly of the Oregon historical society, Sept., 1913, vol. XIV, no. 3,
250-279, contains Willard E. Smith's "Journal while with the fur-traders
Vasquez and Sublette in the Rocky mountain region, 1839-1840." From St.
Louis, the ultimate destination of the expedition and proposed winter quarters,
was Brown's hole. "This hole was the last rendezvous of outlaws who stole
cattle and horses." On September 21, when the party arrived at the "Laramie's
fork," the hunters were within twelve miles of the author's home.

They call themselves Shoshonies. We obtained a few trinkets. They are very good-looking Indians. The men are generally tall and slightly made, the women short and stout." The hunters were now in the valley later to be known as Bridger valley and Washakie valley, where Baptiste, "Mr. Charbenare," was in years to come to make his home with the Shoshones and live beside his brother, Bazil, the adopted son of Sacajawea. After zigzagging over the boundary line of the present state of Wyoming and Colorado as well as into Utah, on July 3, 1840, Smith's party arrived in its boats at St. Louis. The afternoon of this arrival, "Mr. Shabenare went out a short distance from the river bank to shoot buffalo for his meat."

General John Charles Frémont, in the journal of his expedition of 1842, mentions a "Chabonard" who, in all probability, was Baptiste. On July 9, 1842, Frémont had his first glimpse of Long's peak and the snowy summit of the Rocky mountains. On this day he also met some white men hunting for lost horses.

These men were in search of a band of horses that had gone off from a camp some miles down, in charge of Mr. Chabonard . . . about eight miles from our sleeping-place we reached Bijou's Fork, an affluent of the right bank. . . In about two miles arrived at Chabonard's camp, on an island in the Platte. . . Mr. Chabonard was in the service of Bent and St. Vrain's company, and had left their fort some forty or fifty miles above, in the spring, with boats laden with furs of the last year's trade. He had met the same fortune as the voyagers of the North fork, and, finding it impossible to proceed, had taken up his summer's residence on this island, which he named St. Helena. . . Mr. Chabonard received us hospitably. One of his people was sent to gather mint, with the aid of which he concocted a very good julep.

JULY 10TH. We parted with our hospitable host after breakfast the next morning, and reached St. Vrain's fort, about forty miles from St. Helena, late in the evening.[86]

In 1842, Sir William Drummond Stewart organized a party in St. Louis to hunt buffalo. The party began its actual hunt at Fort Laramie, on the Oregon trail in 1843. In this group of hunters with Stewart were Sublette, Captain Jefferson Kennerly Clark, a son of Captain Clark of the Lewis and Clark expedition, and William Clark Kennerly, a nephew of Captain William Clark, for whom he was named. The party included eighty other members, among whom were guides, drivers, and hunters. Among others engaged to join the expedition was Baptiste Charbonneau, who served in the capacity of "a cart driver."

When at Fort Laramie, Baptiste saw young Clark and "at once welcomed him as the son of his old guardian." Fifty or sixty lodges of the Sioux Indians were then at the fort, and some of the chiefs recognized Jefferson Clark because of the strong resemblance to his father, whom they had known on his Pacific expedition, and at once called the young man "son of red-headed father."

In 1906, Captain Kennerly was the last surviving member of the group which accompanied Stewart on this hunt in 1843.[87] Upon his death at St. Louis on Sep-

[86] Frémont, John Charles, *Memoirs of my life,* Chicago, 1887, vol. I, 101-102. It is to be noticed that General Frémont makes no mention of "Mr. Charbonard's" classical attainments or his education, though he does speak favorably of his mint julep.

[87] Mrs. Eva Emery Dye stated in a letter to the author, Dec. 18, 1906, that Captain Kennerly related to her in St. Louis in 1902 at the time of making arrangements for the centennial of the Louisiana purchase exposition, that as a young man he and Clark's youngest son, Jefferson Kennerly Clark, accompanied the Captain Stewart expedition to Fort Laramie in 1843, where they found young Charbonneau, the son of Sacajawea, acting as a guide to hunting parties and overland expeditions. The Indians hailed young Jefferson as

tember 5, 1912, his papers, manuscripts, and a small diary were given to the Missouri historical society.[88] Among this valuable material is a manuscript which contains the following extract:

One of the drivers, Baptiste Charbonneau, was the son of an old trapper and Sacajawea, the brave Indian woman who had guided Lewis and Clark on their perilous journey through the wilderness. . . By singular coincidence he was again to make the journey and guide the son of William Clark through the same region.[89]

It is significant to note that the name of Sacajawea and that of Baptiste Charbonneau are thus spelled, in the Kennerly manuscript describing the buffalo hunt of 1843, precisely as they are today.

One of the most extensive accounts of Charbonneau is to be found in the manuscript of W. M. Boggs, which was prepared in 1905, but remained unpublished until 1930. In this chronicle, covering the period between 1844 and that of 1845, Boggs wrote:

"Red Hair" on account of his resemblance to his father. Kennerly said that he had known Charbonneau as a boy at school in St. Louis.

[88] Kennerly, W. C., "Hunting buffaloes in the early forties," courtesy of Stella M. Drumm, Missouri historical society, St. Louis. This manuscript is written by Captain Kennerly's daughter, to whom he frequently dictated stories or experiences of his early life, and particularly this material, from which was written "Hunting Buffaloes."

Captain William Clark Kennerly wrote a series of letters to the author from Dec. 6, 1906, to Feb. 25, 1907, when the correspondence ceased. Mr. Kennerly gave the following information to the author in a letter of Dec. 6, 1906. "In 1842 Sir William Drummond Stewart organized a party to hunt buffalo and other game; among others engaged to assist was one Baptiste Charbonneau who acted in the capacity of a driver of one of the carts." The company was being organized at St. Louis in 1842, but did not arrive at Fort Laramie until the next summer.

[89] "Sept. 11: We are still at the fort [Laramie]; nothing particular occurs today. There are several chiefs, viz. 'Bull Tail,' 'Red Bull,' 'Little Thunder,' 'Solitary Dog,' 'Dazle Dog Soldier,' etc., etc., that came from the village to see G. Chouteau and myself. We held a council and gave some presents to them; they set off for their village saying that they were perfectly happy now that they had seen their fathers sons." *Ibid,* under date of 1843.

his mother said to be a Black Foot Indian Squaw
his name was Baptiste Charbenau, his Father and
mother accompanied the Lewis & Clark Expidition
in their journey to the Pacific, ohnes via the Columbia
river, as guides, Charbenau & his squaw were very
useful members of the Lewis & Clark Expedition; this
Baptiste Charbenau at Bents Fort was only a "papouse" at
at the time of the "Lewis & Clark" expedition, but his mother
took him the entire route, according to Genl Clarks account
in his published letters—the squaw was as useful as a
guide as the man Charbenau himself being raised in
the country they were passing over—and familiar with the
mountain passes and trails—this Baptiste Charbenau the Hunter
of Bents Fort, was the small Indian Papouse, or half breed
of the elder Charbenau, that was employed by the Lewis
and Clark Expedition as guide, when they descended the
Columbia river to the Pacific Ocean — he had been

educated to some extent, he wore his hair long that
hung down to his shoulders, twas said that "Charbenau"
was the best man on the Plains or in the Rocky mountains
another half breed at the Fort, was "Tessou" his Father was
French and his mother an Indian) but the writer was
not informed of what tribe "Tessou" was in someway related
to Charbenau both of them were very high strung —
but Tessou was quick and passionate, he fired a
rifle across the court of the Fort, at the head of the

FACSIMILE OF BOGGS' MANUSCRIPT
Describes Baptiste and his half-brother, "Tessou," in 1845.

I also learned considerable from the hunters of Bent's fort, particularly from Charbenau, an educated half-breed. His father was a French-canadian, his mother said to be a Blackfoot [?] squaw. His name was Baptiste Charbenau. His father and mother accompanied the Lewis and Clark expedition in their journey to the Pacific shores via the Columbia river as guides. Charbenau and his squaw were very useful members of the Lewis and Clark expedition. This Baptiste Charbeneau at Bent's fort was only a papoose at the time of the Lewis and Clark expedition, but his mother took him the entire route, according to General Clark's account in his published letters. The squaw was as useful as a guide as the man Charbenau himself, being raised in the country they were passing over and familiar with mountain passes and trails. This Baptiste Charbenau, or half-breed of the elder Charbenau that was employed by the Lewis and Clark expedition to the Pacific ocean, had been educated to some extent; he wore his hair long so that it hung down to his shoulders. It is said that Charbenau was the best man on foot of the plains or in the Rocky mountains.

In addition to this commendation of Baptiste, Boggs further pays tribute to the fur company employees:

Such men as these heretofore described were employed by the Bents, and were perfectly reliable and devoted to the interests of the company. The company would entrust them with thousands of dollars worth of goods, and send them to distant tribes of Indians to barter for robes, furs, and peltries, with pack animals to carry the outfit. The traders, thus outfitted, would remain away for months, or until the season for trade was over, and would then return to the fort with the robes and the peltries that they had accumulated, and I have never heard of one of these men being accused of abusing the confidence placed in them by their employers.[90]

Lieutenant George Frederick Ruxton, like Frémont, Boggs, and the others, includes Baptiste in his list of important fur-traders.[91] Thus he writes:

---

[90] Baptiste was an employee and an associate of the higher class fur-traders, which included St. Vrain; Charles, William, and George Bent; Fitzpatrick; Jim Bridger; Milton and William Sublette; Jedediah Smith; etc.

[91] Ruxton, G. F., "Life in the far west," in *Blackwood's Magazine,* LXIII, 1713-1714.

Away to the head waters of the Platte, where several small streams run into the south fork of the river and head in the broken ridges of the "divide" which separates the valleys of the Platte and Arkansas, were camped a band of trappers, on a creek called Bijou. . . They were a trapping-party, on their way to wintering-ground, in the more southern valley of Arkansas. . . There was old Sam Owins—him as got "rubbed out," "rubbed out" by the Spaniards. . . Bill Bent—his boys camped the other side of the trail, and they all were mountain men, wagh!—and Bill Williams, and Bill Tharpe (the Pawnees took his hair on Pawnee fork last spring): three Bills, and them three's all "gone under." Surely Hatcher went out that time; and wasn't Bill Garey along too? Didn't him and Charbonard sit in camp for twenty hours, at a deck of Euker? Them was Bent's Indian traders up on the Arkansas.

Singly and in bands numbering from two to ten the traders dropped into the rendezvous; some with many packs of beaver. . . Fitzpatrick and Hatcher, and old Bill Williams. Sublette came in with his men from the Yellowstone and many of Wyeth's New Englanders were there. Charbonard with his half-breeds, brought peltries from the country below. . . Charbonar, a half-breed, was not lost in the crowd; and last in height, but first in every quality which constitutes excellence in a mountaineer—who was "taller" for his inches than Kit Carson?

In a report made by Lieutenant J. W. Abert on his journey to the upper Arkansas and through the country of the Comanche Indians in the fall of 1845, there are also frequent mentions of "Mr. Chabonard," and his services as a guide from Bent's fort to St. Louis. On August 9, he writes: "Mr. Chabonard called for me to accompany me to Fort Bent on a visit." [92] On the same day Colonel Frémont met with Lieutenant Abert for a council, and also with the Indians. Later Mr. Fitzpatrick joined the expedition, expressing his delight with the usefulness of the guide, "Mr. Chabonard."

During these years, 1846-1847, much is said about "Charbonneaux," who was then serving as guide to

[92] U.S. ex. doc. 438, 30th cong., serial no. 477, Washington, D.C., 1848.

Lieutenant-colonel Philip St. George Cooke. How useful Baptiste was to this conquest of New Mexico and California can only be learned from the numerous extracts taken from Colonel Cooke's journal.[93] From this report one gathers that Charbonneau was not illiterate; that he not only signed his name to a notice, but could also read; that he was a guide and hunter who knew by intuition, like his mother before him when she lead Captain Clark to the mouth of the Yellowstone in 1806, how to discover the gaps and passes in the mountains and the sources of streams. He could also understand and converse in the Mexican language.

Colonel Emory, on October 6, 1846, while en route to San Diego from Santa Fé, writes: [94]

> I saw some objects on the hill to the west, which were first mistaken for large cedars, but dwindled by distance to a shrub. Charboneau (one of our guides) exclaimed, "Indians! They are Apaches." His more practical eye detected human figures in my shrubbery.[95]

The prowess of Charbonneau is further illustrated by an extract from Colonel Cooke's report of November 25, 1846.

> Charboneaux, who had killed an antelope before the column reached the mountain, I found near the summit, while the baggage was slowly crawling up, in pursuit of grizzly bears. I saw three of them far up among the rocks, standing conspicuously and looking quite white in the sun, whilst the bold hunter was gradually approaching them. Soon after he fired, and in ten seconds again; then there was a confused action and we could see one fall, and the others rushing about with loud and fierce cries that made the mountain ring. The firing having

---

[93] Cooke, Lieut.-col. P. St. George, *March from Santa Fé, New Mexico, to San Diego, upper California*, Washington, D.C., 1848.

[94] Emory, Colonel W. H., *Notes on a military reconnoissance, from Fort Leavenworth in Missouri to San Diego in California, 1846-1847*, Washington, D.C., 1848.

[95] Cooke, *op. cit.*, 576.

ceased, whilst the young bears were close by, I was much alarmed for the guide's safety; and then we heard him crying out in Spanish, but it was for more balls, and so the cubs escaped. The bear was rolled down and butchered before the wagons had passed.

In his journal from November 16, 1846, to January 21, 1847, General Cooke mentions the services rendered the expedition by Charbonneau not less than twenty-nine times. He speaks of his skill in the selection of routes, trapping beaver, finding water, establishing camps, discovering passes, scouting, estimating distances, locating smoke signals, hunting bears, fighting Indians, and many other such valuable services. [96]

Cooke's forces reached the headquarters of the Mormon battalion at the mission of San Diego on January 30, 1847.[97] "Thus marching half naked and half fed, and living upon wild animals," wrote Cooke, "we have discovered and made a road of great value to the country." A great deal of credit for the success of the expedition, it would seem, should be given to Charbonneau, who thus guided Cooke's expedition as his mother had guided that of Lewis and Clark, and who now looked again upon the waters of the Pacific which he had seen as an infant at the mouth of the Columbia river in the year 1805.[98]

[96] When hunting for water one day Col. Cooke wrote, "I found here, on the high bank above the well, stuck on a pole, a note, 'No water, January 2 – Charbonneaux.'" Had Charbonneau's mother some time in the past, when the two lived together, told her son about the note of August 5, 1805, placed by Lewis near Beaver's head on a green pole telling Clark and his men the proper course to take to meet the other men? Did he remember that the pole was green and the beaver had cut the pole and carried it off, together with the note? Thwaites, *op. cit.*, vol. II, 312.

[97] Golder, Frank Alfred, *The march of the Mormon battalion*, N.Y., 1928, 207; Brown, James S., *Life of a pioneer*, Salt Lake city, 1900, ch. IV-XII.

[98] It is interesting to note that the name Charbonneau is spelled with a final "x" in Cooke's account. One wonders if perhaps this "x" does not represent

From 1852 to 1885, Baptiste was with his mother's tribe, the Shoshones, in Bridger valley and on the Shoshone reservation in Wyoming. In later life he seems to have deteriorated despite his education, his contact with civilization, and his efficient services in earlier years to explorers, government officials, and fur-traders. Such reversion is not, of course, any isolated phenomenon among the Indians, for it is a problem continually before our government even today. Baptiste thus apparently forgot his "classical education" and "superior attainments," though Indians and white men on the reservation all agreed that even as an old man he used the English language with a limited vocabulary. Certainly the fact that Baptiste reverted in later years to his Indian customs and manner of life does not in any way disprove the fact that it was he who was educated by Captain Clark in St. Louis and accompanied Prince Paul to Germany.[99] Examples without number have occurred of the same sort of reversion both among Indians and whites who have lived under similar conditions among savages or in the wilderness. Culture that is only

a remnant of the "culture" brought from Europe by Baptiste when he returned in 1829.

[99] That the Charbonneau here traced is Baptiste, the son of Sacajawea, is evident. George Bird Grinnell, for example, after enumerating a number of events connected with the wanderings of this Charbonneau, agrees that "while it is true that in no place is Charbonneau's French name mentioned, nor have we any description of his personal appearance, still the fact that he is alluded to as a 'half-breed,' that the statements of Frémont, Boggs, and Sage all agree, and that the time fits perfectly, makes me believe that this man was the son of the 'Bird Woman' who died not very long after 1884 on the Wind river reservation." Grinnell, G. B., "Bent's fort and its builders," in Kansas historical society *Collections*, 1919-1922, 37.

Two exceptions must be taken to Dr. Grinnell's statement that "in no place is Charbonneau's French name mentioned." Prince Paul's *Reise in Nordamerika, 1822-24*, had not then been discovered, nor had the Bogg's manuscript, 1844-45, been published. In these documents the name appears as "Baptiste Charbonneau" and "Baptiste Charbenau."

a veneering is easily rubbed off by constant association
with uneducated Indians and illiterate whites.[100]

---

[100] Friday, an Arapaho, lost from his family when eleven years of age,
was found and taken to St. Louis, where he was educated until he was twenty-
one years of age. Returning to his people on the Shoshone reservation at the
age of fifty, he had lapsed into barbarism. He had forgotten how to read and
write, and "possessed as many squaws as fingers." Lemly, Lieut. H. R., "Among
the Arapahoes," in *Harper's Magazine*, March, 1880, 494; Sage, *Rocky mountain life,* Boston, 1860; Hafen and Ghent, *op. cit.,* 269.

In T. D. Bonner's *Life and adventures of James P. Beckwourth,* N.Y., 1892,
528-529, we read: "An Indian woman, the wife of a Canadian named Chapineau, who acted as interpreter and guide to Lewis and Clark during their
explorations of the Rocky mountains, gave birth to a son. The Red-headed
Chief (Clarke) adopted the infant and on his return to St. Louis took the
infant with him and baptized it John Baptist Clarke Chapineau. After a
careful culture of his mind, the boy was sent to Europe to complete his education. But the Indian was ineffaceable in him. The Indian lodge and his native
mountain fastnesses possessed greater charms than the luxuries of civilized
life. He returned to the desert and passed his days with his tribe."

That Baptiste could converse in half a dozen tongues in his earlier days
made those who saw him and talked with him conclude that he was "well
educated." Jim Bridger was declared to be so illiterate that he could neither
read nor write, yet this old trapper was doubtless "well educated" in the
same sense, in his ability to make use of several languages. Lieutenant Caspar
Collins, in a letter to his mother written from Fort Hallock, Wyoming, on
Oct. 8, 1862, said: "We had Major Bridger with us as a guide. He knows
more of the Rocky mountains than any living man. He came to this country
about forty years ago. He is totally uneducated, but speaks English, Spanish,
and French equally well, besides nearly a dozen Indian tongues, such as Snake,
Bannock, Crow, Flathead, Nez Perce, Pen d'Orille, Ute, and one or two others
I cannot recollect." Hebard and Brininstool, *The Bozeman trail,* vol. 1, 97.
Letter owned by author.

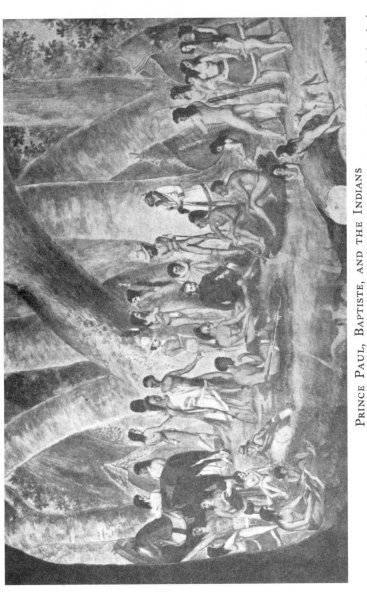

PRINCE PAUL, BAPTISTE, AND THE INDIANS

From an original painting by Möllhausen in Stuttgart, Germany; never before reproduced. Prince Paul, in dark clothing, is seated facing Baptiste, the Indian wearing roached hair, and holding a long pipe in his hand.

Sacajawea among the Comanches and on the Shoshone Reservation

I believe most sincerely in the identity of this Shoshone woman and her being the guide to Lewis and Clark, and from the very first of my acquaintance with her (1874) I was sure of this fact. . . She must have been Sacajawea, for how could an old Shoshone squaw have known of Lewis and Clark, in 1871, if she had not seen them and had not been associated with them at least for some time? Why should she claim, as she did, that she introduced the first white men into this country, unless this was a fact, for in the eyes of her people, this would be considered not a meritorious action but treachery?—JAMES I. PATTEN

CHAPTER IV

Sacajawea among the Comanches and on the Shoshone Reservation

Just when Charbonneau made his reappearance in St. Louis, or what happened to him in the meantime, is not definitely known. We find, however, as already stated, that in July, 1816, he entered the employ of the firm of Auguste Chouteau to engage in a trading expedition along the Arkansas and Platte rivers. This engagement lasted one year. Sometime before 1820 he came back to St. Louis bringing a new wife, named Eagle, of the Hidatsa tribe, with whom Sacajawea apparently made no objection to sharing her home. Later Charbonneau obtained employment with a fur company, taking with him his two wives, Eagle and Sacajawea, and his sons Toussaint and Baptiste. Later still, various members of the family appear to have acted as guides and interpreters at posts near Neosho and Washita.

Somewhere in this region, in what is now western Oklahoma and Kansas, the polygamous old interpreter took to himself another wife. This was a Ute woman, beautiful and youthful enough to become a discordant element in the household, and before long she and Sacajawea were engaged in a bitter domestic feud. During the temporary absence of the two sons, Toussaint and Baptiste, an incident occurred from which Sacajawea emerged triumphant at the expense of her Ute rival.

Charbonneau, having nothing to fear in the absence of his sons, took the part of the younger woman and vented his anger upon Sacajawea by whipping her.

This, as the records of the Lewis and Clark expedition show, was certainly not the first time Sacajawea had suffered similar treatment at the hands of her esteemed husband. But in this instance, not so much because of the whipping itself as because of the disgrace of being beaten by her husband in the presence of the new and younger wife, Sacajawea disappeared from her tepee and left Charbonneau, never to return. When Toussaint and Baptiste returned and learned of Sacajawea's departure and what their father had done, "they made it very serious for Charbonneau and were never friends after that." Apparently they, too, left the old interpreter and were never reunited with him. Charbonneau, on his part, after Sacajawea's disappearance, accompanied a large body of fur-traders to Salt lake where many of the employees of the company were then trapping for beaver and trading with the Indians. The summer following this encampment, Charbonneau crossed the Rocky mountains to the northeast and reached the Wind, Big Horn, Yellowstone, and Missouri rivers, finally arriving at the villages of the Gros Ventre, which he was accustomed to look upon as his home.

After Sacajawea left Charbonneau, she apparently wandered about for some time, finally making her home with a tribe of the Comanches.[101] The language of these

---

[101] "The once roaming banditti of Texas and Oklahoma and New Mexico were Comanches, a branch of the great and widely distributed Shoshoni family. Their language and traditions show that they are a comparatively recent offshoot from the Shoshoni of Wyoming, both tribes speaking practically the same dialect. . . Within the traditionary period, the two tribes lived adjacent to each other in southern Wyoming, since which time the Shoshoni have been beaten back into the mountains by the Sioux and other prairie tribes,

people she could understand, and they in turn could understand her, for they were in fact a branch of the Shoshones, and the two languages differed from each other in about the same degree that high Dutch differs from low Dutch.[102] Here, in the course of time, Sacajawea married a member of this tribe with the aristocratic name of Jerk Meat. With this husband she lived harmoniously for a number of years, giving birth to five children, only two of whom, however, survived. One of these was a son called Ticannaf, and the other, the youngest of the five, a daughter named Yaga-wosier or Crying Basket. Shortly after the birth of this last child, Jerk Meat was killed in battle. From this time on Sacajawea "was not in harmony with her husband's people," and decided to leave the Comanches and seek her own tribe. The Comanches, informed of her intentions, "did not take her seriously." Nevertheless, she so completely disappeared that her whereabouts were unknown for many years, and the Comanches thereafter spoke of her as Wadze-wipe, or Lost Woman. This name, it should be noted, is of Comanche origin, and does not belong to the Shoshone tongue.

When she left the Comanches, Sacajawea took with her her daughter, Yaga-wosier. For food she carried a small parfleche bag filled with dried buffalo meat and, thus equipped, started her long Odyssey in search of her own people. Her Comanche son, Ticannaf, hunted

---

while the Comanche have been driven steadily southward by the same pressure." Hodge, *op. cit.;* Maximilian, *op. cit.,* vol. XXIV, 296; Chittenden, *op. cit.,* 872; Coues, *op. cit.,* vol. I, 98.

[102] Eastman, Charles Alexander, *Report of commissioner of Indian affairs,* department of the interior, Washington, D.C., March 2, 1925. Dr. Eastman was engaged by our government to locate, if possible, the burial ground of Sacajawea. After visiting the Shoshones, Comanches, and Gros Ventres in Wyoming, Oklahoma, and North Dakota, Dr. Eastman made his report.

diligently for her, as did the entire band, but they searched in vain. She was not to be found among the Wichitas nor the Kiowas. She was the Lost Woman.

A number of routes led from the Comanche country to Sacajawea's old home among the Shoshones, and the various authors do not agree as to which of these she followed. It was possible for her to follow up the Missouri to its source in Beaverhead valley where she had been stolen when a young girl, and thence to travel south and east to the Shoshone tribe of Chief Washakie; or, she could leave the Missouri at the mouth of the Yellowstone, following that stream and the Big Horn to Fort Bridger. The most direct route, however, was that used by John Charles Frémont on his second exploring expedition, and ran directly north from the territory occupied by the Comanches, with whom Sacajawea had made her home. This route would also have enabled Sacajawea to avoid Charbonneau's country on the upper Missouri, as she unquestionably wished to do. In Frémont's account of his expedition, moreover, there is a passage describing an Indian woman returning to her people, the Shoshones, which gives every evidence of referring to Sacajawea. This account was written when Frémont was encamped at St. Vrain's fort in July, 1843. The passage is quoted here at length.

Reaching St. Vrain's fort on the morning of the 23rd of July, we found Mr. Fitzpatrick and his party in good order and excellent health, and with him my true and reliable friend, Kit Carson, who had brought ten good mules with the necessary pack-saddles.[103] . . . Through this portion of the mountains also, are the customary roads of the war-parties going out against the Utah and Shoshone Indians; and occasionally parties from the Crow nation make their way down to the

---

[103] Compare Hafen and Ghent, *Broken hand*, 144-145; also Vestal, *Kit Carson, the happy warrior of the old west.*

southward along this chain, in the expectation of surprising some straggling lodges of their enemies. Shortly before our arrival, one of their parties had attacked an Arapaho village in the vicinity, which they had found unexpectedly strong. . . A French engagé at Lupton's fort in Colorado had been shot in the back on July 4th, and died during our absence to the Arkansas. The wife of the murdered man, an Indian woman of the Snake nation, desirous, like Naomi of old, to return to her people, requested and obtained permission to travel with my party to the neighborhood of Bear river, where she expected to meet with some of their villages. Happier than the Jewish widow, she carried with her two children, pretty little half-breeds, who added much to the liveliness of the camp. Her baggage was carried on five or six pack-horses; and I gave her a small tent, for which I no longer had any use, as I had procured a lodge at the fort.

On August 2, while traveling along the most western fork of Laramie river in Wyoming, Frémont wrote:

At this place I became first acquainted with the yampah [Anethum graveolens], which I found our Snake woman engaged in digging in the low-timbered bottom of the creek.[104] Among the Indians along the Rocky mountains, and more particularly among the Shoshone or Snake Indians, in whose territory it is very abundant, this is considered the best among roots used for food.

On the eighteenth, after the expedition had crossed the South pass and was on the old Oregon trail beyond the Big Sandy and Green rivers in the neighborhood of Ham's fork of the Black fork of the Green river, Frémont wrote:

The Shoshone woman took leave of us here, expecting to find some of her relations at Bridger's fort, which is only a mile or two distant, on a fork of this stream. In the evening we encamped on a salt creek, about fifteen feet wide, having today traveled thirty-two miles.

As already stated, Frémont's account of this Snake

---

[104] Note that Sacajawea rendered a similar service to Lewis and Clark in 1805 and 1806. See under dates of Aug. 22, 1805, and May 16, 1806.

or Shoshone woman in all probability refers to Sacajawea. It was not at all strange that Sacajawea should
have adopted the child of a French engagé, even though
the child might not have been her own, for it was customary for a Shoshone woman to adopt a child left
without its parents even though there were no blood
relationship between the woman and the child. Perhaps,
indeed, Sacajawea had herself married this French
trader, but of this there is no evidence. Andrew Bazil,
grandson of Sacajawea, and son of the Bazil whom she
adopted in 1805, told the author in a personal interview
on the Shoshone reservation that his grandmother returned to the Shoshones from the Comanches by the
easiest route, which ran directly from the south through
Colorado into Wyoming and along the Oregon trail,
and that when she returned she had with her two adopted
daughters. James McAdams, a great-grandson of Sacajawea, also confirmed the tradition that Sacajawea returned to her people along a direct route from the south,
and that she brought with her a number of horses.[105]

The Shoshones at this time [1843] were under the
chieftainship of Washakie and were not as isolated as
one might believe, for well-beaten trails radiated from
the valley of the Bridger and the Green, and were constantly in use by hunting parties, Indian raiders, and
even white travelers. These paths led to the sources of
the Missouri, where the lodges of the Lemhi Indians
were located. To this day the Shoshones of the reservation in the Wind river country use these trails, deepened
by generations of heavy travel, in their big game hunting.
At that time the territory contained thousands of buffalo,

---

[105] Interviews of the author with Bazil, 1925; with McAdams, 1929. See
Appendices C, D, and E.

and even today there are elk, moose, deer, and big horn sheep in the regions not frequently traveled. These paths are also still used semi-annually when the Shoshones visit the Indians who live near the sources of the Salmon river where Sacajawea tarried for a week with her people in August, 1805.

It is difficult indeed to realize how migratory the Indians were (and still are), and how far they some-times traveled. In speaking of this trait of the Shoshones, F. G. Burnett, an Indian instructor on the Shoshone reservation for much of the time since 1872, makes this statement:

There are Indians here who have traveled through the mountains and deserts to the California coast, and then have returned through Oregon, Washington, and Montana. Time is nothing to the Indian; his home is wherever his lodge is, and if there is plenty of game or fish, and grass for his pony, he is happy, and it matters little to him, when he takes a notion to move, whether it is north, south, east, or west. There is one thing you can depend on that he will do, and that is that he will move in some direction every three or four days.

The life of Sacajawea after her reunion with her tribe, the Shoshones, is described at length in a later chapter. Among these people she found her two sons: Baptiste, who was now an interpreter, guide, and hunter; and Bazil, the orphan, child of her dead sister, whom she adopted in 1805 when she was a member of the Lewis and Clark expedition. The story of her life from this time on is based largely on the testimony of her friends and relatives on the Shoshone reservation in the Wind river country. Some of this testimony was procured many years ago; some more recently; much of it could never be obtained again, for many of those from whom it came have gone to join their ancestors, carrying with them the fading memory of the trails and hunting-grounds of long ago before the white man came to restrict the Indian's wanderings and to change his customs and habits.

The Shoshone Indians of the Lemhi valley in Idaho, who constituted the tribe to which Sacajawea belonged, in the course of time drifted into Bridger valley in what is now the southwestern part of Wyoming, and set up their tepees along the Bear river and beside the sources and branches of the Green. About 1840 a great Indian leader named Washakie became chief of these Indians in the Bridger valley, and for sixty years filled this high office, winning for himself by his valor, skill in warfare, and constant loyalty to the government of the United States the name of "White Man's Friend, Chief Washakie."[106]

As we have seen, one of the Lemhi chiefs who aided Lewis and Clark was Cameahwait, the brother of Sacajawea. This chief was killed in battle against the Pahkeeps about 1840, and was succeeded by his nephew, Now-ro-yawn [later known as Snag to the Mormons], who had distinguished himself by his bravery in this battle. Fighting beside Now-ro-yawn was his cousin, Shoo-gan or Bazil, as he was more commonly called by the whites, the adopted son of Sacajawea. Bazil became, in time, one of the trusted sub-chiefs under Washakie, to whom he was related, and because of a wound which he received in a battle in 1862 in which Now-ro-yawn was killed, he was known to the Indians as the lame sub-chief of Washakie.[107]

---

[106] See Hebard, Grace Raymond, *Washakie*, 30, 286. Through a common ancestor in Chief Tendoy of the Lemhi Indians, Chief Washakie and Sacajawea were related.

[107] Stuart, Granville, "Montana as it is, 1865," original MS. in the library of the University of Wyoming.

In 1843 James Bridger established his blacksmith shop, post, and fort in the valley of the Blackfork and Green rivers to supply the "immigrants for Oregon and California with necessary supplies." Bridger spoke of this new landmark on the Oregon trail as a "small fort with a blacksmith shop and a supply of iron, in the road of the immigrants." It was not designed for a road house or a saloon, but as a "sanctuary in the midst of the immigrant's journey." It was near this fort, which was completed by the first of August, 1843, that Frémont took leave of the Shoshone woman with her two small children "who expected to find relatives at Bridger fort."

In 1847 the Mormons, under the leadership of Brigham Young, traveled the Oregon trail from Council bluffs to Salt lake. Here they broke the sod, planted seed, and ploughed furrows for irrigation ditches to signalize their arrival in the land of promise. In the meantime, a company of Young's followers had been recruited by the United States government in Omaha, and organized into the so-called Mormon battalion to assist in the conquest of California. With these Mormons Baptiste Charbonneau, Bazil's brother, came in frequent contact while he was serving under General Cooke and the other leaders of the California expedition.

East and north of the Mormon settlement at Salt lake lay the Shoshone reservation where Sacajawea, Bazil, and, in time, Baptiste came to live. Here from perhaps 1850 to 1871, when they migrated to the Shoshone reservation further north, these three made their home, and Bazil at least, from his contact with the Mormons, learned something of agriculture and the cultivation of the soil.

At the time of the construction of the Union Pacific

railroad through Bridger valley it was necessary to secure the permission of the Indians for the right of way in order to avoid serious difficulty and probable bloodshed. The Shoshones naturally objected strongly to the construction through their territory of a railroad, which would drive away the game upon which they depended for their living. Washakie recognized the seriousness of the situation for his people, and therefore sought from the government a new reservation in the Wind river valley where his people might find a new home and where the game would remain undisturbed. The Great treaty, by which this was accomplished, was signed by government officials and Chief Washakie and his sub-chiefs on July 3, 1868. Under this treaty the Shoshones were granted some 2,784,400 acres, all of which lay north of the Oregon trail. Subsequent treaties have reduced this territory to less than 525,000 acres.

On the part of the Indians, the treaty was signed by Washakie and his sub-chiefs, of whom Bazil was one. Since no Indian was then able to read or write, the names of the signers appeared with "his 'x' mark." A thorough search has been made of the files of the Indian office, but no record so far has been found of the minutes of the council at which this treaty was drafted, though such minutes should have been forwarded to Washington. The treaty is, of course, a matter of official record. Prior to this treaty, Bazil had also agreed to and signed the treaty of 1863, and his mark also appears on the treaty of 1872.[108]

With characteristic farsightedness, Chief Washakie cherished the desire that his people might be taught to

---

[108] Kappler, Charles J., *Indian affairs, laws and treaties,* Washington, 1904, vol. I, 153, vol. II, 848, 1020.

FORT SUPPLY, SITE OF FIRST MORMON SETTLEMENT IN WYOMING

Located a few miles from the site of old Fort Bridger. Here, in 1852, at a harvest celebration, Bazil thanked the Mormons for teaching him how to grow crops.

raise crops on some of the land in the new reservation in order that they might have food when the game should have disappeared and the buffalo have been hunted out. Some of the tribe, indeed, had already learned their first lessons in agriculture, even before the move was made to the new reservation, from the Mormon immigrants who had settled in Bridger valley. Here at Fort Supply these followers of Joseph Smith had grown the first crops in southwestern Wyoming. They had also learned to converse with the Shoshones and Bannocks, who had erected their lodges around Fort Bridger, studying the Shoshone language from a Mormon teacher who was married to a Shoshone wife. Here Bazil, among others, had been taught agriculture and the art of irrigating land, and had learned his lesson so well that by 1856 he was able to produce wheat and vegetables. The success of his experiment made him "feel good," and also inspired others to grow potatoes, beets, and peas. Washakie himself also learned the value of reclaiming land by irrigation.

It is only natural that there should have been scant mention made of Sacajawea in the interval between the time that she rejoined her people and the change of the Shoshones to the Wind river reservation; nor is it strange that such meager reference as there is should come from the statements of individuals, including both Indians and whites, rather than from official records; for until the treaty of 1868 the government had little, if any, interest in the Shoshone Indians, and exercised only nominal control over the tribe. Such information as is available, however, clearly shows that Sacajawea exercised great and beneficial influence among her people and was of inestimable service to the whites and to the

American government. It is certain from the testimonies, here printed for the first time, that Sacajawea made her influence felt in the council of 1868 at Fort Bridger, and that she sought to persuade her people to accept the proposed reservation and to live at peace with the whites.

Speaking on this subject, Andrew Bazil, son of the sub-chief Bazil and grandson of Sacajawea, said to the author in 1926:

My father Bazil, my grandmother Porivo [Sacajawea], Chief Washakie, and myself were at the Great treaty, and my grandmother sat back where the women sat in a circle, where I could not hear the words of her speech.

When my grandmother was living, my father used to say to me, "You must respect your grandmother; all the white people respect her and honor her everywhere." My father said he had made peace with the Mormon church on behalf of his people. My father was noted among the Mormons.

My father also had some papers that he carefully kept in a leather bag which he said were very valuable. Later I learned that these papers were given to my grandmother by some great white chiefs.

Barbara Meyers, daughter of Baptiste, and granddaughter of Sacajawea, with a smiling face which resembled that of her grandmother, recalled Sacajawea's presence at the Great treaty.

Yes, Porivo, or Sacajawea, or Wadze-wipe, was at the council of the Great treaty down at Fort Bridger when the Bridger valley territory was exchanged by Washakie and his warriors for the present Shoshone reservation. This Sacajawea was my grandmother, and my father was her son, Baptiste, the papoose who was carried to the big waters toward the setting sun. I was there at the council in 1868, but at that time, I was quite a young woman, and was one of the listeners at the council.

Hebe-chee-chee, in 1929, told the following to the author through the government interpreter:

Yes, I was at Fort Bridger at the time of the Great treaty, when the Bridger country was sold by Chief Washakie for the Shoshone reservation. My uncle (my father's brother), Humpy, was one of the leaders of the Shoshones at the treaty, and one of Washakie's fighters in the council. In the council, Washakie asked my father to suggest what part of what is now Wyoming they should ask for a reservation, and what would be best for the Shoshones. My uncle told Washakie that he should ask for the "warm valley" where there was little snow, and there were hot springs for bathing. . .

I remember that there were a lot of women in a circle at this council. I can not remember whether Sacajawea was there or not. So many women were there she might have been there and not noticed. I was not interested except in the part my uncle was taking.

Enga Peahrora, daughter of Chief Washakie, stood at the open flap of her tepee and spoke of Porivo and her part in the council, called the Great treaty of 1868, as follows:

I knew Porivo, or Sacajawea, at Fort Bridger. She lived with her son Bazil. I was a young girl at the time, perhaps at the age of fourteen or fifteen. She lived with Bazil in an Indian tepee at Fort Bridger.

I knew that Porivo took part in the council at Fort Bridger because I was right there and saw her in the council myself. She had a part in the meeting, and she spoke in the meeting, I know this, because I was there and saw her speak.

Quantan Quay, in a personal interview on the reservation [July 21, 1929], added his testimony:

I was at the council at the time that the treaty was made with our government at Fort Bridger. . . Sacajawea was at this council meeting. I know she was there. I saw her there. Bazil was one of the men speakers and spoke, but Baptiste did not speak nor say a thing.

Edmo St. Clair, son of an employee of the American Fur company when it was operating in the Bridger valley country, knew Sacajawea, Bazil, and Baptiste, particularly the sons, since they were always used as interpreters in dealing with the white traders and Indians. Mr. St. Clair testified:

I met Sacajawea, mother of Baptiste and Bazil, sometime after we had moved to Fort Bridger, and after I had come to know her two sons. This was in 1863.

I was at Fort Bridger when the treaty was made between the government and Chief Washakie and his people in 1868. Bazil, the son of Sacajawea, was one of the signers of the treaty.

I saw Sacajawea at the treaty, and remember very well seeing her in the circle formed by the Shoshone women just back of the circle made by Chief Washakie and his men. They were sitting down. I also saw her standing up and making a short speech of some kind, but I cannot remember now what she said. It has been over sixty years ago. The last time I saw Sacajawea at Fort Bridger was in 1869, a year after the treaty.

Mr. F. G. Burnett, who knew Sacajawea longer and better than any other white man, said in an interview:

At the time of the signing of the Great treaty I was not there, since I did not come among the Shoshone Indians until 1871. It would have been an unthinkable thing under ordinary circumstances for a woman to be allowed to address a council of wise brave lords of creation, but she represented the white men as well as the Indians. There is no doubt that her influence was felt in all important questions that were discussed. Bazil was her mouthpiece, and he was an eloquent speaker. Through him, her influence was felt on all important questions. Bazil was a man of noble and commanding presence. He was fully six feet tall and weighed over two hundred pounds. He had a deep, musical voice, and had a great influence in council. All questions of importance were discussed around the camp fires and in their lodges. Here is where a woman's influence was felt. Many a brave warrior in council has spoken eloquent words of wisdom that his wife or mother put in his mouth while discussing important questions around the camp fire. I have known Washakie and other chiefs to visit Sacajawea's home near the agency and listen intensely to her conversation for hours. . .

When discontent arose for any cause among the Indians, Chief Washakie, his sub-chief Bazil, and Sacajawea could always be depended upon as firm friends of the whites, although the government failed many times to fulfill their promises to them. . . The influence of Washakie, Bazil, and Sacajawea caused all the mountain Indians to remain peaceful during the Indian wars, and saved the government great expense and the lives of many pioneers. Wyoming is under many obligations to these three noble, true, and steadfast Indian friends. . .

What a pity that their influence and worth were not recognized while they were living! There are but a very few men living who knew and appreciated them. Washakie understood English fairly well, but when conversing with Sacajawea, they talked the Shoshone language. . . Those who understood French said that both she and Bazil talked very good French. She and Bazil talked English very well. Sacajawea also talked several Indian languages.

In a letter to the author dated December 9, 1931, the Honorable A. M. Clark, acting governor of the state of Wyoming, commenting upon the book *Washakie,* asks this question: "What was the basic reason for Chief Washakie, under all conditions, ever and persistently remaining a loyal friend to the white people?" In the influence of Sacajawea, as evidenced by the testimony given above, lies the answer to that question. For it is certainly evident that Sacajawea proved of the greatest value to the whites through her influence with her own people. She was able to understand the white man's point of view and to present this to the Indians, at the same time successfully interpreting the Indian's point of view to the whites. Her own people respected her council, and the whites valued her understanding and influence. The influence of Bazil, like that of his mother, was also of great value to the American government.

The domestic relationships of Sacajawea were somewhat complex. She was the mother of Baptiste who, as already frequently stated, was born in 1805 in the Mandan villages just before the Lewis and Clark expedition started for the west. She was stepmother of Toussaint, the son of Charbonneau and the "other Shoshone woman" who died in 1812; and she was the aunt and foster-mother of Bazil, the son of Sacajawea's oldest sister, who was born about 1802. The adoption of Bazil by Sacajawea followed the custom of the Shoshones, by which a sister adopts her deceased sister's children.

At the time of the adoption, on August 17, 1805, near the Two forks of the Jefferson river, Bazil was a "small boy." This expression to the Indians signified a small child who was able to walk, hence it is surmised that Bazil was about three years old at the time of his adoption. The incident of his adoption, as already stated, is recorded only in the Biddle edition of the Lewis and Clark journals.

It will be remembered that after Sacajawea's adoption of Bazil, she continued with the Lewis and Clark expedition, while her newly-adopted son remained with his people, the Shoshones. Apparently, therefore, he knew nothing of his foster-mother until he was a man, grown, and she had returned to her tribe at Fort Bridger, sometime after 1840. From that time on, however, it appears that the relationship between Bazil and Sacajawea was not only formally acknowledged, but was much more intimate and close than that of Sacajawea and her own son, Baptiste. Thus, Sacajawea became known as Bazil's mother, or Bazil umbea, and lived with him as part of his recognized household.

Baptiste, whose history has previously been given in some detail in this volume, undertook the last of his more important missions when he served with the Mormon battalion on its march to California. For twenty years thereafter the records contain almost no mention

Bazil, sub-chief of Washakie

Bazil, adopted son of Sacajawea, is at the extreme left, standing. Chief Washakie is the mounted figure at the right. This is the only known picture of Chief Bazil.

of his name. By this time the trails and passes were well defined and extensively used, and the services of expert guides and interpreters were consequently less and less in demand. During these years Baptiste seems to have devoted himself to hunting and, perhaps in a minor way, serving also as a guide. Apparently he cared almost nothing for the agricultural interests of his half-brother, Bazil. He played but a small part in the historical records and activities of the Shoshones, and, according to Andrew Bazil, almost never spoke in their councils.

Bazil, on the contrary, always held an important and dignified position in the councils of his tribe. As already stated, he was one of the sub-chiefs of Washakie and, as such, signed three of the five major treaties which that great chieftain made with the government of the United States. These treaties were those of 1863, 1868, and 1872. On these documents, Bazil's name appears as Bazeel, though, of course, like most Indians, he was able to sign only with his mark.

Bazil, as already recorded, early recognized the value of studying the agricultural methods of the whites. After he left the Lemhi mission in Idaho he lived until 1871 in close contact with the Mormon settlers in Bridger valley and from them learned much that was useful to his people. The records of the archives of the historical department of the Church of Jesus Christ of the Latter Day Saints, at Salt Lake city, attest to Bazil's friendly relations with these pioneers. As early as 1852 we find him one of the speakers at a harvest festival and pioneer celebration held by the Mormons at Fort Supply, near Fort Bridger. On this occasion he expressed himself as grateful for the training in agriculture he had received, saying in part:

I feel well to see grain growing on the Snake land; now their children can get bread to eat, also butter and milk. Before you came here our children were often hungry; now they can get bread and vegetables when we are not fortunate in hunting meat.[109]

Elder Isaac Bullock, one of the missionaries of Fort Lemhi, writes in the fall of 1856 that

Baziel, one of the Snakes who has lived in the fort with us during the last year, has raised thirty bushels of wheat and some vegetables. He and his squaws have harvested it clean and neat, and appear to feel well satisfied with their prospects for bread this winter.[110]

At a Fort Lemhi banquet of the same year, Bazil proposed the following toast:

I want you to live and never die, that you may raise plenty of the good things we have had to eat today, for they make my heart feel good.[111]

Chief Bazil seems to have been a popular after-dinner speaker, for the three speeches here recorded occurred at three different places—at Fort Supply and Fort Bridger, both then in Utah, and at Fort Lemhi in Idaho.

It is probable, also, that Bazil was actually baptized into the Mormon faith. The records of the Mormon Salmon river mission of November 11, 1855, mention the baptism of sixty-five Indians, among whom appears the name of Snag, a cousin of Bazil's already referred to in a previous chapter, and chief of the Shoshones after Cameahwait. Writes Andrew Jenson, assistant church historian, to the author:

While the mission at Fort Limhi was functioning from 1855 to 1858, Baziel lived there with his wives for about a year. The date of the baptism of Baziel is not recorded in those portions of the manuscript

[109] Hebard, *Washakie*, 75, 119.
[110] *Desert News*, Salt Lake city, Oct. 1, 1856, vol. VI, 366.
[111] Journal history of the Mormon church, July 24, 1856, 9.

records of the Salmon river mission, but it seems hardly credible that this chief remained with the missionaries that length of time and became somewhat prominent among them, unless he had received baptism at their hands.[112]

In 1871, Sacajawea, Bazil and his wives, Baptiste with his three wives, and Chief Washakie likewise with his three wives, migrated into the new reservation in the Wind river valley, to the east and north of the Mormon lands, there to remain with their people for the rest of their lives. Sacajawea died in 1884, Baptiste in 1885, and Bazil in 1886. Chief Washakie lived until 1900. Numerous descendants of these four Shoshones make their homes at the present time on the same reservation, and some of them, both at Fort Bridger and on the reservation, have made valuable contributions to the history of Sacajawea, Bazil, and Baptiste.

The influence of Sacajawea and Bazil, and to a lesser degree of Baptiste, in interpreting the white man to their fellow tribesmen and in urging them to adopt his methods of agriculture, was of the greatest service to the government agents sent to the reservation for this purpose. One of the most important of these government agents was Mr. F. G. Burnett, previously referred to, who was sent to teach the Shoshones and Bannocks how to farm. This position was held by Mr. Burnett with great credit until 1924, and because of his long acquaintance with the Shoshones and his intelligent understanding, his testimony is of particular value and interest. In a personal interview with the author, Mr. Burnett made the following statement:

---

[112] Letter to the author, June 29, 1931. Other information about the Salmon river mission and Fort Lemhi was furnished the author through the courtesy of Joseph Fielding Smith, church historian, in a letter of Sept. 3, 1929, and in excerpts from archives of the Church of Jesus Christ of the Latter Day Saints.

Sacajawea was of the greatest help to the Indian agents, James Irwin and James I. Patten. Into her house about one hundred fifty yards from the agent's office, or into their office at the Wind river agency, she and they were going in and out many times a day and in this way they were kept in close touch with what was to the advantage of the agents to know about the government's wards, the Shoshones. It was she who kept the affairs of the office straight as to information that was to be sent to Washington.

The government interpreter for the Shoshones, during the early years of reservation life, talked very indifferent English, and experienced difficulty in translating the agent's English speeches into the Shoshone language for the Indians. Sacajawea and Bazil, both able to speak English and Shoshone, were of invaluable service as interpreters to the agent during a long and important period of this reservation life.

During the first days when the Indians started to work in agriculture on the Shoshone reservation under my supervision as instructor in agriculture, there was not an Indian or a horse that knew anything about farming. . .

We finally got started with the assistance of Porivo [Sacajawea], Bazil and Baptiste, who had seen the great fields of grain in the south among the Comanches, or with the Mormons in the region of Great Salt lake. Baptiste, too, had seen fields in his travels. With the help these three gave in their native tongue, and the confidence the Shoshones had in Sacajawea and her sons and their ability to tell the Indians what we wished to do, we got under way.

As already stated, Mr. Burnett remembers Bazil as a fine, portly man, nearly six feet tall, who must have weighed over 200 pounds. His complexion was also very fair for a full-blooded Indian. He was crippled in one knee, and when walking, the toes only of one foot touched the ground. He and his mother were much attached to each other, and they lived together until Sacajawea's death. Sacajawea had another son who was identified as the babe she carried on her back on the expedition. He was called Baptiste. He was a small man, and had a complexion as dark as any full-blooded Indian. He was of course, a "breed."

James I. Patten, who was officially identified with the

Shoshone reservation and the Wind river agency as teacher and lay missionary as early as 1871 and for many years thereafter, also corroborates Mr. Burnett's description of Bazil.

Bazil was a sub-chief of the Shoshone tribe, and usually quite active in tribal affairs. He was rather lighter in complexion than Battez [Baptiste], was lame in one of his limbs, five feet eight inches, about, in height, in weight about two hundred seventy-five pounds, with thick lips and a very pleasant and good-natured manner.

He claimed Sacajawea as his mother, and gave her always all the attention and care that a son would be expected to show a mother.

From 1868 to 1875, when supplies were carried by freighters over the Oregon trail from Fort Laramie to Fort Bridger and thence to Salt Lake city, one of the best-known freighters was a man named Jim Faris, who was then well acquainted with the country and its Indian inhabitants. In his statement to Charles Alexander Eastman, Faris made the following comments on Bazil and Baptiste:

Bazil seemed to have had then a great influence with Brigham Young, in fact he made two or three agreements with him.

He also was one of the strong men of James Bridger and Roubideau, for he usually interpreted all their trading with his tribe. I have also known his brother, Baptiste. He was not a leader of the band, but he was assistant to his brother in a way. Bazil once said to me that since he came back here he took the responsibility of guiding his uncle's band. His uncle had been dead before he came back, and it was led by another man, but not successfully.

What Bazil said, I think was true, because ever since I have known him he was always considered the head of Henry's fork Snakes. I know him to be a very reliable and conscientious man. He was practically old or middle-aged when I met him, but in action he was a man of a great deal of physical activity and clear headedness. He was a very useful lieutenant to Chief Washakie. He never claimed very much honor, but it is a fact that he and his mother were the trump card when Washakie made the treaty with the United States in 1868. He did not as a rule volunteer information or tell much about his own life, except that he knew me very well and we talked over a good deal of western life in the past when we smoked in our own cabins.

It appears from what he said he came into this country with Jim Bridger and Roubideau from the southwest. After he arrived here, he devoted his time to his tribe and he was with them all the time, but his brother, Baptiste, became more or less a guide and trapper to the fur-traders and hunters for a time, but he too after a while settled down with his brother's tribe.

Further interesting information regarding the two brothers or cousins was given the author by Barbara Meyers, the daughter of Baptiste.

Baptiste, my father, did not always live with Bazil and did not say very much. He seldom spoke in public nor told of his different travels. My Uncle Bazil was more of a spokesman. My grandmother often spoke to me of having had a French husband and that Baptiste was the son of this French husband. Both Baptiste and Bazil spoke the Ute and French and English languages, as well as, of course, the Shoshone language. . .

My father, Baptiste, often spoke to me of being across the big waters into another country toward the rising sun, and how funny the white people were over in that district. He saw many curious people and often spoke about this period of his life. Baptiste, my father, spoke several languages. At Fort Bridger he used to tell me of his many travels, and at that time when he was at Bridger when the treaty was made [1868] he was sixty-three years old.

From the testimony of those who knew them, at least in later years, Bazil thus seems to have been a much stronger character than Baptiste. Quantan Quay, in describing the two men, says:

Bazil was a man of fine character, physically splendid — a true specimen or type of Indian. He was always gentle in his speech and never loud or boisterous. On the other hand, Baptiste was a treacherous man, because he liked his firewater and used it often.

This opinion is confirmed by Mr. James I. Patten, who thus describes Baptiste as he recalled him:

He was a man of little force or importance in the tribe, about five feet six inches in height, quite dark complexion, stocky build, weight about two hundred pounds, thick lips and his mouth drawn well down at the corners. He was rather pleasant and sociable in manner, liked ease and enjoyed it. He had a wife and several children. He acknowledged Sac-a-jaw-wea as his mother, and that she accompanied the expedition to the coast, but seemed to take but a passing interest in her.

From the statements made above, the conclusion reached in chapter III is further strengthened: that Baptiste in later life suffered the usual fate of the half-breed who deteriorates from adopting the vices of the whites. In earlier years, however, he proved himself of great value to the fur-traders and explorers because of his ability as an interpreter and his knowledge of the west.[113] Returning to his mother's people in later years when changed conditions made his services as guide and interpreter no longer in demand, he lived the remainder of his life somewhat apart from the rest of his tribe – "in a lone lodge camping by himself," as Mr. Burnett records, talking little and mingling little with other people. Bazil, on the other hand, was an active and valued leader of his people and a man whose services and friendship were also greatly appreciated by the whites. The testimony of his contemporaries unanimously ascribes to him exceptional qualities.

The fact that both Bazil and Baptiste claimed Sacajawea as mother and were in turn acknowledged by her as her sons adds substantial weight to the claim that she was the guide of the Lewis and Clark expedition.[114]

[113] See Index for further amplification of this phase of Baptiste's career.

[114] The statements of the Indians and others from which extracts are quoted in this chapter are printed in full in Appendices B, C, and D.

Sacajawea at Fort Bridger and the Reservation

She reached Fort Bridger where she found her two sons. The family reunion was natural and a happy one. Bazil, the older son. . . was exceptionally devoted to her. It was in this family that she lived and died. There are many instances among the Indians where a nephew or step-son has been more devoted to the mother than the real son. That was the case in the relation of Bazil to his mother.

It is the *Ben Hur* of the Indians. A most remarkable romantic life of any age.—CHARLES ALEXANDER EASTMAN [*Ohiyesa*]

CHAPTER V

Sacajawea at Fort Bridger and the Reservation

One of the chief marks of greatness on the part of Chief Washakie, whose name has so frequently been mentioned in these pages, was his ability to look ahead into the future and prepare for the time when the buffalo would be gone and the Indian would be forced to raise his own food or perish from starvation. With this object in mind, Washakie, as we have already seen, succeeded in obtaining the Wind river valley as a reservation for the Shoshone people from the United States government in 1868. The task of teaching the Indians to farm, however, upon this reservation was not without its difficulties. Mr. F. G. Burnett tells the story of the beginnings of this effort in the following paragraph:

We commenced to harness one team to the plow. I told the Indian to drive the horse, but the horse balked. The Indian said to his squaw, "You lead them," referring to the horses, and the Indian would hold on to the plow and at the same time he would have to hold his blanket around his body with his teeth, because he refused to abandon his blanket. At first we got along pretty well. The next horse reared and ran away. The next one had a woman at the plow and the man riding the horse. Finally we got the 320 acres ploughed and had good crops that year through irrigation. We had ten acres of barley, and the rest was in wheat and oats, half and half. Those who measured the grain as it was thrashed vowed that the crop averaged seventy-five bushels to the acre, barley, wheat, and oats equally. That fall we had a little mill with some bolting cloth, which enabled us to do some grinding.

This was the first wheat to be ground by Indians in Wyoming. I am inclined to believe and have always thought that this was the first wheat and first flour in the state.

According to Burnett, as we have already seen, Sacajawea and Bazil rendered great service both in urging the Shoshones to learn to farm and in setting the example. Sacajawea told her people that the buffalo and other game animals would soon be gone, that the whites would become as numerous as grasshoppers, and that the Indians would have to learn to raise wheat and grind grain. Sacajawea also told them how the Mandans on the Missouri raised corn, how good it was, and how it kept away the hunger. The irrigation ditches of the whites seemed to the Indians to lead the water up hill, and Washakie said that only white men and Mormons could do this and that Indians could not. The Indians looked through the surveyor's level or the transit, and wondered how the instrument achieved the miracle, calling it white man's medicine.

Many other difficulties were encountered in the first agricultural work among the Shoshones! Spotted fever took its toll, and the Indian suspected that evil agencies were responsible for this. Mr. Burnett tells how one Indian refused to have his land ploughed or to take care of it. When asked why, the Indian finally admitted, "If I turn water into the gopher's hole, he will come out of the hole and sit up and look at me and I will die!"

That this superstitious fear was not entirely without foundation has been shown by recent tests which have demonstrated that the gopher carries the tick which spreads the dreaded spotted fever in the mountain districts.[115] It was for this reason that the authorities at

115 According to information furnished by Dr. Cecil Elder, research patholo-

Washington, about 1894-95, urged the extermination of the gopher as a dangerous pest. Dr. E. N. Roberts, a trained chemist and son of the Reverend John Roberts of the Shoshone mission, corroborates this fear of the Indians of the gopher, and gives a similar explanation to account for it.

Certain of the Shoshones have told my father that if a gopher comes out of its hole and looks at one, that one is liable to fall ill with the fever. Further, the Indian believes that if he goes out of his tepee in the morning and finds a pocket gopher facing the tepee door, with his head bowed and his forepaws drawn over the face, the Indian or members of his family will become ill and die. The Shoshones believed this to the extent that they would desert their abodes upon such a discovery, and move elsewhere immediately in the hope that they might escape disaster. Hence the Shoshone desire not to disturb the gopher by irrigation, or not to run the risk of being seen by the animal.

The idea of a gopher dying in front of an Indian dwelling is not necessarily "far fetched," because during the season when spotted fever was particularly prevalent, a good many of the gophers also died of the disease, and when ill with it, a gopher would likely wander from his burrow and die in the open and perhaps near an Indian tepee, which he would not ordinarily closely approach.

It is true, as far as I have observed, that white mice, rats, and guinea pigs, when ill from experimental innoculation with virulent bacterial cultures, generally assume a posture which is characteristic — a huddled position, remaining quiet with the feet under them, head down — and generally they die in that position and do not "turn up their toes," so the Shoshone description of a gopher dead from spotted fever sounds accurate and characteristic of rodents dying of such a cause.[116]

gist at the University of Wyoming, the connection between ticks and Rocky mountain spotted fever has been studied since about 1904 when the disease was recognized as a distinct entity by physicians of Bitter root valley, Montana. The proof by Ricketts in 1906 gave his name to the parasitic organism, Rickettsia. Information on the subject is still meager, but it is known that the mammalian hosts of this microscopic parasite include rodents such as ground squirrels, woodchucks, wood rats. The parasites do not kill sheep or cattle.

[116] Personal interview with the author, July, 1929. Dr. Roberts was born

Difficult as were these first problems to overcome, the Shoshones, in the course of time, adapted themselves to agriculture and, as we have seen, Sacajawea and her son Bazil contributed much to the success of this new experiment. It is our purpose in the remainder of this chapter to speak more in detail of the character and activities of Sacajawea as she lived on the reservation as her contemporaries remembered her.

Apparently even in her late years, she was a person of restless spirit who traveled far and wide throughout the west. Thus she was seen at many of the well-known trading-posts such as Fort Laramie and Fort Bridger, and her name appears at irregular intervals in their records.

Charles William Bocker, pioneer of early Wyoming, who died at Laramie on November 20, 1929, prepared a written statement containing the recollections of Sacajawea and of events relating to her life and times. Part of this statement is considered of sufficient interest to be given here unedited.

I came to the Oregon trail from Sweden in 1857, and went over it through Wyoming with an emigrant to Utah, a friend of mother's, a widow. I cannot remember much on the route, but I do remember when we were at Ft. Laramie. From there we went directly to Salt lake, which was the end of our "home stretch." I went to Ft. Bridger in 1858. My mother's cousin lived at Ft. Supply. Ft. Supply was a fort erected by the Mormons not far from old Ft. Bridger. I commenced to work at Fort Bridger for the Judge W. A. Carter family and his brother in 1865, and a part of 1866 and 1867 were spent taking care of cattle and hauling hay cut on Ham's fork or Willow creek.

In 1868 I worked for the Union Pacific railroad, working on the grade, driving spikes in the ties and helping lay the rails. I was working west part of the time toward Promontory.

in the Wind river mission and was a Rhodes scholar from Wyoming.

I frequently saw Jim Bridger at Fort Bridger. I remember that I first met him about 1866, when Judge W. A. Carter and I were walking by Bridger's house where he lived. Bridger, his wife and daughter, all three of them, were in front of the house. Judge Carter introduced me to Jim Bridger, his wife, and daughter at that time. His wife's name was Rutta; the mother was a pretty, fair-looking woman. She was related to Shade Large, who married a relative of Sacajawea's, also to Mrs. Dick Hamilton. All these three women were related – Mrs. Shade Large, Mrs. Dick Hamilton, and Mrs. Jim Bridger – to Sacajawea.

I saw Sacajawea with Bridger's wife walking, talking, and visiting many times.

When I was introduced to Sacajawea at Fort Bridger, by Mr. Carter,[117] I should judge at this time she must have been an old woman of about seventy years. Squaws' ages are hard to tell. She was pretty good looking for an old woman; in fact, quite lovely looking for an old woman, and she could ride horses as well as any of them. She could talk a little English, but got it mixed up. At this time one of the Carters or Mr. Hamilton spoke to me about this Indian woman having been on an expedition with the white men. I heard at that time when I was at Fort Bridger, as many times, that she had been with the white men. Everybody all around everywhere knew it, and it was common talk. Bridger knew it, Carter knew it, Hamilton knew it, the white men knew it, the Indians knew it.

Mr. Bocker also recalled that Sacajawea came to Fort Bridger every year. She had her lodge somewhat north of the old fort, and came with the other Indians to exchange the articles which they had brought for money and trinkets at the Sutler store. During these visits Mr. Bocker became so well acquainted with Sacajawea that he could talk to her in her native tongue. She was commonly called Porivo or chief, the name by which she was known on the reservation, and she usually rode on horseback into the fort, dragging the usual Indian travois behind her horse. This method of travel consisted of

[117] Judge W. A. Carter, 1858, at Ft. Bridger. See Hebard, *Washakie*, 102-103.

having a pole fastened on each side of the pony with cross bars reaching from one pole to the other on which baggage, papooses, or other burdens were carried. Continued Mr. Bocker:

> I remember of buying a pair of moccasins from Sacajawea in 1865 when she came down from her lodge, the articles costing me $1.50 plus a quantity of beads which I purchased for her from the Sutler store; in 1866, I again had a transaction with her on her second visit, when I purchased a buffalo robe from her for three dollars in cash and miscellaneous articles of value to an Indian; in 1867, I purchased from her an Indian blanket for which I attempted to pay her with "shin-plasters," but Sacajawea, not knowing the value of this small paper money issued by our government during the war, refused to accept them and demanded coin or "hard money."

As a result of a newspaper notice of the death of Mr. Bocker in 1929, the author received a letter from Mr. Tom Rivington of Gering, Nebraska, which in turn brought forth much additional interesting information regarding Sacajawea. The letter, printed in part in the Appendix, is full of touches of the old west, the wild escapades of the road agent, and reminiscences of the Indian woman. According to Mr. Rivington, during 1860 and 1861 Sacajawea made her home for part of the time with certain Indians living near Virginia city, Montana. "The white people," he says, "had great admiration for her and did not require her to pay for anything she desired at the store." He also says that Slade, the notorious road agent then operating in Colorado, Wyoming, and Montana, gave Sacajawea money and a pass on the stage, with orders to let her eat without charge at the stations along the road. Rivington, who as a boy "slept in her tent many times," also recalls that once, when Sacajawea was about to board the stage, a notorious character named Plummer, who was both outlaw and

RACE OF THE CHEYENNE MAIDENS

From an original drawing made by Möllhausen, October 26, 1851, at Scott bluffs; never before reproduced. Photographed for the author from the original in Stuttgart, Germany.

sheriff, gave her three sacks of flour to keep her from going. That night the stage was shot up – robbed.

According to Rivington, Sacajawea also lived for a time with the Bannock Indians at Fort Hall, and used also to visit the Blackfeet at Fort Benton. Later she went to Fort Bridger

to live with Jim Bridger's Ute wife. Here is where she got in with the Shoshone Indians. They were the tribe that gave her the name of Sa-ca-ja-we. She made her home with them ever after. She told me that she visited the first time at Fort Laramie in 1856-59-63. She was a woman that was not satisfied anywhere, and the stage companies helped to make her this way as they gave her free rides. She told me she was as far south as the Gila river in Arizona, but she did not like the Apache Indians for they were always at war, but she said the whites made them that way. She was over in California to see the Indians there, but said they were so poor, as the whites had taken all the country away from them, and she had been with the Nez Perce Indians in the state of Washington for several years. She had lived with different tribes up in Canada.

Rivington also recalls that this Indian woman

never liked to stay where she could not see the mountains, for she called them home. For the unseen spirit dwelt in the hills, and a swift-running creek could preach a better sermon for her than any mortal could have done. Every morning she thanked the spirits for a new day. She worshipped the white flowers that grew at the snow line on the sides of the tall mountains, for, as she said, she sometimes believed that they were spirits of little children that had gone away, but reappeared every spring to gladden the pathway of those now living. I was just a boy then, but those words sank deep in my soul. I believed then and I believe now, that if there is a hereafter, that the Indian woman's name will be on the right side of the ledger. Sa-ca-ja-we is gone.

In 1871, as already mentioned, Sacajawea came to the Shoshone Wind river reservation to live with her people. Here she came in constant contact with various whites such as Mr. Fincelius G. Burnett, Reverend John Roberts, and others whose names have frequently been mentioned in this volume. Among other Americans who knew Sacajawea at this time were Mr. and Mrs. A. D. Lane, who were in charge of the store at the agency. In 1929, Mrs. Lane told the author that she

saw Sacajawea many times as she sat in the sun warming her aged bones. She was known to us and the small world in which she lived as Bazil's mother or Bazil Umbea. A niece of Bazil's named Ellen, made her home with us, and often spoke of Bazil's mother and told how this Indian woman led the white men to a great body of water. Sacajawea's cabin, as well as her tent, was about one fourth of a mile east of Mr. Lane's trading store.

Perhaps the American who knew Sacajawea most intimately during these days on the reservation was Mrs. James Irwin, the wife of the United States government agent on the Wind river reservation. From Sacajawea, Mrs. Irwin learned how to speak and understand the Shoshone language, and in turn taught Sacajawea a better use and understanding of English. Mrs. Irwin had had unusual educational advantages, and was an astronomer of some ability as well as a botanist. After a time she began to keep a record of the statements made to her by Sacajawea covering her activities with the Lewis and Clark expedition and her life elsewhere; but, unfortunately, a fire at the agency burned the government records and also destroyed Mrs. Irwin's manuscript, thus causing an irreparable loss to the history of Sacajawea.

Mr. James I. Patten in 1871 became teacher and lay missionary to the Indians on the Wind river reservation, and for many years following served on that reservation. Here he saw and talked with Sacajawea almost daily in

Shoshone and in French and English, both of which languages she spoke "somewhat indifferently." Mr. Patten bears out the statement of the others who met Sacajawea that she was the guide of the Lewis and Clark expedition and that her son Baptiste was the papoose she had carried with her to the coast. In the late fall of 1874, Bazil and Baptiste brought Sacajawea to the agency headquarters for care while they were to be away on a long buffalo hunt. At that time they spoke of her as their mother.

Mr. Patten also remembers that once when he saw Sacajawea carrying a heavy burden, he remarked to Bazil, who had helped her rise with it, that she was pretty old for such a heavy load. "Yes," said Bazil, "pretty old. She is my mother," and mentioned Lewis and Clark. Sacajawea also told Mr. Patten that both Bazil and Baptiste were her sons. Baptiste, though he spoke of Sacajawea as his mother, appears to have had little interest in her. According to the Reverend John Roberts who went to the reservation in 1883 as missionary clergyman of the Protestant Episcopal church, a post which he held until 1932, Sacajawea had many names in accordance with the Shoshone custom. Thus she was called on the reservation "Bah-ribo" or "Water-White-Man," "Wadze-wipe" or "Lost Woman," and "Boo-e-nive" or "Grass Maiden." [118]

A number of the older Indians on the reservation have

---

[118] "She gave Mr. Burnett," says the Reverend Roberts, "the only reasonable derivation of the word Shoshoni – Shont [lots], Shonip [grass], changed according to the Shoshone rule for the sake of euphony to Shot-shoni or Shoshoni. The Shoshones formerly lived in lodges made of grass, and even now the Arapahos call them "the people who live in grass lodges." Among his other activities, the Reverend Roberts has written books, pamphlets, and articles on the Shoshone language, its spelling, pronunciation, and interpretation. His confirmation of Sacajawea was mentioned above. See also Appendix B.

also told their recollections of Sacajawea or Porivo to the author. In 1926 one of these, known as Grandma Herford, who was then about ninety-eight years old, told the author that she had met Porivo when she was herself a girl some twelve years of age, soon after Porivo's return to the Shoshones.[119]

I remember her telling my mother that when she was traveling with a large body of men over whom army officers were in charge, that the people became very hungry and killed some of their horses, and even dogs, for food. This meat Sacajawea did not eat, nor did the Shoshones.

Quantan Quay, a name which means "She Held My Hand," also living on the Shoshone reservation, told his recollections of Sacajawea in the musical Indian tongue. He said that he knew the woman guide and her sons very well, and that the two men acted as interpreters with the whites near Fort Bridger and later traded in furs. He recalled that once when a band of his people were away all summer hunting in the Wind river country, they heard on their return that Bazil's mother had come back to Bridger. He also said that he had heard many times that the father of Bazil and Baptiste was a Frenchman, and that he had been left among the Utes.

The tradition was wide-spread among the Indians, according to Quantan Quay, that Sacajawea had led a body of men in the early days to the waters of the west.

I have no reason to doubt that she was the real Sacajawea of the Lewis and Clark expedition, because both her sons were buried and are still buried here near her.

Quantan Quay also told of seeing Sacajawea at the council of 1868, and of hearing Bazil speak.[120]

---

[119] This would have been around 1840. "The Shoshones," the Reverend Roberts writes to the author [Mar., 1928], "do not know their own ages. The Arapahos do; the Flatheads do."

[120] Quantan Quay married a cousin of Bazil's, and hence spoke of him as

Frequent mention has been made of Mr. Burnett, and frequent citations covering phases of Sacajawea's life have been quoted from his statements to the author. Like Mrs. Irwin, he was intimately acquainted with Sacajawea, and learned from her and her family how to use the Shoshone language. According to Burnett, Sacajawea and Bazil both spoke French. It was in 1871 that Sacajawea told him that she had been the guide with the Lewis and Clark expedition, and gave him many of the details of the experiences of the expedition. He recalled especially her description of the difficulties she experienced in approaching close enough to the Shoshones, when the expedition reached their territory, to convince them that the white men were their friends – thus substantiating the statement already made that Sacajawea on this, as well as on other occasions, saved the party from attack by her presence. This is further borne out by the statements of a few very old Indians living in 1902 west of the mountains, who told how they hid in the grass and bushes, behind stones and trees, or in canyons watching the expedition, and were prevented from destroying the party only by the presence of the woman with the papoose on her back. According to Mr. Burnett, Sacajawea was modest in her behavior and could not easily be induced to talk. Sometimes, however, she would tell him some of her recollections of her associations with Lewis and Clark. One of these ran as follows:

I remember very distinctly that one day about 1872 a group of us including Doctor James Irwin, Charlie Oldham, some other white men, and a group of Indians were sitting in a circle with Sacajawea.

his brother-in-law, according to the Indian custom. He was an Indian war pensioner, and wore upon his black coat a bronze medal with a red ribbon given him for his services. Of this medal he was very proud.

She was talking about her trip across the mountains, telling her story in the English language, and turning always to Bazil for verification, always speaking to him in French. She told that when she was out across the mountains with the Lewis and Clark people, word came to camp one day that a big fish had been found on the great sea, and that she begged the white men to allow her to go down and see the fish. She told about the fish she had seen, and the Indians at once whispered to each other, then called out, "Ishsham! Ishsham!" which being interpreted means "A lie! A lie! Squaw a liar!" The Indians were incredulous and could not believe a fish could be as large as she indicated. They asked her how long it was. She indicated by a space that was from fifty to sixty feet, the distance between the hitching-post and her tepee, and again the Indians could not believe it saying, "White man, is this the truth?" I answered that there were fishes called whales that were as long and even longer than she indicated. At this the Indians burst out of one accord and said, "Ishsham! Ishsham! White man a liar!" But Sacajawea stuck to her story, and again appealed to me for verification as to the size of the fish, saying, "White man, is squaw a liar?" [121]

At the time of this incident, Mr. Burnett had not read any of the accounts of the Lewis and Clark expedition, and knew nothing of the story recorded in the journals of the discovery of the carcass of a whale on the shores of the Pacific, nor of the account by Lewis and Clark of Sacajawea's request that she be allowed to see the remains of this monstrous fish. He could easily, of course, guess that the Indian woman referred to a whale by her description.[122]

---

[121] As a matter of record, the fish Sacajawea saw at the Pacific coast was over 100 feet long, with a mouth from ten to twelve feet wide. Much of the blubber had been removed from the frame of the whale though the skeleton was intact. Thwaites, *op. cit.*, vol. III, 314.

[122] "Information which I received about the expedition of Lewis and Clark was obtained from Sacajawea," says Mr. Burnett. "I wrote to both my father and mother innumerable times about Sacajawea, and my father was acquainted with Lewis, but a very few years ago all of these records were destroyed as being without worth or value."

Sacajawea further told of the dark or brown people who lived on the rock at the edge of the big water, and who slipped into the water at the approach of the white men. Lewis and Clark in their account call them more accurately seals. The Indian woman also, according to Mr. Burnett, told of lashing two canoes together to make a larger boat, no trees being found large enough to make into boats to hold the instruments and supplies of the voyagers to the Pacific.[123] This method of transportation is frequently mentioned in the journals of Lewis and Clark.

Mr. Burnett also gave a personal description of Sacajawea. She loved to dress like the whites and sometimes did so, but not often, because she did not like the ridicule of the others. Burnett described her as

not dark in looks, but rather as light as a half-breed, medium of size, a very fine-looking woman and much thought of by the other Indians. She weighed about one hundred forty pounds, was about five feet three inches tall. She was pleasing in appearance, a woman full of brightness and smartness, and you would have taken the son, Bazil, as the elder of the two.[124]

Of the various attempts in statuary to represent the Indian woman guide of Lewis and Clark, Mr. Burnett preferred the one by Henry Altman of New York, in which an Indian woman is represented on horseback. Of this statue he said:

It comes nearer to being like Sacajawea as I knew her than any of the pictures or statues that I have seen. Sacajawea was as she is represented in the picture, small and squat and brown in color, although she was light complexioned for an Indian. The statue of Sacajawea

[123] Thwaites, *op. cit.* Entry under date of Aug. 3, 1806.

[124] Sacajawea's usual silence about Charbonneau is explained by Mr. Burnett as not unnatural. "It is contrary to custom for an Indian woman to talk about her man or any man."

in Portland, Oregon, is to my mind beautiful, but it is a typical representation of a Sioux woman rather than of Sacajawea, a Shoshone. Sacajawea was really very good looking, in fact, handsome, as many Shoshone women are.

Further confirmation of Sacajawea's life among the Comanches was also obtained from many of the older Indians on the reservation. In fact, nearly everyone interviewed by the author among the Shoshones mentioned the fact that Sacajawea had lived for a time with the Comanches.

When Andrew Bazil,[125] for example, the grandson of Sacajawea, was interviewed by the author as he halted in his work in one of the finest hay fields on the reservation, he replied:

I remember very well my grandmother's story of her life among the Comanches. I used to get her to talk Comanche because it sounded funny. It was different from the Shoshone language, although they understood each other. I have cousins in that tribe, descendants of my grandmother, Porivo, who come to see me and I go to see them, but they did not know of her past when she came to them.[126] They supposed

---

[125] On the reservation, July 21, 1929. See Appendices C and D.

[126] When Andrew Bazil was asked if he had recently had a visitor from his Comanche cousins, he said that he had, a Comanche woman named Ta-soonda-hipe, the granddaughter of Porivo, Bazil's cousin, whom he called his sister after the Shoshone custom. The name Ta-soonda-hipe is variously spelled Tah-cu-tine or Ta-ah-cutine. Translated, it means "Take Pity On." Tah-cu-tine lived in Lawton, Oklahoma. Many years ago, according to Andrew Bazil, an Indian from the reservation by the name of White St. Clair visited the Comanches and discovered that there were relatives of Porivo among the Comanches. Soon after this discovery, Ta-soonda-hipe, the daughter of Ticannaf, son of Sacajawea and her Comanche husband Jerk Meat, made her first visit to the Shoshone reservation, and since that time they have visited back and forth almost annually.

Ta-soonda-hipe, said Andrew Bazil, came chiefly to visit the grave of her grandmother. She said that "her mother had told her that at one time in the travels of Porivo, the men she was with became very hungry, and that our grandmother, Porivo, carried with her a parfleche full of dried meat or pemmican, as the white people call it. This she shared with the white men." A parfleche is a flat skin box made of stiff-dressed rawhide with ends folded

she ran away, leaving a son, who was the son of her Comanche husband. On account of her disappearance, they called her "Wadze-wipe" or "Lost Woman." While she lived with this tribe, she was called "Porivo" or "Chief," because the whites looked up to her as a big woman and respected her. When she came back here she was still called by that name, although it was not a Shoshone word.

Bazil also stated that he had heard from other Indians that his grandmother had run away from the Comanches, and that it was they who gave her the name Wadze-wipe. "I received this information when I was in Oklahoma, and I visited the very scene from which my grandmother ran away from her Comanche husband." Bazil was at that time planning to go again to Oklahoma.

Hebe-chee-chee, an Indian seventy-eight years old, who was born in the Wind river valley, remembered Sacajawea at Fort Bridger, and recalled the story of how she ran away from the Comanches and returned to the Bridger country with some white people.

She left a son among the Comanches and during recent years a daughter of that son visited us here on this reservation. I know this visitor well as she was a close friend of Andrew Bazil. One time when she was on the reservation she explained to me that she was a grand-daughter of Sacajawea. The tradition was very common among this tribe of Indians that Sacajawea had led a large body of white men to the west to a body of big waters. All of this was a tribal tradition, never questioned, but accepted by all of her tribe and the Bannocks and white people.

Barbara Meyers, daughter of Baptiste,[127] also said:

over to keep the dust out and the contents in. It was used to carry dried meats and other foods. Pemmican is a food made of strips of dried meat pounded into fine material, and mixed with dried fruits, such as choke cherries. This concoction, if kept dry, can be preserved for four or five years.

[127] Barbara Bazil Meyers died on the Shoshone reservation, Dec. 5, 1931, and was buried by the Rev. John Roberts, who assisted both at the burial of Sacajawea, 1884, and that of the elder Bazil, 1886.

My grandmother often spoke to me about being with the Comanche Indians for several years, and of her travels and exploits. My father also often spoke of having traveled with a large body of white men when they were hungry and making pemmican of buffalo meat, that is, pounding it up fine and mixing it with tallow and fat.

Ta-soonda-hipe, to whom extended reference has just been made, died in 1929, shortly after a visit to her grandmother's grave on the Wind river reservation. She told the author that Sacajawea was the wife of Jerk Meat, and when he died, she ran away with her youngest child, Yaga-wosier, finally reaching her people, the Shoshones, in southwestern Wyoming.[128] The Comanches mourned her as dead for many years. According to Ta-soonda-hipe, it was not until Comanche boys from Oklahoma attended the Carlisle school in Pennsylvania and met the Shoshone boys from Wyoming, that it was learned that Sacajawea had successfully reached her people.

One of Sacajawea's great-grandsons, named James McAdams, contributed certain interesting information regarding the lost medal which Sacajawea had received from the government for her services. This medal bore Jefferson's head and his name, and had a gold rim about it.

I have seen it many times. At Salt lake the people, when they saw this medal, said to Porivo or Chief, "Something grand!" and they gave Sacajawea and her people who were with her a big feast in honor of her wonderful achievements for the white people when they were on their way to the big waters.

My great-grandmother Sacajawea gave Bazil, her son, some precious papers, and these papers were put in a leather wallet, which

[128] The daughter whom Sacajawea took with her from Oklahoma to Fort Bridger, as already explained, was named "Yaga-wosier," or "Crying Basket." In time she married and had a daughter who still lives on the Shoshone reservation. See Appendix E.

were then in the possession of Bazil and were buried with him. Mr. Eastman [Dr. Charles A. Eastman] dug up the bones of Bazil, but found them deeply embedded in wet earth, and the bones and the writing in the wallet were only dirt or mud, though the wallet was in good shape, made of thick, heavy leather and being about the size of a woman's pocket-book, perhaps four by six inches. I helped to bury the bones of my grandfather by the monument or marker of Sacajawea in the Wind river Indian cemetery a short time after.[129]

McAdams said further that he had often seen the wallet Sacajawea carried, for she always carried papers with her "to show she was worth something." According to McAdams, the wallet also contained a letter from Brigham Young, which he thought might have been a recommendation of some kind. McAdams, like Andrew Bazil, credited Sacajawea with introducing the sundance among the Shoshone Indians. He also said that Baptiste had told him of seeing Sacajawea at Fort Bridger, and that Bazil had said that he saw her and said to her, "Here is my mother back again." He added that Sacajawea called her French husband Schab-a-no. He also had heard the story of her leaving Charbonneau because he had treated her roughly and had brought home a Ute wife with whom Sacajawea could not agree.

She further told me several times of the fact that one of the "Big Soldiers" on the march in which she took part, wanted her son to educate him as his ward. Whenever she told this story she would throw out her arms and then clasp them close to her breast, saying, "I wanted to hold my son right here." [130]

---

[129] See also Index.

[130] The statements of Indians and others from which extracts are quoted in this chapter are printed in full in Appendices B, C, D, and E.

Sacajawea's Death and Burial

But most of all the lone Sacajawea is an object of interest. Her figure in the story of Lewis and Clark is very pathetic and engaging. It is doubtful if the expedition could have pushed its way through without her. – JAMES K. HOSMER

CHAPTER VI

Sacajawea's Death and Burial

While Sacajawea was in the agency, as stated elsewhere in this volume, a number of white people who in one capacity or another were likewise attached to the reservation, made her acquaintance. One of these was Bishop George Maxwell Randall who, following the assignment by President Grant to the Protestant Episcopal church of spiritual oversight of the Shoshone Indians, came to the reservation in 1873 and established there a mission for the Shoshone and Bannock Indians. Bishop Randall was a man of eloquence and courage, and one or two incidents related by Mr. Burnett, illustrative of the character of this first bishop to the agency, are well worth recording here.

On August 19, 1873, according to Mr. Burnett's account, Bishop Randall was holding services in a schoolhouse (later known as the Bishop Randall chapel), which was ultimately moved to the Wind river cemetery near the spot where Sacajawea lies buried. Here it now serves as a sort of mortuary chapel.

The schoolhouse was about two or three hundred yards from our residences, and of course the Indians were hostile to the Shoshones and the white men, and were almost continually trying to get us. We never went anywhere, even to church, without our arms. On entering the church, we would stack our guns in the corner, but would keep on our cartridge belts and revolvers. Later it was learned that on this night we and our schoolhouse were surrounded by a large war party, which sneaked up to the little wooden building and peeped through the windows. The red men saw the guns stacked in the corner and learned that we were all fully armed, which fact made the red men conclude that the white men were putting up some kind of a game on them, so they slipped away and left us, all of us being unaware of their close presence to us.

Three months after this event, Dr. James Irwin, our Indian agent at that time, was transferred to the Pine ridge agency, where the Indians informed him that they had us surrounded in the schoolhouse that night in 1873. They asked Dr. Irwin why we were there. They also asked, "Who was the Big Chief with the big voice who was talking to the white men?" The bishop was dressed in his ecclesiastical robes, different, of course, from the clothes worn by the ordinary white man. Hence, he was the chief of the gathering. . . Not only were there white men in the congregation, but there were some Shoshone Indians and a few of their women, among whom was Sacajawea.[131]

In the baptismal records of Bishop Randall appear the names of four of Sacajawea's great-grandchildren who were baptised in the mission room on August 19, 1873.[132] Three of these were children of "Battez" and

[131] A letter from Rev. John Roberts, May 27, 1931, contains an account of the same incident. Bishop Randall started home the day after this event, traveling 150 miles in an open wagon to the railroad. The exposure brought on an illness from which he died, Sept. 28, 1873, in Denver. Mr. Roberts describes him as "a typical city clergyman who dressed as such, even when on his visitations to the remote missions of his vast diocese. Though not strong physically, he was a gentle, saintly man with the courage of a lion, who never faltered in danger, however imminent."

[132] Sarah Mathilda Trumbull Irwin and her husband, Dr. James Irwin, are buried in a small cemetery near their old home on the reservation. Appropriate stones mark the resting place of these two pioneer missionaries. Mr. Patten and Mrs. Irwin not only served as "sponsors in baptism" for the Indians, but in 1872 acted in the same capacity for various white people of Lander, South pass, and Fort Stambaugh, near Fort Washakie. This information was obtained from the records of the Protestant Episcopal church in Denver, book I, 477, through the courtesy of the very Rev. Benjamin D. Dagwell of St. John's cathedral.

"If Sacajawea had been baptized after 1871, the entry in the register would have been under the name of Bazil's mother or of Boenive or of Wadze-wipe

one a child of "Bazil." The sponsors of these and other
Indian children were Mrs. S. M. Irwin and J. I. Patten.
The names of the two sons of Sacajawea, as used by
the Indians, were so near alike in pronunciation that it
was difficult to know of which they spoke. "Pasce" was
Bazil, and "Patseese" was Baptiste, according to Mr.
Burnett; and in the record, various spellings of the two
names appear.

Other whites on the reservation from whom intimate
details of Sacajawea's life were secured were Dr. James
Irwin and Mr. James I. Patten, who early were identified with the work of the Episcopal church among the
Indians of the reservation. The Reverend John Roberts,
who in 1883 was put in charge of the mission established
by Bishop Randall, carried on his work for fifty years
among the Shoshones and therefore became one of the
chief authorities on the history and customs of that people. He was called "White Robes" by Chief Washakie
and is still held in such respect that even today when he
passes a group of Indians sitting on the ground gambling,
they always arise and say with a bow, "How do you do,
Father Roberts?"

In the parish records kept by Mr. Roberts appears
the official record of the death of Sacajawea. The certified copy of the entry, furnished by Mr. Roberts and
later verified by the personal examination of the author,
reads as follows:

(Date) April 9, 1884, (Name) Bazil's mother (Shoshone), (Age)
One hundred, (Residence) Shoshone agency, (Cause of death) Old
age, (Place of burial) Burial ground, Shoshone agency, (Signature
of clergyman) J. Roberts.[133]

or of Bah-ribo, not Sacajawea. But no such baptismal record appears." Statement of Rev. John Roberts.

[133] Wind river reservation church register of burials, no. 1, 114.

Mr. Roberts conducted a Christian burial ceremony over Sacajawea's grave in the cemetery of the Shoshone reservation on the day she died. Sacajawea had no last illness. She was found lifeless in her tepee on the morning of April 9, 1884. She was in her "shakedown" of blankets and quilts, and death had apparently come during the night. To the end of her life she retained her vigor and health, and she died alone, as she had so very often lived.

One of Sacajawea's close neighbors at the agency gave the following account of the incident, which clearly describes the circumstances of her death:

One morning word was received that Bazil's mother was dead. Mr. Lane, the Indian trader, said, "I'll go to the tepee." At the door of the tent Bazil arrived with tears running down his face. Speaking to me, he said, "Mrs. Lane, my mother is dead." I saw Bazil's mother taken from the tepee wrapped in skins and sewed up for burial. The body was placed on her favorite horse, the horse being led by Bazil. Probably the body was to be taken to where the coffin was, for she was buried in a coffin according to the statement by Reverend Roberts and others. At the time of Sacajawea's death Bazil had two wives, and they all lived together, Sacajawea with them all the time and, at times, Baptiste was there also.[134]

The cemetery where Sacajawea lies buried is a forty acre tract of ground enclosed by a strong, durable fence made of cedar posts and twisted, barbed wire. When Sacajawea was buried, a small wooden slab was placed at the head of her grave. After this was worn away or removed, a small boulder was placed to mark her head and another to mark her feet. Today, however, a substantial cement stone column commemorates the spot. On the inclined face of this is a bronze tablet bearing the following inscription:

---

[134] Interview with the author, 1929.

SACAJAWEA'S GRAVE, SHOSHONE INDIAN RESERVATION CEMETERY, WIND RIVER, WYOMING

The Reverend John Roberts, missionary clergyman to the Indians, and Andrew Bazil at the graves of Sacajawea and her adopted son, Bazil, father of Andrew Bazil. Sacajawea was buried on the day of her death, April 9, 1884, the Reverend John Roberts officiating. Bazil died in 1885, and was reburied January 12, 1925, with both Indian and Christian services.

SACAJAWEA
DIED APRIL 9, 1884
A GUIDE WITH THE
LEWIS AND CLARK EXPEDITION
1805-1806
Identified 1908 by Rev. J. Roberts
Who Officiated at Her Burial

This cement marker, which was placed on Sacajawea's grave by Mr. H. E. Wadsworth, Shoshone agent, was built with the assistance of Sacajawea's descendants, and the tablet was the gift of the Honorable Timothy F. Burke of Cheyenne, Wyoming, in 1909.

The family of Sacajawea was not to be separated, even by death, for more than a few years. In 1885 Jean Baptiste Charbonneau died on the reservation. His body, according to Mr. Lahoe, the government interpreter for the Shoshones, who knew both Baptiste and Bazil and assisted at their burials, was taken by a few Indians and carried into the mountains west of the agency and there let down between two crags about forty feet high. After the body had been lowered by a rope, a few rocks were thrown down upon the corpse, one of which struck the skull and crushed it.

With the death of Baptiste in 1885, the last survivor of the Lewis and Clark expedition had once more joined the other members of that gallant company.[135] In view of the persistent belief that a medal given Toussaint Charbonneau by Lewis or Clark was worn by Baptiste at the time of his death and was buried with him, a search was made in recent years for the body; but an examination of the side of the mountain where the corpse had

---

[135] Wheeler, *Trail of Lewis and Clark*, vol. I, gives this distinction to Patrick Gass, who died in 1870. Sacajawea and her son Baptiste share this honor.

been left in 1885 showed that a mountain slide had for-
ever buried from sight the bones of the man who as a
child traveled on the back of his mother to the Pacific
with the first expedition of whites to cross the continent.

In 1886, Bazil, the adopted son of Sacajawea and
formerly a sub-chief under Washakie, also died. He was
buried after the Indian custom. Wrapped in a sheet and
blanket, the body was taken by a few Indians up to a
stream called Mill creek, and there placed in a new
gulch which was dug into the bank and which caved
down and covered the body.[136]

When Bazil was buried, a leather wallet or some similar receptacle containing a number of valuable papers,
letters, and documents whose exact contents were unknown, was buried with him. These papers had at one
time belonged to Sacajawea, and she had carried the
packet containing them with her at all times. At her
death, in accordance with the usual custom, these papers
had been given to Bazil as the oldest son. It was reported
that the leather case contained letters written by Lewis
and Clark, together with certificates of good character
given to Sacajawea by President Brigham Young of the
Mormon church, but the exact nature of the papers was
known only slightly to persons outside of Sacajawea's
immediate family. When the United States government
wished to make an appropriation to erect a monument
over Sacajawea's grave, Dr. Charles Alexander Eastman, a Sioux, instituted an official search for this wallet
together with the papers which it was reported to contain, for the discovery of this would serve to identify
the grave and settle the controversy as to where Sacajawea was buried.

---

[136] One reason for this procedure was that the ground was deeply frozen.

In the fall of 1924 Andrew Bazil, the grandson of Sacajawea, volunteered to locate the site of his father's grave, made nearly forty years before, and gave permission to have the grave opened. He recalled that his father was buried with the papers, and that he had stated that they belonged to Sacajawea and many of them had been obtained from the members of the Lewis and Clark expedition, of which she was a member. The wallet was found, as many predicted it would be, in Bazil's grave lying underneath the skull. The contents of the bag, however, had been so ruined by moisture and the passage of time that nothing could be deciphered. It was only possible to determine that the papers discovered had had writing on them at the time of Bazil's burial. The skeleton was found to be in poor condition. An old saddle lay across the feet, and beside the skeleton was a handsome pipe of peace. On January 12, 1925, the bones were reinterred beside those of Sacajawea, but because of the inclemency of the weather, it was impossible to hold a formal ceremony beyond the reading of the prayers for the dead.

In August, 1915, the author made a pilgrimage to the cemetery of the Wind river reservation for the purpose of paying humble tribute to Sacajawea. There she placed a few flowers upon her grave – wild sun flowers, purple wood asters, and sweet-smelling clover picked from the side of Andrew Bazil's irrigation ditch. This silent city of the dead was a part of the old hunting ground of Sacajawea's sons and of her tribal ancestors. The cemetery – barren, beggaring description – stands on an open desert tract of land surrounded in the distance by the Wind river mountain range with its ragged, eternally snow-capped peaks. Around these few sacred acres was

a five-strand barbed wire fence with an old-styled, seven-
step stile over it. There were no evidences of life; the
land—devoid of trees, shrubs, flowers, and grass—was
as quiet and dead as the mortal bodies of the braves who
were there taking their last sleep. Here and there the
cemetery was dotted with spears, long and straight,
placed at the heads of departed chiefs in order that those
who were in their new happy hunting-grounds might
continue their activities with the same instruments of
war they had used when upon the earth. On these spears,
flying, fluttering in the wind, were bright pieces of cloth,
giving the appearance of a gala day. On many of the
graves was placed some chosen piece of property—the
one most loved from the possessions of the dead—which
could again be used in the new land to which the departed one had gone.

Among these sacred grave decorations, iron bedsteads
held the most prominent place, for many of them were
placed around the graves, the head and foot boards and
the two sides making a small fence to protect the grave.
Many wagons were likewise given an honored place,
though the boxes and tongues had been removed from
them. In 1915 there was but one marble tombstone in
the entire cemetery; this was over the grave of an infant
but three days old, and bore the inscription "Coffin the
same as white man." [137] The last view from the old-
fashioned set of steps remains vividly in one's memory,
weird, fascinating, oppressive, suggestive of the crowd-
ing of one civilization upon another.

Gradually, however, the primitive method of grave
marking is being displaced by white tombstones, by an
occasional iron marker for the World war heroes, a

[137] Hebard, *Washakie*, 298-302.

bit of grass, flowers mostly of bright-colored paper, or an isolated tree. A well-beaten path from the wooden stile to Sacajawea's grave makes no guide post necessary. Annually thousands of people journey to this last resting place of the woman who served as guide to the Lewis and Clark expedition.

With the account of the death of Sacajawea and her two sons, the present volume logically draws to its close.[138] It is believed that the evidence here presented proves conclusively that the central figure of the volume was in reality the famous guide of the Lewis and Clark expedition, and that she was the mother of Baptiste and the foster mother of Bazil. All of this is substantiated by the testimonies of those – both men and women, whites and Indians – who knew Sacajawea on the reservation and who heard first hand the account and tradition of her services with the exploring party. Added to this testimony is that of Charles Alexander Eastman who, as already stated, made a thorough and detailed search

[138] Attending a funeral of one of the descendants of Sacajawea was Maggie Bazil Large, daughter of Bazil. At that time in her ninetieth year, Maggie Bazil nevertheless exhibited great energy in an emergency, for as the coffin was being lowered, the ropes became twisted, hindering the ceremony. An ancient, white-haired woman sprang forward, took the ropes in her own hands, and, bracing herself, successfully lowered the box to its resting place with a dexterity that challenged the skill of the young men present. She seems to have possessed something of the alertness, power to do, and energy of her grandmother.

Maggie Bazil married a well-educated Missourian, Mr. Shade Large, who came to Wyoming long before it was a state, ultimately settling on the Utah-Wyoming line. He taught his wife to sign her name, and she discarded Indian dress for that of the white women. The original homestead is still in the possession of the family. Two daughters of Maggie Bazil Large's son, Charles Large, have received a high school education. One of them attended the University of Wyoming in 1924 and submitted a paper to the author in a class in Wyoming history entitled "My Great-grandmother," that is, Sacajawea. Those who knew the grandmother of these girls, Maggie Bazil, agree that she was "very pretty" in her youth, another trait she had in common with Sacajawea.

on behalf of the United States government for the grave of Sacajawea, and who formally declared on March 17, 1925, in the city of Washington, that Sacajawea's last resting place was on the Shoshone Wind river reservation in Wyoming.[139] This decision, as Dr. Eastman says, must be accepted on the basis not only of the tribal tradition, but of other evidence that corroborates that tradition so strikingly that its truth cannot be questioned.[140]

In addition to the evidence already cited in this volume, it should also be pointed out that in more than a century and a quarter which has elapsed since the Lewis and Clark expedition, no claim has been advanced on behalf of any other person as a rival to Sacajawea; and in spite of repeated efforts by careful investigators, no evidence has been discovered that points to anyone except the heroine of the Shoshone valley as the guide of Lewis and Clark.

If the objection is raised that no effort was made by Sacajawea to proclaim herself to the world as the guide of the expedition, this is easily answered. Although Sacajawea, as a matter of fact, willingly told her story both to whites and Indians when they asked her about it, she was naturally not inclined to boast of an exploit

[139] Eastman, Charles A., *op. cit.*, 1925. Perhaps it should be mentioned here that Dr. Eastman's work in tracing the history and final resting place of Sacajawea, done at the request of the government, had no connection with the present author's work, but rested on independent testimony gathered by him. That the two researches corroborate each other in many particulars is but further testimony to the reliability of each.

[140] Olin D. Wheeler to the author: "I think you have made a very complete and thorough presentation of the proposition, and one which to my mind makes a very strong argument in favor of your position. In fact, the more I think of this, the more I feel that it is going to be extremely difficult to disbelieve the fact that the little Indian woman finally made her way back to her old home, died, and was buried there."

which, by bringing the first white men into the territory of her people, eventually destroyed their hunting
grounds and brought an end to their freedom. In other
words, that which might be regarded as worthy of great
praise among the whites, would be bitterly condemned
by the Indians, and naturally she did not care to court
such unpopularity.

As to the argument that if it had been the real Sacajawea who died on the Shoshone reservation nearly fifty
years ago, there would have been a great deal of publicity
given to the event and the death of such an important
character would have aroused wide-spread interest instead of being lost in obscurity, one has only to cite the
case of a vast number of other famous characters in
history whose fame experienced a similar eclipse. To
cite the fate of Columbus will be sufficient for our purpose. When this first of explorers died only fourteen years
after his great voyage, it was written:

The event made no impression either upon the city or upon the
nation. . . The world at large thought no more of the mournful
procession which bore that wayworn body to the grave than it did
of any poor creature journeying on his bier to the potter's field.

As time passes and a new century dawns since the
young Indian woman guided the Lewis and Clark expedition on its historic way, it is believed that the desire
to commemorate her faithfulness and integrity will grow
and prompt the erection of further monuments to her
name. History has frequently had to seek the last resting
places of its heroes to do them honor. How many places
claimed the blind poet after death, who, when living,
had to beg for his very food:

Seven cities warred for Homer, being dead,
Who living had no roof to shield his head.

Expenditures for Toussaint and Baptiste Charbonneau

APPENDIX A

Expenditures for Toussaint and Baptiste Charbonneau[141]

Abstract of expenditures by William Clark, governor of Missouri territory, as superintendent of Indian affairs, from January 1 to December 31, 1820.

DATE OF PAYMENT – Jan. 22, 1820. No. of vou. – 118. Payments, to whom made – J. E. Welch. Nature of disbursements – for two quarters' tuition of J. B. Charboneau, a half Indian boy, and firewood and ink. Amount – $16.37½.

March 31. L. T. Honoré. For boarding, lodging, and washing of J. B. Charboneau, a half Indian, from 1st January to 31st March, 1820. Amount – $45.00.

April 1. J. & G. H. Kennerly. For one Roman History for Charboneau, a half Indian, $1.50; one pair of shoes for ditto, $2.25; two pair of socks for ditto, $1.50; two quires paper and quils for Charboneau, 1.50; (one Scott's lessons for ditto, $1.50; one dictionary for ditto, $1.50; one hat for ditto, $4.00; four yards of cloth for ditto, $10;) . . . one ciphering book, $1; one slate and pencils, 62 cents for Charboneau.

April 11. J. E. Welch. For one quarter's tuition of J. B. Charboneau, a half Indian boy, including fuel and ink. Amount, $8.37½.

---

[141] American state papers, *Abstract of expenditures by Capt. W. Clark as superintendent of Indian affairs, 1822*, Washington, 1834, class II, vol. II, no. 5, 289.

May 17. F. Neil. For one quarter's tuition of Toussaint Charboneau, a half Indian boy. Amount—$12.00.

June 30. L. T. Honoré. For board and lodging and washing of J. B. Charboneau, a half Indian boy, from 1st April to 30th June. Amount—$45.00.

Oct. 1. L. T. Honoré. Nature of the disbursements—For boarding, lodging and washing of J. B. Charboneau, from 1st July to 30th September, 1820, at $15 per month. Amount—$45.00.

Testimony of Indian agents, missionaries,
and teachers among the Shoshones

APPENDIX B

Testimony of Indian agents, missionaries, and teachers among the Shoshones

TESTIMONY OF DOCTOR JOHN ROBERTS [142]

Shoshone agency, Wyoming, November 25, 1905
DR. GRACE R. HEBARD

MY DEAR MADAM: I do not think that Sacajawea's picture was ever taken, but some of the old people tell me that one of her grand-daughters looks very like the heroine did in former days. There are several of her descendants living on this reservation. She was 100 years old when she died. It was the age given to me at the time, and I so made entry of it in our parish register of burials. She was not educated. She understood French well. Her sons both used French often. They knew but little English. . . A son of Baptiste told me that his father often told him that his [Baptiste's] mother carried him when a baby on her back when she showed the way to "the first Washington" across the Crow Indian country to the big water toward the setting sun. Baptiste's father died "long ago" near the site of the present White rocks Ute agency, Utah. He had lots of papers that were burned at his funeral, according to the custom of Shoshones and Comanches.

The old lady was wonderfully active and intelligent, considering her age. She walked alone and was bright

---

[142] Episcopal missionary among the Shoshones from 1883 to 1932.

to the last. You ask, would she wish to return to her people to live in danger and poverty with them rather than remain in the Mandan country? Yes, if she were a Shoshone or a Comanche [they are the same people]. Their language too is identical. She could never be happy away from her people. I believe she would have died of homesickness away from them for a long time. Such has been my experience during my sojourn here with them for 23 years. Sioux, Arapahos, Cheyennes can be weaned from their people, but a Shoshone or Snake Indian, never. Believe me with great respect, faithfully yours,

JOHN ROBERTS

On July 5, 1926, the Reverend John Roberts, in a letter to the Honorable A. J. Mokler, stated: "Sacajawea in her younger days seems, as you state, to have had her full share of trouble, but in her old age she was more fortunate. Her latter years on the reservation were passed in peace and plenty. Her wants were well provided for in every way. The log cabin in which she died was put up for her by the government–it was rough, but comfortable. The rations given her weekly by the United States Indian agent were ample–plenty of beef, flour, bacon, beans, rice, coffee, tea, sugar, baking powder, and tobacco [she loved her pipe]; and plenty of blankets, quilts, and clothing were issued to her annually. This liberal provision by the government was supplemented by the never-failing products of the hunt; venison to eat, pelts and buckskin to wear. . . The old lady, during her latter years spent among her people under the flag she had upheld for so many years, had a good time and enjoyed ease and comfort."

TESTIMONY OF JAMES I. PATTEN [143]

Denver, Colorado, September 7, 1926

I, James I. Patten, certify that I was for a period of years one of the Indian teachers on the Shoshone reservation, Wyoming.

During my long period of years on the reservation, I not only daily saw Wadze-wipe or the "Lost Woman," Sacajawea or the "Boat-pusher," Bah-ribo or "Water-White-Man," but I had personal conversations with her frequently, for she not only spoke the Shoshone language, which I understand, but could converse somewhat indifferently in French and English.

This Indian woman not only told me that she was with Lewis and Clark on the expedition to the Pacific ocean, but that her son Baptiste was a little papoose whom she carried on her back from the Mandan villages across the shining mountains to the great lake, as she called the Pacific ocean.

From this testimony, which she gave me in the way of conversation, I never questioned her information and thoroughly believed that she was the Shoshone Indian guide woman to the expedition.

About this time I had read one of the publications of the Lewis and Clark expedition, and was entirely convinced from their description of the Shoshone Indian woman guide whom they called Sacajawea in the journals or in the book which I read, that the Sacajawea of the reservation and the Indian guide of the expedition were one and the same person.

Attest of witnesses   JAMES I. PATTEN

J. G. Viner
L. Davidson

[143] Teacher and agent, 1870-1884.

Further statements of Mr. James I. Patten give the following information: "Bazil was a sub-chief of the Shoshone tribe and usually quite active in tribal affairs. He was rather lighter in complexion than Battez, was lame in one of his limbs, five feet eight inches in height, in weight about two hundred seventy-five pounds, with thick lips and a very pleasant and good-natured manner.

"He also claimed Sac-a-jaw-wea as his mother, and gave to her always all the attention and care that a son would be expected to show to a mother.

"It was a question never definitely settled at the agency, which one it was who was born at the Mandan village, or whether their father was the same, but according to the most reliable information obtained, Bazil was the oldest.

"Bazil died and was buried at the agency in 1886. The death of these two, the last of the generation who knew much of Sac-a-jaw-wea's history, makes it impossible to secure further facts.

"The Shoshone Battez [Baptiste] was the son born to Sac-a-jaw-wea shortly after the arrival of the expedition at Mandan.

"He died at the agency several years ago [1885]. He was a man of little force or importance in the tribe, about five feet six inches in height, quite dark complexion, stocky build, weight about two hundred pounds, thick lips and his mouth drawn well down at the corners. He was rather pleasant and sociable in manner, liked ease and enjoyed it, had a wife and several children. He acknowledged Sac-a-jaw-wea as his mother and that she accompanied the expedition to the coast, but seemed to take but a passing interest in her.

"At the time of the grand annual buffalo hunt in 1874

to the Big Horn mountains [Wyoming], Chief Washakie did not use Battez and Bazil as guides, because guides
were the foremost young men of the tribe; he always
picked young men to go ahead and spy out the buffaloes.

"I can remember Sac-a-jaw-wea's personal appearance but very dimly, as it was a good many years ago
that I first saw her. She was with Bazil one day when
the Indians were drawing their weekly rations at the
agency warehouse. Bazil and I were walking together
towards where the Indians were, and when we had
passed into the yard we saw an aged Shoshone woman
lying on her back, her shoulders resting on a fifty pound
sack of flour around which was looped a strap or rope,
the ends of which were brought over her shoulders and
held in her hands in front. She was just ready to rise
with her burden, and Bazil assisted her to her feet and
she trudged off. I told Bazil I thought the load too heavy
for such an old person to carry. "See, she is staggering,"
I said. "She is quite old and weak." Bazil replied, "Yes,
pretty old. She is my mother," and spoke of her connection with Lewis and Clark.

"This was my first sight of her, and under the circumstances, not very distinct. However, I gained a
glimpse of her poor old wrinkled face, which in young
life must have been very fair. Her eyes I could not see;
her features were regular, her height was not over five
feet, and she was of good form. The second time I saw
her was on the day we were preparing to take the trip
into the Basin country in 1874, when Bazil brought her
up and gave her over to the care of Agent Irwin while
the hunt lasted. She was ill then and too infirm to walk,
and lay in her small tent all the time."

TESTIMONY OF F. G. BURNETT[144]

Fort Washakie, Shoshone reservation, Wyoming
September 5, 1926

I mined in South pass in the fall of 1868, 1869, and 1870; then on the first of May, 1871, I was employed as boss farmer on the Indian reservation under Doctor James Irwin.

I moved over to the Shoshone Indian reservation, or agency, on the fifteenth day of May, 1871. The soldiers, under Captain Torry, moved to the present site of Fort Washakie about the last day of July, or the first day of August, in 1871.

I took my wife with me. She was the first white woman there, and the Indians were so hostile that we were afraid and slept in the fort until the soldiers came in the last of July. The first of June, Dr. James Irwin, his wife, and two daughters came to the agency. Then the Shoshones, under Washakie, the Pokatellas, and Bannocks came to the reservation some time in September, the fall of 1871. It was the Shoshones' and Bannocks' reservation then. I am almost sure, but not positive, that Sacajawea, with Bazil and family were with them.

There were twenty-four log houses, a story and a half high, built for the Indians. The one nearest the agency was given to Bazil and family, they being, Bazil especially, able to interpret and to use good English, none of the whites at that time being able to understand the Shoshone language. From that time until she died, 1884, I was intimately acquainted with Sacajawea and Bazil and family. Baptiste was not there. The first I remember of Baptiste being on the reservation was in 1874. The first I became acquainted with Sacajawea and

---

[144] Teacher and agriculture adviser, 1871-1932.

Bazil was by visiting their family in their house, and they instructed me in the Shoshone language.

At that time, on account of the Sioux and Arapahos being so hostile to the Shoshones and the whites, the Shoshones were unable to remain in the valley in the summer, so they would go back over the mountains. Washakie was forced to this by all other three tribes, any of which was numerically stronger than the Shoshones. Charlie Oldham and I took the census in the fall of 1871, and there were less than twelve hundred Shoshone Indians in the tribe.

Sacajawea's house was the nearest of the twenty-four houses to the agency. The house was one and a half stories high, built of logs, with a shed on the north side. There was one room upstairs, and one room downstairs, along the front. The shed was divided into two rooms, one the kitchen and one for the bedroom. It was the front room downstairs where I generally had my meetings with Sacajawea and Bazil, when they were teaching me the Shoshone language. They being in the house nearest to the agency, and having more protection, remained continuously throughout the year, and did not cross back and forth over the mountain to the west. They lived there constantly until she died, from 1871 to 1884.

Up to a few years before she died, Sacajawea looked as young as her son Bazil; she might have been a sister, or his wife. Bazil looked fully as old, if not older than Sacajawea.

Sacajawea was a typical Shoshone woman, rather light complexioned for an Indian. I judge her height was about five feet and five inches. She was not fat, as the Shoshone Indian women generally are at that age. It seems to me that her hair was quite long, and slightly grey, and that she did it as the Shoshone women at that time generally did it. She wore a blanket, and an Indian costume such as all the Indians wore before they were issued annuities by the government. The true Indian costume was made of buckskin.

I did not understand French, but there were four more there who were French half-breeds, and when they visited with Sacajawea and Bazil, they always conversed in French. Sacajawea understood and talked with them in French, as also did Bazil. Other Indians told me that "Sacajawea was conversant in several different languages."

I first knew that she was with Lewis and Clark during the winter of that first year, 1871, when she spoke of being a guide for the Lewis and Clark expedition. I had never read the history of the Lewis and Clark expedition, though of course knew of it from conversations with different ones who had talked about and read about it. In no way did I know definitely about the expedition.

Now I might say for Doctor Irwin and his wife, that in becoming acquainted with them, I became interested in the life and history of Sacajawea, and from that time all during her life, Mrs. Irwin, Charlie Oldham, an old schoolmate of mine, and I visited her in her house, and Mrs. Irwin wrote, from Sacajawea's description, a history of the Lewis and Clark expedition and the part that Sacajawea had taken in the expedition.

I remember distinctly how interested Mrs. Irwin was in Sacajawea's description of the expedition. Mrs. Irwin was well educated. The paper on which she wrote this history was legal cap, with a red line down the side, and it was more than twenty-five sheets; rolling it up, it made quite a large roll. I cannot definitely state the number of pages. The last time I saw it, it was kept with an autographed letter from President Lincoln to Dr. Irwin, for services rendered by him on the field of the battle of Shiloh. The last time I saw it, it was at the office of the agency, which was burned. I can't remember the date, but it seemed that part of the records were saved. We hunted diligently for the letter from President Lincoln and the manuscript, realizing even then that they were very valuable. Some years after, at the request of Mrs. Irwin's daughter, I hunted for the letter and manuscript, but was unable to discover either one.

I never had any doubt but that she was the real Sacajawea of the Lewis and Clark expedition, nor did anyone who heard her of our small group. She told me that when she was coming back and was on the western side of the Rocky mountains, Mr. Clark wished to leave the main party of the expedition and come over on to the Yellowstone river. He requested Sacajawea to guide him down to the Yellowstone to its junction with the Missouri. I remember her telling about trees large enough to make canoes, and timber being scarce on the river of Clark fork.[145] They overcame the difficulty by making two small canoes, decked them over, loaded their goods on these, and then traveled down the river to its junction, where they met the Lewis division of the expedition.

I remember very distinctly of her telling me where and when she was taken prisoner, and from her description of the place, I am almost sure it was on the Madison fork of the Missouri. She and some other women and children were out gathering berries some distance from the main band; and she was captured with another young Indian woman, so she told me.

---

145 Thwaites, *op. cit.*, vol. IV, 319, under date of Aug. 3, 1806.

At this time of meeting and talking with Sacajawea, I had never read a book on the expedition, nor had I read any magazine articles on it. During the period of the Civil war, and following that war, I was not in a place where I could gain access to books, newspapers, or magazines. I had never read anything about the expedition during the period of my acquaintance with Sacajawea, and even to this day, September 5, 1926, I have never read a book on the Lewis and Clark expedition, but I have since then read magazine articles on the expedition.

Her people, the Shoshones, appeared to think that she did right in guiding this company of white men, because the Shoshones were always friendly to the whites.

Sacajawea was always modest and never bragging when she spoke about being helpful to Lewis and Clark. Sometimes we had difficulty in inducing her to talk, on account of her diffidence.

I am making this statement word by word to a stenographer, and what I have said has not been dictated to me or suggested by any one else.

Done on this fifth day of September, in the year of our Lord, 1926, in old Fort Washakie on the Shoshone reservation, in the office of the superintendent, R. P. Haas.

Attest to signature　　　　　　　F. G. BURNETT
J. E. Compton

San Joaquin, California, January 22, 1929
DEAR MISS HEBARD: I was disappointed in being unable to procure additional data relating to the history of Sacajawea, all of her intimate acquaintances, both

men and women, having passed away, i.e., Wah-witch or Susan Perry, Judge Ute, and Mell. Mushurah, all having passed away during 1928, these being the last of her intimate friends. Sacajawea rarely spoke of Charbonneau. When she did mention his name, it was with bitterness and in remembrance of his temper and abuse. Many times I have listened to her stories of journeys back and forth from the Shoshones to the Comanches, and many times of her relationship to the Comanches. She and others who were related to the Comanches held that they were the true Shoshones, and that Washakie and his band were half-breeds and a tincture of Bannock, Umatilla, and other western tribes. There is yet a division and jealousy between them.

I have a vague memory of what Sacajawea related to me of her visits to St. Louis, Mo., and of Baptiste having been sent to school, and upon his return from Germany he told unbelieved stories of people who wore wooden shoes, and described great cities. The Shoshone name for a German is "Wo-be-namp-Tiko," meaning "Wooden-Shoe-White-Man." If Sacajawea ever spoke of having married a Comanche, I do not remember it. She always spoke of Charbonneau as being a bad man who would strike her on the least provocation. She thought a lot of Clark who on the Lewis and Clark expedition took her part and would not allow Charbonneau to abuse her. I am disappointed in not being able to relate more of the history of this wonderful woman, but remember that it has been 45 years since she passed away.

F. G. BURNETT

I, F. G. Burnett, being duly sworn, declare the following to be an exact and true statement of my remembrance of Sacajawea, the Shoshone Indian woman guide of the Lewis and Clark expedition, 1804-1806:

I first saw Sacajawea in the year 1871, when she came to the old Shoshone agency at Wind river, Fremont county, Wyoming, with her son Bazil. From that time until her death I knew her intimately, as I was at the time in the government service at the agency.

She was known at that time among the Shoshones as Wadze-wipe, meaning "Lost Woman," evidently with reference to her disappearance and long absence.

She must have been close to 80 years of age when she arrived at the agency, but was a remarkably healthy and well-preserved woman – about 5 feet 5 inches in height, and of somewhat light complexion for an Indian.

Reverend John Roberts, an Episcopalian clergyman, still living at Wind river, Wyoming, also knew her well, and I believe officiated at her funeral. At any rate, he can point out the grave in the Episcopal burying ground, and can give the date of her death from his records at the mission. Her son, Bazil, also died and was buried at the old agency, and some of his mother's documents, perhaps bearing on her history, were placed in the grave with him. His son, Andrew Bazil [grandson of Sacajawea], is still living at the agency and might be induced to permit the disinterment of his father's remains so that search might be made for the papers referred to.

In 1871 the government built 24 small houses at the old agency for the use of friendly Indians. Among these houses was a small dwelling located just east and a little south of the store building now occupied by John Burns at Wind river. In this house lived Sacajawea and her son, and it was there that I visited her many times and listened to her stories of her adventures. She spoke fairly good English, though French was the language most familiar to her. She also knew several Indian dialects and was an adept "sign talker."

Mrs. Irwin, wife of the Indian agent at that time, wrote a history of Sacajawea's life from the latter's reminiscences, but unfortunately this manuscript was lost, together with other valuable documents belonging to the Irwins, in a fire which destroyed the old agency office at Wind river – a log house located just east of the row of the present employees' quarters there.

Sacajawea, with another Indian girl, was captured when perhaps 9 or 10 years old by a band of Sioux in a fight with the Shoshones on the Madison river. She became the wife of a French-Sioux half-breed called Charbonneau.

At the time she accompanied Lewis and Clark on their expedition to the Pacific, she carried her son Baptiste on her back as an infant, and as I remember her saying she joined the party of white men at a Mandan village on the Missouri river. She told me that she saved the life of one of the leaders of the expedition [Lewis or Clark] near the place where they abandoned their canoes. She spoke of the scarcity of food after the expedition had crossed the Rocky mountains, and said that the white men had eaten horses and dogs – a most abhorrent diet to a Shoshone. She said that she had survived on roots she had found and fish she had caught, but would not admit that she had shared the horse and dog flesh. She also mentioned many narrow escapes from drowning in making the trip through the rapids and falls of the Snake river and the Columbia. She said she saw quite a number of the "people who lived in the water," but could never get close enough to speak to them. At every attempt to get near them, they would get frightened and disappear. She evidently referred to seals. She also told me of the rough water near the mouth of the Columbia and of the tremendous waves which several times nearly swamped the canoes of the party. She mentioned the great fish which some of the Indians caught in the big water. The Shoshones would never believe this fish story. When asked how large it was, she said "as high as the ceiling of this room," and about as "long as from the door of his house to the hitching rack outside." This would be about 60 or 65 feet. They could understand the "people who live in the water," as some of them had seen seals on their visit to the Columbia Indians, but the whale story was "a lie." [146]

She told of the hardships the expedition had experienced on its return to the eastern slope of the mountains, and said that she had guided Clark to the Clark's fork of the Yellowstone river, where they had great difficulty in finding timber large enough to build canoes. They decided at last to make two small canoes and connect them together. With this craft they voyaged down the river until they met the other expedition division. [147]

In all my conversation with Sacajawea, she never voluntarily mentioned the name of Charbonneau, so I assumed that she was not very much attached to him and probably never saw him after the expedition.

Her son Bazil was a fine, portly man, nearly six feet tall, and must have weighed over 200 pounds. He was crippled in one knee, and when walking, the toes only of one foot touched the ground. His knee was stiff and he walked on the toes only of this foot. He and his mother

---

[146] Thwaites, *op. cit.*, vol. III, 211, 314.

[147] Thwaites, *op. cit.*, vol. III, 247.

were much attached to each other and, as before stated, they lived together until Sacajawea's death. Another Indian who has been named as a son of Sacajawea, and identical with the babe she carried on her back on the expedition, was called Baptiste. He was a small man, and had a complexion as dark as any full-blooded Indian. Sacajawea lived with Bazil, and called him son.

F. G. BURNETT

Subscribed and sworn before W. H. Tuttle, *notary public,* of Fresno county, California, on March 2, 1925.

Jackson, Wyoming, September 28, 1931
MISS GRACE RAYMOND HEBARD

DEAR MISS HEBARD: In answer to your letter of Sept. 21st. If Charbonneau had endeavored to parcel Sacajawea out to men for immoral purposes, he would have had trouble.[148] In all my acquaintance with Shoshone women I never knew one of them to allow her person to be used in this way. She would have been disgraced and killed by her relatives. If they had not killed her they would have cut off her nose and expelled her from the tribe. In all probability his attempt to do this was the cause of her hatred of him. She rarely ever mentioned him in her stories of the expedition, and when she answered a question as to whether Charbonneau was with her at the time mentioned, she always spoke of him with hatred and disgust. Sacajawea would not submit to be thus disgraced, which was what caused Charbonneau to beat her and why Clark took her part. Some tribes might commercialize their women, but the Shoshones never. The Shoshones were a moral, truthful, and brave people. Infidelity was a disgrace.

---

[148] Thwaites, *op. cit.,* vol. II, 349, under date of Aug. 14, 1805.

If Sacajawea had allowed her body to be commer-
cialized, she would not have been honored and loved by
Chief Washakie and all of her people. She would have
been ostracized and banished from the tribe.

Captain Clark evidently protected Sacajawea from
the advances of white men, and no Shoshone would
make improper advances to her. Yours sincerely,

F. G. BURNETT

TESTIMONY OF TOM RIVINGTON [149]

Bocker [150] was not the only one that lost his money.
Slade [151] held out on other drivers. If a horse lost a shoe,
Slade charged the lost shoe up to the driver. As a rule
the drivers did not protest, for if Slade was out of humor
about something they knew he would go for his gun. I
saw Slade bluffed once at Fort Laramie. Wild Bill [152]
drove from Fort Sedgwick to Fort Laramie. He had
orders to get there at a certain time. Well, he did get
there on time, but just as he stopped, one horse fell dead
and three others died inside of two hours. Slade was
at the fort. He told Hickok that he would have to pay
for the dead horses. There were a lot of Indians at the
fort. Slade gave a handful of money to some Indian
children. To the Indian woman that was with Lewis and
Clark, Slade gave $10.00 and a pass on the stage to Fort
Bridger. She wanted to visit the Ute Indians. Slade had
given orders to let her eat at the stage stations and ride
on the stage free of all charges whenever she wanted to.

[149] From letters to the author, written Mar. 4, 10, and 24, 1930.

[150] Charles William Bocker, pioneer on the Oregon trail.

[151] Joseph Slade, the notorious road agent operating in Colorado, Wyoming,
and Montana.

[152] "Wild Bill" Hickok, gunman and sheriff of the western frontier, buried
by the grave of "Calamity Jane" in South Dakota.

In 1860 and 1861 she, Wadze-wipe, made her home part of the time with a bunch of Indians up by Virginia city, Montana. I got acquainted with her then. I was just a boy, but I have slept in her tent many times and did run errands for her. The white people in those days had a worship for her. She did not have to pay for anything at the store, for they gave her these things. She went to Fort Benton to visit the Blackfeet Indians, and she would go to Fort Hall down in Idaho on the Snake river to visit the Bannock Indians. The stage company did not charge her for eats, or the ride either. I remember one evening she was going on the stage. Plummer,[158] the then sheriff, bought and gave her three sacks of flour to keep her from going. That night the stage was robbed and shot up. She did live with the Bannock Indians at Fort Hall for a while. A scout for the government by the name of John Reshaw wanted her to be his wife. Right then she grabbed a ham bone of an elk and brought it down on his head. When he got his bearings he went from there. Then she went to live with Jim Bridger's Ute wife at Fort Bridger. Here is where she got in with the Shoshone Indians. They were the tribe that gave her the name of Sa-ca-ja-we. She made her home with them ever after. She told me she visited the first time at Fort Laramie in 1856-59-63. She was a woman that was not satisfied anywhere, and the stage companies helped to make her this way as they gave her free rides. She told me she was as far south as the Gila river in Arizona, but she did not like the Apache Indians for they were always at war, but she said the

---

[158] Henry Plummer, one time road agent serving as sheriff in the country around Virginia city and Bannock, combined the duties of this office with outlaw depredations quite successfully until vigilance committees ended his activities.

whites made them that way. She was over in California to see the Indians there, but said they were so poor, as the whites had taken all the country away from them, and she had been with the Nez Perce Indians for a long time up in the state of Washington for several years. She had lived with different tribes up in Canada.

You wanted to know how I knew the woman named Sa-ca-ja-we. Well, I lived with her at Virginia city, Montana, in 1862, and I made several trips with her to visit different Indian tribes. In the fall of '62 we went to Fort Hall to see the Bannock tribe. Then we came to Fort Laramie to see the Indians there. The old army officers all knew her and would give her presents. She could understand English pretty well, but would not talk it. I would tell her what the men said. Jack Slade could talk to her in her language. At this time Slade gave her ten dollars and a pass on the stage. From here she went to see the Pawnee and Omaha tribes.

She never liked to stay or live where she could not see the mountains, for them she called home. For the unseen spirit dwelt in the hills, and a swift running creek could preach a better sermon for her than any mortal could have done. Every morning she thanked the spirits for a new day. She worshipped the white flowers that grew at the snow line on the sides of the tall mountains, for, as she said, she sometimes believed that they were the spirits of little children that had gone away, but reappeared every spring to gladden the pathway of those now living. I was just a boy then, but those words sank down deep in my soul. I believed then, and I believe now, that if there is a hereafter, that the good Indian woman's name will be on the right side of the ledger. Sa-ca-ja-we is gone.

TOM RIVINGTON

Shoshone Indian Testimony

APPENDIX C

Shoshone Indian Testimony

TESTIMONY OF EDMO LeCLAIR

I came to Fort Bridger while I was a boy, and lived there a great many years. I knew Sacajawea very well. She came to Fort Bridger after I did. My father was an employee of a fur-trading company stationed at Fort Bridger at that time, so I became very well acquainted with many of the Indians who came to the fort to trade furs and buy supplies. Many of them stayed near the fort all the time. I knew Bazil and Baptiste, the sons of Sacajawea, better than the rest of the Indians, because they always acted as interpreters for the other Indians whenever they had any hides to sell or trade. I became very well acquainted with Sacajawea in the years that passed.

I was at the meeting [treaty of 1868], and remember it very well. Bazil, the son of Sacajawea, was one of the signers of the treaty. Sacajawea was at the meeting. I remember very distinctly seeing her sitting in the ring just back of the ring formed by Chief Washakie and his men, with a number of other Shoshone women who were present at the meeting. I remember seeing Sacajawea standing up and making gesticulations with her hands and making a short speech to Chief Washakie and his men. But I am unable to recall the nature of her speech at this time, considering that it was nearly sixty years ago. But I do know that she spoke at that meeting, because I saw her at the meeting and I saw her get up from where she was sitting and, standing, give a short address.

I further know that Sacajawea was well respected both by Chief Washakie and the Shoshones and the white people who were in and around Fort Bridger.

The treaty was signed by Chief Washakie and his people out in the open air: I have been able to call the names of most of the signers of the treaty of 1868, knowing them personally.

Witnesses   EDMO LECLAIR
Frances Jones
J. E. Compton

TESTIMONY OF DICK WASHAKIE[154]

As I first knew Sacajawea, or Porivo, she was a woman of medium height, and medium build. She was not very heavy. She had a kind disposition, and a very slow form of speaking, the common accent of speech as the Comanches are in the habit of using. She had lived so long with the Comanches she had acquired their form of speech. I did not know Porivo while she was young, but this was when she was an old lady at Fort Bridger, and until her death she retained this form of speech.

My father respected Sacajawea or Porivo very highly, above the ordinary Indian woman. One reason is because Baptiste and Bazil were very close and intimate friends of my father. Baptiste and Bazil were both sub-chiefs under Chief Washakie, my father. I may relate that Andrew Bazil is the grandson of Sacajawea, or Porivo, and we are today very close friends on account of the associations and friendship of our fathers.

---

[154] Son of Chief Washakie.

Baptiste and Bazil could not talk the Shoshone language very plainly. They used a brogue between French and Shoshone language, and used the accent of the French.

The Shoshone Indians always believed very strongly in Sacajawea, and what was said about her in regard to her voyages that she had taken, and also what she said about her trips.

DICK WASHAKIE [thumb print]

Certified September 5, 1926

James E. Compton, *U.S. interpreter*

Grace Raymond Hebard

TESTIMONY OF ENGA PEAHRORA [155]

I knew Porivo, or Sacajawea, as she was known, at Fort Bridger. She lived with her son Bazil. I was a young girl at that time, perhaps at the age of fourteen or fifteen. She lived with Bazil in an Indian tepee at Fort Bridger.

As I knew her, she was a woman of medium height and of small stature, and had a kind disposition; always willing to do what was right. As far as I know, she always had kind feelings toward the white people, and they had a great liking and respect for her, often times giving her food and clothing. I do not know of her ever having any disposition of hard feelings toward the white people.

I knew that Porivo, or Sacajawea, took part in the council at Fort Bridger, because I was right there and saw her in the council myself. She had a part in the meeting, and she spoke in the meeting. I know this, as I was there and saw her speak.

This is as near as I can remember, it has been many

[155] Daughter of Chief Washakie.

years ago and my memory is becoming dim, but I do remember that she was very highly respected and thought of by the residents of Fort Bridger.

The council, as I understood at that time, was in regard to the government transferring the Indians to the present reservation. I was at the meeting or council, and I understood at the time it was in regard to the reservation, and the other Indians told me it was about this.

What I have said is absolutely the truth. I am not trying to pretend at all. I am telling the truth.

ENGA PEAHRORA [thumb print]

Certified September 5, 1926, by

J. E. Compton, *U.S. government interpreter*

Lela McDowell, *stenographer*

Matt McGuire, *merchant, Fort Washakie, Wyoming*

Grace Raymond Hebard

Peter Peahrora, *who speaks and understands both English and Shoshone*

David Perry, *who speaks and understands both English and Shoshone*

TESTIMONY OF GRANDMA HERFORD [156]

I personally knew Porivo, or Sacajawea, very well. She was called Porivo by the Shoshone people, which means "Chief." I first met Porivo when I was about 12 years of age. That was soon after her coming to the Shoshones. She claimed my mother as a sister in accordance with Indian customs of those days, though perhaps no blood relationship existed. Sacajawea made many visits to our home and oftentimes remained several days at a time. I, being a young girl at the time, paid little atten-

---

[156] At the time this testimony was given, Grandma Herford was believed to be about one hundred years old.

tion to the conversation that passed between Sacajawea and my mother. I remember in one instance that Saca-jawea told my mother (I was present at this instance), that while she was traveling with a large body of people in which army officers were in charge, the people became very hungry and killed some of their horses and even some of the dogs for food.

I also saw Sacajawea wearing a beautiful medal around her neck, a little larger than the size of a dollar, which she said that army officers had given her. She told of many experiences which I cannot recall at this time, as my memory is getting very faint.

Sacajawea claimed that she had two sons who were at Fort Bridger among the Shoshones before her arrival at the Shoshones, Bazil and Baptiste by name. I knew both of these men in later years.

I truly believe that Porivo or Chief woman is the true and identical Sacajawea that guided and was interpreter for the Lewis and Clark expedition; because she told of many experiences which she had encountered during her past life, otherwise no other person could have told of those experiences unless they had some similar experience. I remember she mentioned something about Clark, but I cannot recall what it was now.

GRANDMA HERFORD [thumb print]

Witnessed, November 29, 1926, by

James E. Compton
Charles Snyder
Viola Snyder

TESTIMONY OF QUANTAN QUAY [157]

I may be eighty-five years old. I was born in the

[157] Testimony given the author in an interview on the Shoshone reservation, July 21, 1929.

Bridger country. I knew Baptiste and Bazil, sons of Sacajawea or Porivo, very well. These two Indians seldom came up on a hunting expedition in this region in the very early days before this reservation was set aside for the Indians. These two people, Baptiste and Bazil, generally stayed at or near Fort Bridger and often traded with furs from visiting Indians and resold the furs to the traders and trappers. Both Baptiste and Bazil acted as interpreters for other Indians who were trading their furs. On one occasion a band of my people hunted in the Wind river mountains and remained in the mountains all summer, and in the fall when they were in the Bridger country I heard that Bazil's mother had come back to Bridger while we were away. I did not at that time see Bazil's mother, but I was told by my people that she had arrived, but I afterwards knew her very intimately. One reason I became very friendly with Sacajawea was because I claimed that Bazil was my brother-in-law by reason of my having been married to a cousin of his, and for this reason I went to Bazil's camp and visited very often.

The tradition was generally known by every Shoshone about Sacajawea and her life, that she led a large body of people in the early days to the waters in the west, and this tradition was a generally-accepted statement among her people. I have often visited the old lady when she lived with Bazil. I have no reason to doubt that she was the real Sacajawea of the Lewis and Clark expedition, because both of her sons were buried and are still buried here near her. I was at the council at the time that the treaty was made with our government at Fort Bridger, giving this Shoshone reservation to the Shoshones who were at Fort Bridger, making this reservation their

SUSAN PERRY AND THE AUTHOR

On the Shoshone reservation, Wyoming, September 5, 1926. Te-ah-win-nie, one hundred years old, is seated on a pile of "squaw wood" recounting her experiences with Sacajawea.

future home. Sacajawea was at this council meeting. I know she was there. I saw her there. Bazil was one of the men speakers and spoke, but Baptiste did not speak nor say a thing.

QUANTAN QUAY [thumb print]

TESTIMONY OF SUSAN PERRY [158]

Baptiste, the son of Porivo, "Water-White-Man" or "Guide-to-the-White-Man-up-the-River," married two of my sisters.

I remember very well the medal which Baptiste, the son of Porivo, used to wear on a string around his neck. It was a very beautiful medal, and had a beautiful silver edge all around the circumference of it, with a man's face on it. Baptiste was wearing the medal the last time I saw it, but I think when he died, the medal was buried with him.

The first time I saw Porivo was when I was eighteen years old. I was quite a young lady then, and Porivo was quite an old lady. This was at Fort Bridger, a long time ago. I saw her before the treaty at Fort Bridger, in 1868, before the Indians and white men made friends. At the time of the treaty I was at Fort Bridger and she was there too. I know that she was at the council, but I was a young girl then and I do not remember what she said at the council.

Porivo never told me personally that she had a French husband, but the other Indians told me that she had a French husband.

Porivo told me that at one time, when she was with the soldiers, that the men were all very hungry. She had a parfleche full of dried meat or pemmican, and she

[158] Testimony given Sept. 5, 1926, when Susan Perry was more than one hundred years old.

took down her pack and opened it for the men, and they ate the pemmican.

I do not know how she came to the Shoshones, but I understood from other Indians that she ran away from the Comanches. I do not know how she came to the Shoshones, but I do know that she was the identical person whom I knew at Fort Bridger, and whom the white men called Sacajawea.

I was at her funeral when she died. She had a very large funeral because she had many relatives on the reservation. Many of these relatives have now died.

SUSAN PERRY [thumb print]

Attest of witnesses

J. E. Compton, *U.S. interpreter*
Lela McDowell, *stenographer*
Mr. and Mrs. Matt McGuire
Grace Raymond Hebard

TESTIMONY OF ANDREW BAZIL[159]

I am the son of Bazil, grandson of Porivo or "Chief Woman," also called "Pohe-nive" or "Grass Woman." I was about nine years old, as near as I can remember, when I saw my grandmother Porivo, Bazil's mother, for the first time. She was active, smart, and bright. She spoke French and she was free to go to the white people when we met any of them, especially the white people at Fort Bridger. She was respected and looked up to by the Shoshone Indian women. As far as I know, my grandmother was always interested in the tribal affairs and often took part in the councils. I remember her telling that her first husband was a Frenchman. Also she used to tell with pride that somewhere she had fed the white

---

[159] Testimony given Jan. 15, 1925, to Dr. Charles A. Eastman. Permission given author to quote, Sept. 5, 1926.

people with buffalo meat when they were very hungry, and spoke of them as having to eat dog after that which she would not eat because her people never ate dog.

I remember very well her story of her life among the Comanches. I used to get her to talk Comanche because it sounded funny. It is different from the Shoshone language, although they understand each other. She never told very much about her French husband, neither did she tell much about her life with the Comanches. She seemed to want that part of her life unknown, except occasionally, she would tell something of the Comanches, but I have learned from the Comanche descendants of hers who told me of her life there. I have cousins in that tribe who come to see me and I go to see them, but they did not know of her past life when she came to them. The strange part of it was she all at once came up missing. They supposed she ran away, leaving a son who was the son of her Comanche husband. On account of her disappearance they called her "Wadze-wipe" or "Lost Woman." While she lived with this tribe she was called "Porivo" or "Chief," because the white people looked up to her as a big woman and respected her.

When she came back here she was still called by that name, although that was not a Shoshone word. Later she was called "Pohe-nive" or "Grass Woman" by the Shoshones. My grandmother told at one time that she ran away from the Comanches and joined the white people and went with them up the big river, but I do not know what river that was. My father tells the story that when he was 15 or 16 years of age, his father and mother lived among the Ute Indians and somehow or another became separated, and his father married a Ute woman and his mother gradually drifted to the Comanche Indians.

My father told me that his father and mother had both left him and he had grown up among the Utes, and when he and his brother were young men they drifted back among the Shoshones. He never saw his father again, but his mother came back to Fort Bridger, Wyoming, long years afterwards when he was married and had children, and his mother was a gray-haired woman at that time.

When my grandmother was living, my father used to say to me, "You must respect your grandmother, all the white people respect her and honor her everywhere. Some day she will be useful to her people." It was my father who got the missionary, Reverend John Roberts, to bury her in the white man's graveyard because she was a friend of the white people, although at that time the Indians did not care to bury their dead in a white man's graveyard because they did not believe in the white man's religion.

I remember my father saying that the wife of the second Indian agent we had was writing the life story of my grandmother, but a fire destroyed all the agency records in 1884-85, and these papers were destroyed at that time.

My father said he had made peace with the Mormon church on behalf of his people, the Shoshone Indians. My father was noted among the Mormons. When he was old he often went to Salt Lake city, Utah, and he was usually honored. Bazil was the name he went by. His brother was called Baptiste. My grandmother had no other children among this tribe, but she raised one or two girls after she returned here.

My father's name was prominent at Fort Bridger, Wyoming. He was the first interpreter at that place and

ANDREW BAZIL AND BARBARA BAPTISTE
Grandchildren of Sacajawea.

was employed by the fur-traders to carry goods for them among the Ute Indians. He never said that he met his French father among the Utes. He must have been dead before that.

Both my father and his brother got married among the southern branch of the Shoshones, of which he became a leader. I do not know personally, because I was small then, but I have heard my father and other Indians say at the time Chief Washakie made a treaty with the white people at Fort Bridger, Wyoming, my father and my grandmother both took part in it. They were influential in getting their people's agreement. I have seen a large medal worn by my father on special gatherings, and sometimes his brother Baptiste would wear the medal, because they thought a great deal of each other.

My father also had some papers that he carefully kept in a leather bag, which he said were very valuable. Later I learned these papers were given to my grand-mother by some great white chiefs.

My father was a very close friend of Brigham Young, the chief of the Mormons. In the early days, my father and his band of Shoshones often went to visit the Mor-mons, and Brigham Young always gave my father and his band plenty of food and clothing. One time my father made an agreement with the Mormons to establish a school where the Indians could learn English and the Mormon children could learn the Indian language and customs. In fact, my father made lots of agreements with Brigham Young.

My grandmother introduced the sun-dance among this tribe when she came back, and my father Bazil was made leader of that dance by my grandmother. I am today considered the leader of that dance because my grandmother originated the dance here. We did not have that dance among the Shoshones before that. It belonged to the plains Indians.

My grandmother seemed to be very careful to keep her early part of her life to herself. My father and his brother were always known from childhood until their death by just one name of Bazil and Baptiste. This is all I can say.

ANDREW BAZIL [thumb print]

Attest of witnesses

J. E. Compton, *U.S. interpreter*

Lela McDowell, *stenographer*

Grace Raymond Hebard

Sacajawea among the Comanches

APPENDIX D

Sacajawea among the Comanches

INTERVIEWS WITH COMANCHE INDIANS

Dr. Charles Alexander Eastman's investigation of the history of Sacajawea, and the testimony gathered by him from some of the Shoshones led him to investigate the tradition of Sacajawea's sojourn among the Comanches, with the discovery there of descendants of Sacajawea by her Comanche husband, who could verify the story from a new angle. Dr. Eastman obtained material from Ta-soonda-hipe or Tah-cu-tine, granddaughter of Sacajawea, and from other Comanches.

In the author's various researches she engaged the services of Mrs. Edith Connelley Clift. Mrs. Clift is the daughter of William Connelley, for many years secretary of the Kansas historical society, and is herself technically trained in the methods of historical research. Her search in St. Louis and elsewhere for new material on Prince Paul of Würtemberg, and on Clark, Charbonneau, Sacajawea, and Baptiste involved the examination of old newspapers, court records, letters, manuscripts, and documents. Mrs. Clift was also engaged to search for material on the Fort Bridger treaty of 1868,[160]

---

[160] Material on the treaty of 1868 at Fort Bridger is meager. In a letter to the author on Aug. 5, 1929, from the U.S. bureau of Indian affairs, is this statement: "Because of the removal of the office several times in the last decade, it is believed that this file has been lost, or it may be that it has been transferred, without record, to congress." Whatever the cause, it is difficult to get any information beyond the names of the signers to the treaty.

and among the Comanche Indians for further light on Sacajawea's life there. What she found served to strengthen the testimony already gathered by others from both Comanches and Shoshones.

Mrs. Clift was joined in Oklahoma by her husband, Mr. W. H. Clift, who is well acquainted with the Comanches, and deeply interested in Indian history in that locality. With letters of introduction from Curator Thoburn of the Oklahoma historical society, and from Mr. Croft, Indian agent at Lawton, Oklahoma, the two interviewed many older Comanche Indians, getting sworn statements from them and thumb print signatures. Information was gathered from the following Indians: We-sa-poie, mother-in-law of Tah-cu-tine, the daughter of Ticannaf, son of Sacajawea and Jerk Meat; Mum-su-kih, brother of Tah-cu-tine's first husband; Woo-wa-kih, sister of Mum-su-kih; and other kin of Sacajawea or her husband, Jerk Meat.

Mrs. Clift's letter of recent date to the author says: "In scouting from Lawton in a radius of one hundred miles, I found constant information, with variations, of Sacajawea's existence among the Comanches. The main facts were always the same.

Apparently only one white man was living in 1932 who was at Fort Bridger on July 3, 1868, when the treaty was signed. This was Alfred Alexander Taylor, governor of Tennessee from 1920 to 1923. Governor Taylor was interviewed by Mrs. Edith Clift, and said to her, "My dear young lady, if I had known that it would have made the great difference that it apparently has made in several instances where I could have testified, I would have paid attention, of course. But how was I to know? I was only seventeen years old, and it was a great lark for me, and I was more interested in collecting Indian ponies, shooting antelope, and hunting for moss agates than in any history-in-the-making."

A "chum" of Governor Taylor's on his trip as far as Cheyenne was Henry M. Stanley, of darkest Africa fame, who had attached himself to the treaty commission as a New York correspondent, but who turned back at Cheyenne, returning on the recently-constructed Union Pacific railroad.

"Everywhere, in some form, the story of Sacajawea and her years among the Comanches persists as tribal knowledge. One old woman states that it was a band of wandering Mexican traders – not soldiers – with whom Sacajawea journeyed northward. All the Comanches to whom I talked insist that she had at least one child by a Mexican husband while journeying on the plains.

"Sacajawea never spoke a word that is known today to any of the Comanches about her former life, or Baptiste. That is unknown territory to them."

We-sa-poie, mother-in-law of Tah-cu-tine [Ta-soonda-hipe], remembered a woman who came among the Comanches when she herself was but a girl. The newcomer was called Wadze-wipe. We-sa-poie testified that she was about ten years old when this woman left with her baby. "She came to live with the Comanches before they came to Oklahoma, when they lived on a big river near the plains where there were buffalo [panhandle of Texas country on the Big Canadian]." This Indian witness further said that Wadze-wipe "looked like any Indian woman, not so large. Her skin was like an Indian or Mexican." She described the oldest boy of Sacajawea as being about twenty when his mother left the Comanches, leaving her son behind. Mr. Clift found We-sa-poie one of the best witnesses, other historical testimony definitely verifying her statements, and her memory excellent and exact.

Woo-wa-kih was a small child when the strange Indian woman came from the north to join the Comanches. "None of the tribe knew anything about her past life. She married a Comanche who was killed in battle. She grieved for her husband, and told the Comanches she was leaving. She intended to go some definite distance, for she took her youngest child, a daughter, and some dried meat in a leather pouch, and disappeared. The Comanches knew she intended to go north. They knew that on her way she was found in a starved and suffering condition by a party of Mexican traders. One of these she married." Of this woman's history before and after her sojourn with the Comanches, this witness knew nothing.

Mum-su-kih, an aged Comanche living near Walters, brother of Tah-cu-tine's first husband, remembered from his childhood a strange woman who was the object of considerable curiosity among his people. She married a Comanche. After the death of her husband she took her small child and wandered away from the tribe. She was found in a starving condition, without food or water, by a party of Mexican soldiers, one of whom she married. Her oldest son, Ticannaf, hunted for his mother but could not find her.

Fred Tice-ah-kie, testifying along the same general line, added, "They heard no more of her until just before the World war, when a Shoshone named Jim McEllum [McAdams] came here to Oklahoma from Fort Washakie, Wyoming. He told them that a lost woman had come among his people many years ago and had lived with them until her death. The old people to whom McEllum talked identified the woman as the one who had left the Comanches so many years ago and gone toward the north carrying her little girl with her."

It is to be noted that no Comanches knew of Sacajawea's experience with the Lewis and Clark expedition. So far as her earlier life was concerned, she seems to have been a veritable Sphinx. Mr. Clift mentions a rather unfriendly name given Sacajawea at first by the

WE-SE-PAIE, GEORGE KO-WE-NA AND WIFE, AND HI-WE-NAH

We-se-paie is the mother-in-law of Tah-cu-tine, Sacajawea's Comanche grand-daughter. George Ko-we-na is Tah-cu-tine's nephew. Hi-we-nah is the first cousin of Tah-cu-tine. From these Indians much valuable testimony concerning the lost years of Sacajawea's life was obtained.

SACAJAWEA'S COMANCHE KINSFOLK

Hi-we-nah's eldest daughter, second from left, and her family. Mr. and Mrs. W. H. Clift, also pictured, conducted interviews among these Comanche Indians, blood relations of Sacajawea.

Comanches, "Nyah-Suqite," "The Flirt." She was young, good-looking, a stranger, attracting the jealousy of Comanche women. In time she won or earned a different and more respectful name, Wadze-wipe.

ANDREW BAZIL VISITS THE COMANCHES [161]

We had a visitor lately, a Comanche woman, whose name was Ta-soonda-hipe, my sister, as the Indians commonly call those whom white people call cousins. She was the granddaughter of Porivo, who was the mother also of my father. Many years ago there was an Indian from this reservation by the name of White St. Clair, who went to visit the Comanche Indians in Oklahoma. It was while visiting there that he discovered that we had relatives there on the part of our grandmother, Porivo, or Sacajawea. Soon after this discovery, my sister, or, in English, my cousin as I knew she was later, came to visit me first. From that time on, we have visited back and forth almost annually.

Her many visits here have been mainly to visit the grave of her grandmother, Porivo. We have talked about our grandmother many times. It was in this way that we became so well acquainted. She truly believes that our grandmother was with, or led, a large body of men on a long journey. This sister, or cousin, that visited here, Ta-soonda-hipe, told me that her mother had told her that our grandmother, Porivo, told her these stories many times — how she had been with this large body of men, and how she led them across the country to a large body of water. . .

I have learned from my cousin that my grandmother

---

[161] Testimony given to the author Sept. 5, 1926.

came to the Comanches from somewhere in the east and that it was from the Comanches that she came to the Shoshone Indians. I heard later from Indians that she, my grandmother, Porivo, had run away from the Comanche Indians, and I understood that it was the Comanches that gave my grandmother Porivo the name of Wadze-wipe, or the Lost Woman, because she had run away from them or disappeared so mysteriously. I received this information when I was in Oklahoma, and I visited the very scene from which my grandmother Porivo or Sacajawea ran away from her Comanche husband's people.

ANDREW BAZIL [thumb print]

Attest of witnesses

    James E. Compton, *interpreter*

    Lela McDowell, *stenographer*

    Grace Raymond Hebard

TA-SOONDA-HIPE VISITS THE SHOSHONES [162]

My name is Tah-cu-tine [Ta-soonda-hipe]. I am a Comanche woman 66 years old, wife of Powwe-Tipi, and I am the daughter of Ticannaf, son of Porivo. The story of my grandmother, Porivo, is told in this way.

She married Jerk Meat and had five children. My father was her second son. About the time when my father had three children, my grandmother disappeared. My grandfather Jerk Meat had been killed, and my grandmother was very unhappy and also had some trouble with her husband's people. She declared she wouldn't live with the Comanches any more. The people thought she was not serious, but one day she departed,

[162] Quoted by permission of Dr. C. A. Eastman from testimony secured by him Feb. 15, 1925, at Lawton, Oklahoma.

nobody knows where, and took her youngest little daughter. She took some dried meat in a parfleche. The people worried about her and hunted all over for her, but could not find her. My father hunted for her for a long time, even went to other tribes to see if she had gone there, but nothing was heard of her. A long time afterwards we heard that she lived among the white people, but we did not know whether that was true or not. We all thought she was killed or perished somewhere. It was after the reservation life, when the Comanche boys went to Carlisle school, a boy by the name of Howard had met a boy by name of McAdams from the Shoshone tribe at Fort Washakie. This boy McAdams asked Howard if any relatives of Porivo lived among the Comanches. He told them he thought there were some. When Howard came back here from school he told us about it, and learned all that McAdams had told him about Porivo, my grandmother being at Fort Washakie and died there. We could scarcely believe it, but McAdams spoke of her children's names here on this reservation, then we knew it must be her. Since then, by correspondence, we came in communication with her grandchildren at Fort Washakie. I have visited there once or twice, and her grandson Andrew Bazil, son of Bazil, has visited us here once, and some of her great grandchildren, namely, the McAdams, have been here quite often.

We never knew that my grandmother had been married before she married my grandfather here, and we never knew that she had any children anywhere else but here, until as I stated above.

We never knew that my grandmother had married a white man by the name of Charbonneau and guided some soldiers across the Rocky mountains to the sea. And we never suspected that she was among any other tribe of Indians before she married my grandfather, Jerk Meat.[163]

TA-SOONDA-HIPE [thumb print]

TESTIMONY OF JAMES McADAMS

I went to the Carlisle Indian school in Pennsylvania in 1881, and was there for six or seven years. Porivo I knew intimately; she was my great-grandmother, and Bazil was my grandfather. I lived with Porivo, or Sacajawea, when I was a little boy and lived at Wind river, at the Wind river agency on the Shoshone reservation. I was about six years old when I first went to live with my great-grandmother, Sacajawea. My folks, when I was a small child, left me to live with Bazil, my grandfather, and Sacajawea, my great-grandmother. I lived with her until I went to Carlisle. I probably lived with her four or five or more years. I am today sixty years old, in this July, 1929. Sacajawea was not so very big, but she was kind of fleshy and very good-looking. She talked French. Both of her sons, Bazil and Baptiste, talked French. I only knew of these two children, but she had a son born and who lived in Oklahoma. She never brought him up here to the Shoshone reservation. He died in Oklahoma. She herself distinctly told me a number of times that she had relatives in Oklahoma. She said to me, "You have relatives down with the Comanches in the south."

While I was at the Carlisle Indian school in Pennsylvania, I saw some Comanche Indians, and I asked them

[163] Tah-cu-tine, or Ta-soonda-hipe, died in Oklahoma in the late fall of 1929, shortly after she had visited Andrew Bazil and had decorated the grave of her grandmother, Sacajawea.

about Sacajawea, or "Pohe-nive" or the "Grass Woman," "Porivo" or "Chief," "Wadze-wipe" or "Lost Woman." These boys, Comanche Indians from where Oklahoma is, said they knew of Porivo and the Lost Woman, who had lived with the Shoshone Indians in the north, although she, Sacajawea or Porivo, considered herself a Comanche Indian or as belonging to the Comanche branch of the Shoshone Indians. This was the beginning of the direct connection of Sacajawea of the Comanches and of the Shoshones under Washakie, and the connection of our Sacajawea with the Sacajawea of the Lewis and Clark expedition. Sacajawea told me many times that she worked for the soldiers away off into the country clear to the big waters to the west. She said, "I took soldiers or went with soldiers." On the trip to the big waters, in coming back, there was a war party against the soldiers. Sacajawea drew out her blanket and by signs she made with the blanket, the Indians knew she was a friendly Shoshone and the soldiers were not molested. Bazil and Baptiste lived with her. They all three used to go together and were as one family.

I knew Chief Washakie very well. Washakie had twelve chiefs. Washakie and these chiefs came to visit Sacajawea and Bazil, who also was a chief. Washakie and his head-men, or chiefs, thought that Sacajawea was a great woman. Sacajawea went at different times to Utah to the Utes. Here the trading-post and people looked at her medal which she wore, with Jefferson's head and his name on said medal. This medal had a gold rim around the outside. I have seen it many times. At Salt lake the people, when they saw this medal, said to Porivo or Chief, "Something grand!" and they gave Sacajawea and her people who were with her a big feast in honor of her wonderful achievements for white people when they were on their way to the big waters.

My great-grandmother Sacajawea gave Bazil, her son, some precious papers, and these papers were put in a leather wallet, which were then in the possession of Bazil and were buried with him. Mr. Eastman [Dr. Charles A. Eastman] dug up the bones of Bazil, but found them deeply imbedded in wet earth, and the bones and the writing in the wallet were only dirt or mud, though the wallet was in good shape, made of thick, heavy leather and being about the size of a woman's pocketbook, perhaps four by six inches. I helped to bury the bones of my grandfather by the monument or marker of Sacajawea in the Wind river Indian cemetery a short time after Mr. Eastman had found what was left of Bazil. When Sacajawea was in Utah, Salt lake, she received a good recommendation from the people and she often showed this recommendation, which she kept in her wallet that she gave to Bazil, saying that the writing was a recommendation by "Big Officers." These recommendations were for Sacajawea, although after her death Bazil carried them until his death. Bazil was the older son of Porivo. I have seen this package many times. It was a small leather case, not much larger than a large woman's hand. She always took or carried some papers with her so as to show she was worth something, so as to show that she had a sort of fine recommendation in regard to who she was and what she had done.

Did Sacajawea ever tell me with whom she left the Comanche Indians and how she came back? When she was tired of the Comanche country and the Comanches, she went to see her sons Bazil and Baptiste, and came toward where Fort Bridger is now located. She came from the south with horses, and found her two sons at Bridger. When she arrived at Bridger, Baptiste told me that he had seen her when she appeared at Fort Bridger, and Bazil said that he also saw her and said to her, "Here is my mother back again." And so they gave the first sun-dance that the Shoshones ever had. Sacajawea introduced the sun-dance to her Shoshone Indians in Bridger valley, and she acted as a chief of this first sun-dance. She died while I was at school. I went to Carlisle first in 1881.

Bazil got shot. He was a warrior of Washakie's. Baptiste was a quiet sort of a fellow and did not say much. Bazil was an interpreter, and Bazil and Baptiste both talked French. Sacajawea, Porivo, often talked to her boys in French. I often heard the three talking in French together. Sacajawea spoke of having lived with Charbonneau, a "Frenchman," and said that she used to have a Frenchman for her husband. He was "pretty rough" at times in his treatment of her, and she ran away from him after he had whipped her. He had at this time a Ute woman for wife, also Sacajawea. Sacajawea and the Ute woman could not agree. Sacajawea did not like the new wife, the Ute woman, and was jealous and so she left.

Schab-a-no she called her husband. She told me of this that I have just related to you at the Wind river agency where she and her two sons and I lived in her reservation log cabins and her tepee. She always called Bazil her own son. He was a fleshy man and tall, and Baptiste was medium-sized, short and dark. Bazil was lighter than Baptiste.

After the death of Sacajawea how did the Indians feel toward her? The Indians never thought much about her work with the white men out to the coast, because the importance of that expedition had never been brought to the attention and the minds of the Shoshone Indians, even though it was realized that Sacajawea had done an unusual thing and the white men were under obligation to her as a guide and interpreter. There was another reason why the Indians did not exalt over her work – the fact that the Indian men did not like to see a woman go ahead of them. Even Washakie himself and his followers did not desire that Chief Washakie should be placed on the top shelf and Sacajawea occupy a more prominent position in the esteem and appreciation of what Sacajawea had done. This does not mean that there was any hatred or dislike by Washakie and his followers and the other Shoshones, but it was a natural thing that the men should not rejoice in a woman's being a chief.

Sacajawea also told at one time of traveling with soldiers that were starving, and the soldiers killed horses for meat. She also told of another time, of soldiers killing game when they were about starving. She further told me several times of the fact that one of the "Big Soldiers" on the march in which she was, wanted to take Baptiste and educate him as his ward. Whenever she told this story she would throw out her arms, and then clasp them close to her breast, saying, "I wanted to hold my son right here." In this way she opened up her arms as if to surround him and hold him closely to her so that he could not be taken away. She did not want him to go off. Porivo was a good-natured woman, always jolly. She stated to me that she left a boy or son, Ticannaf, down in the south with the Comanches.

I found when I visited the Comanches her granddaughter, whose name was Tah-cu-tine, which means

STATUE OF SACAJAWEA, BY HENRY ALTMAN, 1905

"This statue of the Shoshone princess more nearly represents the real Sacajawea," says Mr. F. G. Burnett, who knew Sacajawea and frequently saw her astride a horse. The papoose cradle is in accordance with the style used

White Spot, the woman that was on the Shoshone reservation in the fall of 1926. The fact that Sacajawea got away or left the Comanches in the south gave her the name of Wadze-wipe. This means Lost Woman, but it was not a Shoshone word, but a Comanche word, and at the time that she returned to the Shoshones at Fort Bridger she was not at first called by this name, Wadze-wipe. Among the Shoshone people after her return she was generally known as the old Comanche woman — Yanb-he-be-joe. She came back to the place where the Shoshones were located in the Bridger valley in order to be near her sons. I do not know the date when she came back from the Comanches. The Shoshones do not keep track carefully of the dates of their movements. I have seen the papers containing her letters and history wrapped with a buckskin string on her chest in a leather case.

As to the medal which Charbonneau had, it must be remembered that he wore it and then he died, then Sacajawea wore it and died, then Baptiste wore it and died, and finally Bazil wore it and died, and the Shoshone people declared it was no good, for everyone who wore it had died. It may be buried with someone who did not belong to the family, and it was, as I stated, about three inches in diameter. It was a "Hoodoo," and may have been buried to hide it or secrete it so that the "Hoodoo" might be broken. It was probably destroyed or it was thrown away as "bad medicine," because these four people of the family who had worn it had, as a result, died. Nobody wanted it and would not accept it as a gift. Sacajawea is buried up at the Shoshone cemetery near Wind river. My mother was Nancy Bazil and sister of Andrew Bazil. My mother is buried at the Shoshone cemetery, and Bazil's bones are buried by the body of Sacajawea – all three are buried very close together. I assisted in burying the bones of Bazil in the cemetery as above indicated.

Our tribe all know and have no doubt but that Sacajawea was the original Indian woman from where she said she was, that is, a member of the Lewis and Clark expedition. Personally, I would like to ask, what is all of this fuss about? She cannot be buried in other places. She is here on the hill in the cemetery. She can only be buried in one place. The story of her life with Lewis and Clark and among the Comanches and elsewhere was always the same and it was never any different – there was never any change or variation. She always spoke of the big waters, that is, the water that goes on around the world. I wish to also state that I know Mr. F. G. Burnett, who knows much about Sacajawea from his association with her and her family, for I at one time lived with him.

My old great-grandmother Sacajawea told me repeatedly that I had some relatives down in the south and that her own name was Porivo and also Wadze-wipe. As I stated before, when I went on to the Carlisle school and had talked with the people from the Comanches about my great-grandmother who was a relative of some of the Comanche Indians at Carlisle, I came back to the Shoshone reservation for a while and then went down to see the Comanches, where in personal interview many of the facts that Sacajawea had given me were verified. The people in the south said to me, "We will take you over and show you about Porivo – about a relative of hers," which they did. The Comanches had thought up to that time that the white men had stolen Wadze-wipe.

When I met the Comanches in the south, they said, "We shake hands with you," and said to me, "you are as my son." That was because I had stayed with Sacajawea for a number of years. There is no fraud in the statement which I am making you, nor is there any fraud in this matter of identification of Sacajawea, the interpreter for Lewis and Clark. It is a true story. Fraud is not with the Indians in matters of this kind. They do not put up a story just to have it startling and out-of-place. What the early Indians say on this reservation and among the Comanches and elsewhere relative to their old stories is true and can be accepted. This I know from my long contact with Indians and particularly the old ones. After I had known Sacajawea for many years here on the Shoshone Indian reservation, she spoke of being with the white men when she helped to turn a boat over. Porivo means "Chief," not "Chief Woman," and "Pohe-nive" means "Grass Woman." Something that she had done in her life gave her the name of Pohe-nive. I was the first Shoshone Indian from this reservation to go down to the Comanches to find about my relatives who had been lost years and years. I repeat again, the Co-manches never called her Chief Woman, but Porivo, Chief.

JAMES MCADAMS

Certified July 21, 1929, by
James E. Compton, *U.S. interpreter*
Grace Raymond Hebard

Sacajawea's Names

APPENDIX E

Sacajawea's Names

The Shoshone woman who guided Lewis and Clark had a plurality of names. This is not surprising, since it was customary among Indians of all tribes to confer upon individuals such names as were suggested by their participation in some unusual event or by their conduct under unusual circumstances. Sometimes these names were given in derision, but more frequently they were bestowed as a tribute to the individual concerned. Thus Washakie, chief of the Shoshones, received his name, which meant in the Sioux tongue Rattler or Gambler's Gourd, because he made rattles out of bladders by placing in the latter small stones then inflating the bladders and tying them to sticks. These bladders, when dried, made a noise loud enough to frighten the horses of the enemy.[164] The famous Sitting Bull was so called because he "made medicine" while sitting in his tent. Crazy Horse received his name because a wild horse dashed through the village during his birth. Rain-in-the-face owed his name to the fact that, having painted his face red and black when engaged in a fight with Indian boys, it became streaked and covered with blood.

Frequently in translating such a name, the interpreter or translator gives to it a wholly erroneous and sometimes an exactly opposite meaning from its true interpretation. Thus, the Indian words "Tasunka-Kokipape,"

---

[164] Hebard, *Washakie*, 48, 51.

translated "Young Man Afraid of his Horse," actually meant that the sight of the Indian with his horse inspired his enemies with fear. Dr. McLaughlin cites the instance of the woman, called as a compliment "Beautiful White Cow," who became as a widow "Mrs. Spotted Horn Bull."

When and where Sacajawea received her name has heretofore been set forth. Sacajawea is a pure Shoshone name and consequently could not have been given at the Mandan villages. It is also certain that the name did not originate with the American commanders of the expedition.[165] It is possible that the name was given to Sacajawea in her early childhood by her people, the Lemhis, who occupied the territory near the extreme sources of the Missouri and across the crest of the Rocky mountains at the source of the westward-flowing Salmon river. This tribe, of course, had no written language, and thus the pronunciation and spelling of the word Sacajawea has long been a matter of some dispute. The spelling used in this volume is supported by long usage, a careful analysis of the records of the Lewis and Clark expedition, and by the modern Shoshone pronunciation.

An examination of these three sources will not be out of place at this time. On April 7, 1805, the name Sacajawea first appears in the Lewis and Clark journals as Sah-kah-gar-we-a. This word was apart from any sentence context, and was written down as if to make a special entry of the name as nearly as Clark could render

---

[165] Mr. John Rees points out in *Shoshonis contribution to the Lewis and Clark expedition:* "The word Sacajawea is used in Lewis's and Clark's journal before the party arrived at Three forks, but all evidence shows that these were put there after the captains returned from the trip, either when they rewrote them at St. Louis, or when the journals were emendated, erased, or interlined to assist Biddle in preparing the manuscript for publication."

it in his phonetic spelling, seemingly written as a memorandum for future usage, which appears some six weeks later in the Lewis journal in the statement, "a stream was named after our interpreter, the Snake woman, Sah-ca-gee-me-ah." If we assume, as later evidence seems to justify, that Clark's "g" was pronounced in combination in the same way that it was pronounced alone [that is, with the customary "dg" or "j" sound], and that his "r" was the southerner's soft "r," we have in this first entry essentially the word as it is now generally accepted, i.e., Sacajawea. On May 20, a stream was named for the Indian woman, Sah-ca-gee-me-ah, and in the entry of August 17, 1805, she is called Sah-cah-gar-weah; again on August 28, 1806, she is spoken of as Sah-car-gar-weah. All of these three entries are by Lewis.

On April 28, 1806, we find Clark omitting the "r" for Sah-cah-gah-weah, and Lewis writing Sahcargar-weah, a name he again uses on May 16. Thus the two captains do not entirely agree with each other, nor even with themselves, in the spelling of the name. But, if by logical deduction, we find that Clark, like most southerners, elided the "r," there is no essential difference in the spelling employed by the two men, nor is there any confusion possible except as to whether the "g" in the third syllable was hard or soft. The one entry, which mentions the naming of the creek after the Indian woman, uses the syllable "ger" in which the "g" is certainly soft. Thus we arrive without much difficulty at essentially the modern pronunciation.

But the name Sacajawea receives additional support from other sources that have previously been mentioned. It will be recalled that Shannon, a member of the expedition, assisted Biddle in the preparation of the Lewis and Clark journals for publication. Inasmuch as the Biddle edition profited not only from the contributions of Shannon but also was edited under the personal supervision of Captain Clark himself, it is illogical to presume, as some have done, that the text of this edition was merely a garbled version of the actual journal. It is indeed far more likely that such changes as were made in the Biddle edition from the actual journal entries, particularly in the case of proper names, were authorized only after careful consideration by both Clark and Shannon. Shannon, as elsewhere explained, had by this time received part of his college education and was furthermore unusually gifted with the ability to discriminate between fine shades of sound. It is certainly to be expected that he should have made a sincere and honest effort to see that the proper names which appeared in the Biddle text were spelled correctly. Thus, when the word Sacajawea appears in the Biddle edition, one can find no conceivable reason for rejecting it out of preference for such forms as Tsakakawea, Sakakawea, or Sacágawea, as some writers have proposed.

In the same way that George Shannon spelled the name Sacajawea in the Biddle manuscript and doubtless as he himself pronounced it, so it is pronounced today by the Shoshones on their reservation in Wyoming. The word is most musical, as sounded by the Indian lips, with slight accent, and with the "jaw" sounding much as "jar."[166] "The orthography," says Mr. Roberts, missionary to the Shoshone Indians since 1883, "is 'ja,' the pronunciation 'jah' as in 'jar.' 'Sac' is boat, canoe, or raft; 'a' is the; 'ja-we,' launcher; 'Sack-ah-jar-we,' the

---

[166] Author's visits to Shoshone reservation, 1915, 1926, 1929, 1931.

canoe launcher. All the 'a's' in the word are like the 'a' in far. The last 'a' is silent, although we on the reservation pronounce all the syllables including the last one, stressing 'jah.' It is not 'jaw.'"

In a personal letter to the author, Mrs. Eva Emery Dye, author of *The conquest,* supports the conclusion reached by Mr. Roberts. "Other confirmation comes," she writes, "from Judge Shannon of Fowler, California, who to me emphasized the statement that his father, George Shannon of the Lewis and Clark expedition, pronounced the name as Sacajawea, accenting the 'jaw' as 'jar.' This accounts for Clark's 'Sacarjarwea.' Clark was nothing if not phonetic."

The spelling Sacajawea has been in use now for a century and more, and would seem to be firmly established. It has become familiar to readers of journals, children's stories, accounts of the Lewis and Clark expedition, and in historical works. But both the spelling and pronunciation of Indian names in the United States has been notoriously uncertain and confused. The correct spelling both of Chicago and Milwaukee, for example, was in dispute for years.[167] One reason why the territory of Wyoming was not called Cheyenne, after the tribe of Indians who inhabited it, was that in 1868, when the new territory was about to be named and organized, the word Cheyenne was spelled and pronounced in so many different ways by different congressmen that congress, in desperation, moved that "the territory be given a name that is easy of pronunciation and with a known way of spelling." Hence, it was called Wyoming. Iowa has been spelled in a hundred different

---

[167] Pointed out to author by W. M. Camp of Chicago, author and historian. See Hodge, *Handbook of American Indians,* vol. I, 258, 863.

ways, but is now accepted as Iowa, and the other ninety-nine, from "Aiaouez" to "Zaivovis," were rejected. The fact that the word Sacajawea is, therefore, both spelled and pronounced in a variety of ways is not to be regarded as in any sense peculiar or unusual.[168]

The journals of Lewis and Clark, of course, call Sacajawea by other names. She is spoken of as "the Indian squar," the "wife of Charbono," "the Indian woman," "our interpreter," "the Bird Woman," "interpretress," "squaw" and "squar," "the Snake woman," "the interpreter's wife," and even "Janey." "The Indian woman" seems Captain Lewis's favorite term, for he uses it twenty-seven times in his records. Captain Clark speaks of Charbonneau's wife as "your wife Janey," in his letter to the French-canadian in 1806; and when in November, 1805, a vote was taken as to where Fort Clatsop should be located for winter quarters, at the end of the list of voters, after the name of York, Clark's servant, appears the name of "Janey," who voted "in favor of a place where there is plenty of potas."

It is perhaps significant that both Lewis and Clark speak of Sacajawea by this name chiefly when the expedition is in the country of her own people. Thus between May 20 and August 20, 1805, when the explorers are in the region from which Sacajawea had been stolen, she is spoken of by this name nine times in the journals, and afterwards a lapse of eight months ensues before she is mentioned again by this name and then it seems

---

[168] Sacajawea peak in Wyoming was so named and so spelled on Oct. 1, 1931, by the United States geographic board, but at the next meeting in November, the board changed the spelling to Sacagawea. This decision was based on the spellings of Lewis's and Clark's original journals, and on the mistaken assumption that Sacajawea was a Hidatsa name meaning Bird Woman, a conclusion not here accepted. There appears to have been no consultation with the Shoshone Indians or those acquainted with their language.

to have been called forth by her meeting with a Shoshone woman and a Snake boy. Apparently, therefore, when she is with her tribal group, Sacajawea is known to Lewis and Clark by her Indian name. On all other occasions they speak of her as the "squaw," Charbonneau's wife, the interpretress, or some similar name of general identification.

Mr. John Rees, who accompanied Dr. Elliott Coues over the Lewis and Clark trail in 1893, and who knew the Shoshone Indians and their language intimately for over a half-century, believed that Sacajawea was greeted with signs of joy by her own people as she drew near them on the banks of the stream, and that the word Sacajawea, or "Boat Launcher," symbolized the motions of launching a canoe. Firm in his conviction that the meeting between Sacajawea and her tribe was an actual reunion, and that Sacajawea and these people had a common language, Mr. Rees provided that a painting should be prepared under his personal direction representing the mutual recognition, through the sign language, of Sacajawea and the Shoshone Indians. This painting he presented to the author of this book.

The name Sacajawea is found elsewhere in earlier records, though but rarely outside of historical journals.[169] Captain William Clark Kennerly, nephew of Captain Clark, in a personal account of a hunting trip into Wyoming in the early forties dictated to his daughter, mentions both "Sacajawea" and "Baptiste Char-

---

[169] Recently, in 1931, an old issue of the *Big Horn River Pilot* for July 23, 1902, vol. VI, no. 25, was found in an old trunk. In it the name of Sacajawea appears. The paper is issued at Thermopolis, Wyoming, where are located the Hot springs donated by Chief Washakie of the Shoshones to our government. The article, unsigned, may be from the pen of the Rev. James I. Patten, first teacher to the Shoshones in the early seventies.

bonneau."[170] Captain Kennerly lived in the home of Captain Clark for a number of years, and was a well-educated man. His spelling, however, it is only right to add, may have been influenced by the Biddle text.

In later years, Sacajawea also had many names. Among these were Wadze-wipe or Lost Woman; Bahribo or Guide of White River Men; Pohe-nive or Grass Maiden; Bazil's mother of Bazil Umbea; Porivo or Chief; A-va-je-me-ar or Went-a-long-way; Nyah Suwite or Constant Lover; and Yanb-he-be-joe or the Old Comanche Woman. Some of these names are Shoshone and some Comanche.

Authorities for the spelling and interpretation of the name Sacajawea, and for the other names which from time to time were bestowed upon her, are as follows: Mr. Fincelius G. Burnett, in the United States government employ from 1871-1926, who daily came in contact with Sacajawea on the Shoshone reservation during the years 1871-1884; Mr. James I. Patten, United States government teacher, religious instructor, and Indian agent to the Shoshones from 1872-1880; Dr. John Roberts, an Oxford graduate, missionary-clergyman to the Indians from 1883-1932; Mr. James E. Compton, one of the first graduates from the Carlisle Indian school, and United States interpreter for the Shoshones; Dr. Charles Alexander Eastman [Ohiyesa], a Sioux and a college graduate, appointed in 1925 by the United States department of Indian affairs to visit the Shoshone, Gros Ventre, and Comanche reservations on which Indians might still be living who had known Sacajawea personally or who knew of her by Indian tradition; and Mr. W. H. Clift of Oklahoma, who

---

[170] Kennerly, W. C., "Hunting buffaloes in the early forties."

lived for many years in the territory of the Comanche Indians and who was well acquainted with their language and with them. All of these six men are recognized authorities in the orthography, pronunciation, and significance or interpretation of Indian names. Their testimony, accordingly, must be recognized as authoritative and competent.

Sacajawea's Memorials

APPENDIX F

Sacajawea's Memorials

On May 20, 1805, Lewis and Clark named a creek in what is today Montana, for Sacajawea. It is now known as Crooked creek.

Mrs. Eva Emery Dye, 1902, wrote *The conquest,* and by this publication "rediscovered" Sacajawea.

Bruno Louis Zimm, 1904, designed a statue to be placed in the Louisiana purchase exposition grounds, St. Louis. This was modeled after an Indian girl named Virginia Grant from the Shoshone reservation, Wyoming, to represent her kinsman, Sacajawea. The papoose on her back is modeled after a child of Sitting Bull.

Sacagawea peak, the top of the ridge of Bridger mountain in Montana, overlooking the valley of the Gallatin, Jefferson, and Madison rivers, was named and the location suggested by Mr. O. D. Wheeler.

Henry Altman, in 1905, made a statue representing Sacajawea, with her child, astride an Indian pony. In this statue the child is carried in a "papoose cradle," with his back to that of his mother, according to the true Indian custom.

Alice Cooper, in 1905, designed a statue which was placed on the Lakeview terrace of the city of Portland, Oregon. This was erected by "the women of the United States in memory of Sacajawea and in honor of the pioneer mothers of old Oregon."

In 1904, Rollin Bond, a bandmaster of the city of

New York, wrote an intermezzo score named "Sacajawea," which contained a number of typical tunes descriptive of the activities of the Shoshone woman.

Edward Samuel Paxson, in 1906, produced an oil
painting called "Sacajawea," which is now hanging
on the walls of the library building of the state university
of Montana. The same artist painted a number of historical murals for the capitol at Helena and for the
county court house at Missoula. One of particular significance in the capitol building is that representing
"Lewis and Clark at Three forks."

In 1909, a concrete shaft with an imbedded bronze
tablet was erected as a headstone for the grave of Sacajawea in the cemetery of the Shoshone reservation. The
location of the grave was designated by the Reverend
John Roberts, who officiated at the burial of Sacajawea
on April 9, 1884. The shaft and bronze were donated by
the Indian agent, Mr. H. E. Wadsworth, and Mr.
Timothy H. Burke.

Cyrus Edwin Dallin, in 1910, designed a statue of an
Indian girl leading and pointing the way for Lewis
and Clark.

Leonard Crunelle, in 1910, designed a statue in bronze
representing Sacajawea. This was erected by the Fede-
rated club women and the school children of North
Dakota, and is located in the capitol grounds at Bismarck.

In 1912, a silver service set, decorated with emblems
representative of Sacajawea, the gift of the state of Wyoming, was presented to the battleship "Wyoming" by
Honorable Joseph M. Carey, governor of that state.

The Montana Daughters of the American revolution,
in 1914, placed a granite boulder with a brass tablet

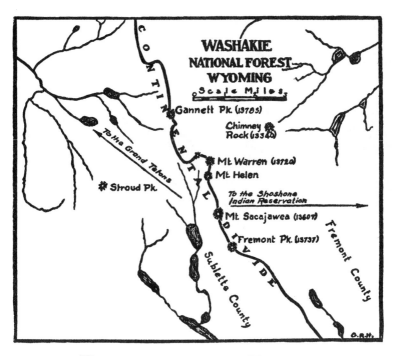

WASHAKIE
NATIONAL FOREST
WYOMING
Scale Miles

Gannett Pk. (13785)

Chimney
Rock (13340)

Mt. Warren (13720)
Mt. Helen

Stroud Pk.

To the Shoshone
Indian Reservation

Mt. Sacajawea (13607)

Fremont Pk. (13737)

CONTINENTAL DIVIDE

To the Grand Tetons

Sublette County

Fremont County

WASHAKIE NATIONAL FOREST, WYOMING
Locating Mount Sacajawea.

"In Patriotic Memory of Sacajawea" near the Three
forks of the Missouri.

In the historic valley of the Beaverhead river, near
the Two forks of the Missouri where Sacajawea discovered her people, a pageant was staged in August,
1915, to portray the historic events in the life of Sacajawea. The episodes of the drama were written by Mrs.
Laura Tolman Scott and presented by Montana Daughters of the American revolution, and was held on the
site where the canoes of the Lewis and Clark expedition
were beached, where the "interpretress" of the Lewis and
Clark expedition discovered her people, the Shoshones.

A boulder with bronze tablet was dedicated November 15, 1914, at Armstead, near where the Horse prairie
and Red Rock rivers unite, by the Montana Daughters
of the American revolution. This was the meeting place
of Chief Cameahwait and his sister, Sacajawea, on August 17, 1805.

At the back of the speaker's desk in the house of representatives, Helena, Montana, is a mural of heroic size
painted by Charles Marion Russell representing the
meeting in 1805 of Sacajawea and her brother.

Lake Sacajawea in Longview, Washington, is named
for the Shoshone guide.

In 1924 Sacajawea was introduced to a radio audience
through a song entitled "Sacajawea," lyric by Mr. Porter
Bryan Coolidge of Lander and music by Frederick
Bouthroyd of Leicester, England. Mr. Coolidge's home
overlooked Sacajawea's tepee home on the Shoshone
reservation.

In 1925, Mr. Tullius P. Dunlap presented a painting
bearing the title "The Shoshonis naming Sacajawea,"
picturing the incident which took place at the meeting

of Sacajawea and her people in the Beaverhead valley.

An airplane named "The Spirit of Sacajawea" made its initial flight in July, 1927, over the ancient home of the buffalo and the Shoshone Indian hunting ground in the Shoshone national forest, Wyoming.

In the public square of Charlottesville, Virginia, stands a group monument representing Meriwether Lewis, William Clark, and Sacajawea.

U.S. Forest Ranger Alfred G. Clayton of Wyoming recommended in 1930 that a peak 13,737 feet high on the continental divide of the Wind river range between Frémont peak and Mount Warren, should be named Mount Sacajawea. This was so named officially on October 1, 1930.

The Bishop Randall bronze tablet on the outer wall of the log building known as the Bishop Randall chapel, Shoshone cemetery, Wyoming, records the fact that on August 19, 1873, this missionary bishop baptized eleven Shoshones, "four of whom were the great-grandchildren of Sacajawea." This tablet was placed and unveiled with religious ceremony, August 22, 1931.

Dedicated to the Toledo choral society in 1932, a cantata was produced, "The Bird Woman, Sacajawea, a Legend of the Trail of the West." The text was written by Evangeline Close, the music by William Lester.

In 1932, two granite monuments were placed in the Shoshone Indian cemetery in memory of Bazil, son of Sacajawea, and Barbara Baptiste Meyers, a daughter of Baptiste and granddaughter of Sacajawea.

Another evidence of appreciation for the services Sacajawea rendered to the Lewis and Clark expedition was made by the formal dedication on August 14, 1932, under the auspices of the Daughters of the American revolution and the U.S. forest service, of the Montana and Idaho inter-state Sacajawea national monument. The preserve is situated at Lemhi pass on the summit at 7,500 feet of the continental divide at the boundary between Montana and Idaho, where in August, 1805, Sacajawea guided the explorers over the Rocky mountains to the west. This formal linking of one hundred forty acres of contiguous territory commemorates the joint interest in Sacajawea and the long existing good-will between the two states.

Bibliography

Bibliography

ABBOT, N. C. Montana in the making (Montana, 1931).
> Sacajawea's services recognized.

ABERT, Lieut. J. W. See *Emory, Col. W. H.*

ALTER, J. Cecil. James Bridger (Salt Lake city, 1925).
> Description of Shoshone Indians in the country about Fort Bridger from 1843, when Sacajawea returned to her people from life in the Comanche territory, to the time of government ownership of the fort.

AMERICAN STATE PAPERS. Abstract of expenditures by Capt. W. Clark as superintendent of Indian affairs, January to December, 1820 (St. Louis, 1820).
> Contains statements of expenditures for the education of Baptiste and Toussaint Charbonneau Jr.

BANCROFT, H. H. History of the northwest coast (San Francisco, 1884), 2 vols.
> Pages 1-87 concern the Lewis and Clark expedition.

—— Nevada, Colorado, and Wyoming (San Francisco, 1890).

BARRY, J. Neilson. Original letters and manuscript, in possession of the author.

BAUSER, Friedrich. Original letters, photographs, and copies of manuscripts from archives of Paul Wilhelm, Herzog von Würtemberg.
> Bauser, archivist at Stuttgart, Germany, discovered the documents for the author which record the education for six years of Jean Baptiste, Sacajawea's son, by Prince Paul of Würtemberg.

BAZIL, Andrew. Original typed testimony, in possession of the author.
> Thumb-marked depositions taken on the Shoshone reservation by Dr. Charles A. Eastman, under direction and with the authority of the United States commissioner of Indian affairs, 1925, and by the author, 1926 and 1929. Andrew Bazil is a son of Bazil, the nephew whom Sacajawea adopted in August, 1805, at the headwaters of the Missouri.

BECKWOURTH, J. P. Life and adventures of James P. Beckwourth, mountaineer, scout and pioneer, and chief of the Crow nation of Indians, edited by T. D. Bonner (New York, 1856).

BIDDLE, Nicholas. See *Lewis and Clark expedition.*

BOCKER, C. W. Original manuscripts, in possession of the author.

Certified accounts made December 12, 1926, describing Sacajawea who, when at Fort Bridger, sold her beadware to Bocker.

BOGGS, W. M. Manuscript about Bent's fort, Kit Carson, the far west and life among the Indians, 1844-1845, edited by Le Roy Hafen: in *Colorado Magazine,* vol. vii, number 2, pages 45-69.

Reprinted as a separate. Reveals the identity of Toussaint Charbonneau Jr., the half-brother of Baptiste.

BRACKENRIDGE, Henry M. Views of Louisiana; together with a journal of a voyage up the Missouri river in 1811 (Pittsburgh, 1814).

Reprinted in Thwaites's *Early western travels,* vol. vi (The Arthur H. Clark Company, 1904-1906). Charbonneau receives frequent mention as an interpreter.

BRANCH, D. E. Westward; the romance of the American frontier (New York, 1930).

Describes the Lewis and Clark journey, and its importance in establishing the boundaries of the Louisiana purchase.

BROOKS, Noah. First across the continent (New York, 1901).

A popular account of the Lewis and Clark expedition.

BROSNAN, C. J. History of the state of Idaho (New York, 1918).

Includes map of the Lewis and Clark expedition. Chapter v devoted to Sacajawea.

BROWN, James S. Life of a pioneer (Salt Lake city, 1900).

An autobiography by a member of the Mormon battalion under Gen. Cooke on the march to San Diego, 1847. On this journey Baptiste served as interpreter and guide. Brown recounts meeting Chief Washakie of the Shoshones on the Oregon trail.

BULLOCK, Isaac. Original letter, in possession of the author.

Written from Fort Supply about Bazil and his agricultural crop, October 1, 1856.

BURNET, John C. Original letters, manuscripts, photographs, and typed personal interviews, in possession of the author.

Information gained during a half-century of residence among Sacajawea's tribe, and given to the author in 1926, 1929, 1931.

BURNETT, Fincelius G. Original letters, manuscripts, and typed interviews, in possession of the author.

Burnett, boss farmer for the government and resident on the Shoshone reservation from 1871-1931, became intimately acquainted with Sacajawea, her two sons, and their numerous descendants.

BUTSCHER, Louis G. Translation of manuscripts, Prince Paul journals and life.

CAMP, William C. Original letters, in possession of the author.

By the Indian historian, and dated 1916.

CAMPBELL, W. S. Kit Carson, the happy warrior of the old west (New York, 1928).

A biography. Carson and Baptiste were at times in the same group of fur-men.

CAREY, Gov. Joseph M. Original manuscript, in possession of the author.

Describes Sacajawea decorations on the silver service donated by Wyoming to the U.S.S. "Wyoming," December 21, 1912.

CARTER, William A. Manuscripts and letters from Fort Bridger.

Contain information concerning Chief Washakie.

CATLIN, George. Letters and notes on the manners, customs, and condition of the North American Indians (London and New York, 1841), 2 vols.

The original contained more than three hundred colored plates by Catlin. Reprinted several times, with both plain and colored plates. When Catlin was at the Mandan village in 1833, the ancient chief gave him information about the Lewis and Clark visit in 1804-1805.

CHANDLER, Katherine. Bird-woman of the Lewis and Clark expedition (New York, 1905).

A supplementary reader for pupils of the second and third grades; illustrated.

CHARDON, Francis A. Fort Clark journals of the upper Missouri outfit, 1834-1838 (American fur company. MS.).

Owned by the American fur company, for whom Charbonneau served as an interpreter. This original manuscript records on October 27, 1838, Charbonneau's marriage, at eighty years of age, to a young wife of fourteen.

CHITTENDEN, H. M. The American fur-trade of the far west (New York, 1902); 3 vols.

A valuable history of pioneer trading posts and early fur companies of the Missouri valley and Rocky mountains. Contains an account of Prince Paul and his travels up and down the Missouri; also a map. This datum is not entirely accurate in the light of recent research work in German archives.

CLARK, W. P. Indian sign language (Philadelphia, 1885).

Account of tribal histories and race peculiarities, with brief explanatory notes.

CLIFT, Edith Connelley. Original manuscript of researches made for the author, in possession of the author.

Covers researches made among the Comanche Indians, the tribe in which Sacajawea took refuge and with whom the Shoshone woman lived for many years.

CLIFT, W. H. Original letters, manuscripts, and photographs, in possession of the author.

Obtained through interviews with descendants of Sacajawea, 1930-1931, at Lawton, Oklahoma.

COLLINS, Caspar. Original letter to his mother, Mrs. William O. Collins, October 8, 1862, in possession of the author.

Describes Jim Bridger who, though illiterate, possessed the ability to converse in several languages. Collins met Bridger when helping to defend the frontier, now Wyoming.

COMANCHE INDIAN TESTIMONY. Original typed interviews, in possession of the author.

Obtained direct from Ta-ah-cutine, We-sa-poie, Mum-sa-kin, Woo-wa-kin, Fred Tice-ah-kie, George Ko-we-na, and Hi-we-na by Mr. and Mrs. W. H. Clift. All of these Indians testified that they were descendants of Sacajawea, or Porivo as she was known among the Comanches of Oklahoma.

COMPTON, James E. Original manuscripts and typed interviews, in possession of the author.

United States government interpreter for the Shoshone Indians of Wyoming. He acted as interpreter for Dr. C. A. Eastman and the author, Shoshone reservation, 1925, 1929.

CONNELLEY, William E. Original letters and manuscripts, in possession of the author.

As secretary of the Kansas historical society, Connelley assisted the author and furnished much important data.

COOKE, Col. P. St. George. See *Emory, Col. W. H.*

COUES, Elliott. See *Henry and Thompson; Larpenteur, Charles; Lewis and Clark expedition.*

CRAWFORD, Helen. Sakakawea: in North Dakota historical society *Quarterly,* vol. i, number 3.

Of particular value on Prince Paul and his visit to North America in 1822-1824.

DEFENBACH, B. Red heroines of the northwest (Caldwell, Idaho, 1929).

Deals with three women, Sacajawea, the Dorian woman, and Jane, who made possible three expeditions into the west. Contains some new material on Sacajawea's life on the Shoshone reservation. A combination of historical accuracy and imaginary romance.

DESERT NEWS [Salt Lake city], October 1, 1856, vol. vi, page 366.

Contains a statement of Bazil's appreciation of the agricultural teaching of the Mormons.

DE SMET, P. J. See *Smet, P. J. de.*

DODGE, G. M. How we built the Union Pacific railway (Washington, 1910).

Chief Washakie, signer of the treaty with the United States government for the right of way for the railroad, was aided by Bazil and Sacajawea, who addressed the white men concerning the grant of land for the reservation.

—— Union Pacific railroad: report of chief engineer for 1866 (Washington, 1868).

DYE, Eva Emery. Conquest; the true story of Lewis and Clark (Chicago, 1902).

This novel, based on historical facts, gave to the public for the first time Sacajawea's story. The author discovered the Shoshone woman, and gave her life and personality.

—— Original letters and manuscripts, 1902-1932, in possession of the author.

EASTMAN, Dr. Charles A. Original letters, written in 1925, in possession of the author.

—— Report of commissioner of Indian affairs, March 2 (Washington, 1925).

The report of Eastman, inspector and investigator appointed by the department of interior, office of Indian affairs, locating the final resting place of Sacajawea. Includes accounts of his visits to the reservations of the Gros Ventres of North Dakota, the Comanches of Oklahoma, and the Shoshones of Wyoming. Eastman, after his research, concluded "that after Sacajawea returned to her people at Fort Bridger [Wyoming], she lived the remainder of her life with her sons in peace until her death, April 9, 1884, at Fort Washakie, which is her final resting place." The commissioner of Indian affairs accepted this report and agreed with the conclusions drawn.

—— See *Gros Ventre Indian testimony; Hidatsa Indian testimony; Shoshone Indian testimony.*

ELDER, Cecil. Original manuscript, in possession of the author.

Treatise on tick fever, compiled at University of Wyoming, 1930.

EMORY, Col. W. H. Notes of a military reconnoissance, from Fort Leavenworth in Missouri to San Diego in California, 1846-1847 (Washington, 1848).

Includes reports of Cooke, Johnson, and Abert. Baptiste acted as guide, hunter, and interpreter for this army of the west, from Santa Fé to the Pacific.

FERRIS, W. A. Life in the Rocky mountains, 1830-1835: in *Wonderland,* 1901.

Also published in the *Western Literary Messenger.* Mentions in 1830 the "Charbineau" who was an infant with the Lewis and Clark expedition.

FITZPATRICK, Thomas. See *Hafen, Le Roy.*

FLOYD, Sergeant Charles. New found journal of Charles Floyd, a

sergeant under Captains Lewis and Clark, edited by James D.
Butler: in American antiquarian society *Proceedings,* 1894, pages
225-252.

> Floyd died before the expedition arrived at the Mandan villages, hence
> no mention is made in his journal of Charbonneau, Sacajawea, or Baptiste.
> This manuscript has also been published in the Wisconsin historical society
> *Publications,* vol. xxii, 1916, and republished, 1904-1905, in Thwaites's edi-
> tion of Lewis and Clark journals.

FORREST, Earle R. Original letters, manuscript, and photographs, in
possession of the author.

> Contain information relative to Patrick Gass and his two daughters.

FRÉMONT, Maj.-gen. John C. Memoirs of my life (Chicago, 1887),
vol. I.

> Frémont piloted Sacajawea, during his journey through Wyoming in
> 1843, to her Shoshone people at Fort Bridger.

FULLER, George W. History of the Pacific northwest (New York,
1931).

> Deals with orthography of the name Sacajawea, pages 73-75, 352. This
> new material on the Shoshone woman guide is treated with scholarly at-
> tention, and is accurate and documented.

GASS, Patrick. Journal of the voyages and travels of a corps of discovery, under command of Captain Lewis and Captain Clark,
1804-1806 (Pittsburgh, 1807).

> Narrative of the expedition by one of the men employed during the
> journey. It has been reprinted, Dayton, 1847; and with an introduction
> and index, Chicago, 1904, by James K. Hosmer.

GHENT, W. J. The early far west (New York, 1931).

> Story of western America from the coming of the first Spaniards to
> California statehood. Considerable information given on the Lewis and
> Clark expedition and Sacajawea.

GOLDER, F. A. See *Standage, Henry.*

GRINNELL, G. B. Bent's fort and its builders: in Kansas historical
society *Collections,* 1919-1922.

> Extensive data relative to Baptiste and his services as guide and in-
> terpreter.

—— Story of the Indian (New York, 1900).

> Collection of stories related to the author.

GROS VENTRE INDIAN TESTIMONY. Original typed interviews, in possession of the author.

> Testimony reported by Mrs. Weidman and Dr. C. A. Eastman, March
> 2, 1925.

HAFEN, Le Roy and W. J. Ghent. Broken hand (Denver, 1931).

Thomas Fitzpatrick's life and leadership in the frontier fur-trading. An account of Friday, an Arapaho, educated and uneducated.

HALE, Horatio. Ethnology and philology: in Wilkes's *United States exploring expedition during the years 1838-1842* (Philadelphia, 1844-1874), 20 vols.

HEBARD, Grace Raymond. Pathbreakers from river to ocean (The Arthur H. Clark Company, 1933).
Contains a chapter on the Louisiana purchase and the Lewis and Clark expedition.

—— Pilot of the first white men to cross the American continent: in *Journal of American history,* vol. i, number 3.
Records the discovery of Sacajawea's grave.

—— Washakie (The Arthur H. Clark Company, 1930).
Account of the treaty with the Shoshones in 1868, of Washakie the chief, and of Sacajawea who took part in the discussion in the council tents.

HENRY, Alexander and David Thompson. New light on the early history of the greater northwest, 1799-1814, edited by Elliott Coues (New York, 1897), 3 vols.

HIDATSA INDIAN TESTIMONY. Original typed interviews, in possession of the author.
Testimony reported by Chief Wolfe, Mrs. Weidman, and Dr. C. A. Eastman, March 2, 1925.

HISTORICAL DICTIONARY of Canadian and French half-breeds of the west, edited by J. P. Garneau (Quebec, 1912).
Records Sacajawea's marriage.

HITCHCOCK, James R. W. Louisiana purchase and the exploration, early history, and building of the west (Boston, 1903).

HODGE, Frederick W. Handbook of American Indians north of Mexico (Washington, 1907-1910), 2 vols.
United States bureau of American ethnology *Bulletin,* number 30.

HORNER, John B. Oregon (Portland, 1921).
Contains high school material and many illustrations on the Louisiana purchase, Lewis and Clark, and Sacajawea.

HOSMER, James K. History of the Louisiana purchase (New York, 1902).

JENSON, Andrew. Bannock stake (Salt Lake city, 1890).
Pamphlet containing brief sketch, pages 156-159, of Salmon river mission, Fort Lemhi, Idaho, where Bazil lived with the Mormons.

—— Original letter, June 29, 1931, in possession of the author.
Information about Bazil from the assistant church historian of the Church of Jesus Christ of the Latter Day Saints, Salt Lake city.

JOHNSON, Albert W. Original letters and reports, in possession of the author.

> Contain research work done during 1928-1931 by Johnson for the author concerning Prince Paul and his Indian boy.

JOHNSON, Capt. A. R. See *Emory, Col. W. H.*

JUDSON, Katharine B. Montana, the land of shining mountains (Chicago, 1909).

> An historical reader for children, dealing with early Montana history and Sacajawea.

KAPPLER, Charles J. Indian affairs, laws, and treaties (Washington, 1904), 2 vols.

KENNERLY, William Clark. Hunting buffaloes in the early forties (Original MS., dated 1843).

> Diary dictated to his daughter. In the archives of the Missouri historical society.

—— Original letters, in possession of the author.

> Information from St. Louis, 1906-1907, relative to Baptiste who was engaged on a buffalo hunt as "driver of carts."

KROEBER, A. L. Shoshonean dialects of California: in California university *Publications in American archaeology and ethnology,* vol. iv, number 3.

> Contains vocabularies and dialects.

LANE, A. D. Original typed interview and testimony, given near the Shoshone reservation, Wyoming, July 22, 1929, in possession of the author.

> Narrate personal, daily acquaintance and contact with Bazil and Sacajawea, 1871-1884.

LANGFORD, N. P. Vigilante days and ways (Boston, 1890), 2 vols.

> Records conditions prevailing in Montana at the time Bazil was shot by bandits.

LARPENTEUR, Charles. Forty years a fur-trader on the upper Missouri, 1833-1872, edited by Elliott Coues (New York, 1898), 2 vols.

> A valuable personal narrative.

LAUT, Agnes C. Blazed trail of the old frontier (New York, 1926).

> Part iv contains drawings by Charles M. Russell of Lewis and Clark's "farthest north." A log of the upper Missouri historical expedition under the auspices of the governors and historical associations of Minnesota, North and South Dakota, and Montana for 1925.

—— Pathfinders of the west (New York, 1904).

> Story of the adventures of Radisson, La Vérenderye, Lewis, Clark, and others who discovered the great northwest.

LEMLY, Lieut. H. R. Among the Arapahos: in *Harper's Magazine,* March, 1880.

LEWIS AND CLARK EXPEDITION. Two authentic accounts have been published: the original Biddle edition, frequently reprinted; and the complete publication of the original journals under the editorship of Reuben G. Thwaites. The latter is by far the most complete and valuable publication. The Biddle edition includes some material gathered orally by Biddle from Clark and Shannon (one of the members of the expedition), which did not appear in the original journals.

Counterfeit editions were published prior to the Biddle edition: in 1809, 1811 (German), 1812 (German), 1812, 1813, and later reprints thereof in 1840 and 1851.

Patrick Gass, one of the members of the expedition, published his journal first in 1807, and it was reprinted in 1808, 1810, 1810 (French), 1811, 1812, 1814 (German), 1847, 1852, 1859, and 1904.

Charles Floyd, John Ordway, and Joseph Whitehouse, members of the expedition, also kept journals which have been published, and are listed herein under their names.

The Biddle edition was first published at Philadelphia, 1814, in 2 vols., 8vo. It was also published in London, 1814, in 1 vol., 4to, and republished as follows: London, 1815, 3 vols.; London, 1817, 3 vols.; Philadelphia, 1817, 2 vols.; Dordrecht, 1816-1818 (Dutch). It was many times reprinted after 1842 by Harpers and other publishers.

In New York, 1893, was published the excellent edition edited by Elliott Coues, in 4 vols., 8vo. This edition followed the Biddle text, but was very extensively annotated. The long-lost original journals came to light while this edition was in preparation, and Dr. Coues added many extensive notes therefrom.

In New York, 1904-1905, under the editorship of Dr. Reuben G. Thwaites, the original journals of the Lewis and Clark expedition were published verbatim for the first time, to which a large amount of manuscript material from other sources, including notebooks, letters, etc., and the journals of Floyd and Whitehouse, was added. It was published in 8 vols., 8vo, and in a special edition of 15 vols., 4to. This is without exception the most complete and valuable account of this important expedition.

The best and most complete bibliography of the various editions of the Lewis and Clark expedition is given in the Thwaites's edition, vol. 1, pages lxi *et seq.* This is complete to the date of its publication, 1904.

LUTTIG, John C. Journal of a fur-trading expedition on the upper Missouri, 1812-1813, edited by Stella M. Drumm (Missouri historical society, 1920).

New information concerning the education of Toussaint Charbonneau Jr. and Jean Baptiste by Captain Clark.

McGuire, A. J. Sacajawea: Indian girl who led Lewis and Clark (Portland, 1905).

McLaughlin, James. My friend the Indian (Boston, 1926).
Describes the transfer of a portion of the Shoshone reservation to the United States government.

MacLeod, W. C. American Indian frontier (New York, 1928).
Contains the rise of the reservation system, the Indian country of the great plains, the revolt of the Indians from 1864 and the Sand creek fight, to Chief Joseph's great trek of 1877. Includes numerous maps and historical illustrations.

Mallary, Garrick. Picture writings of the American Indian: in Bureau of American ethnology *Tenth annual report* (Washington, 1893).

—— Sign language among North American Indians: in bureau of American ethnology *First annual report* (Washington, 1879-1881), pages 263-552.

Maximilian, Prince of Wied. Travels in interior of North America, 1833, translated by H. E. Lloyd, edited by R. G. Thwaites (The Arthur H. Clark Company, 1904-1906), 3 vols.

Mokler, A. J. Transition of the west (Casper, Wyoming, 1927).
Reviews testimonies given by different authors as to the character of Sacajawea.

Montana historical society. Contributions (Helena, 1876-1923), 9 vols.

Newton, L. L. See *Wyoming state journal*.

New York Herald, July 5, 1868.
Notice of the Fort Bridger treaty of July 3, 1868.

Ordway, John. Journals of Captain Meriwether Lewis and Sergeant John Ordway, 1803-1806, edited by Milo M. Quaife: in Wisconsin state historical society *Collections,* vol. xxii.
Ordway was a member of the Lewis and Clark expedition.

Patten, James I. Original letters and manuscript, in possession of the author.
Certified information relative to Sacajawea, Bazil, and Baptiste, all known personally by Patten, 1871-1884.

Paul Wilhelm, Friedrich, Herzog von Würtemberg. Reise in Nordamerika wahrend den jahren 1822, 1823, und 1824 (Erster theil Mergentheim. Gedruckt von Johann Georg Thomm, 1828).
One copy only, written but not published.

—— Erste reise nach dem nördlichen Amerika in den jahren 1822 bis 1824 (Stuttgart und Tubingen, J. G. Cotta'schen buchhandlung, 1835).

Pages 259, 348, 379.

—— Original unpublished transcript of a fragment of Prince Paul's travel diary, in possession of the author.

From a manuscript in the Würtemberg library, roll ix, pages 521-523; discovered and transcribed for the author by Friedrich Bauser; translated by Prof. Louis C. Butscher. This extract again associates Jean Baptiste and Prince Paul.

RANDALL, Bishop G. M. Baptismal records of the Shoshone Indians, 1872-1873 (Wind river reservation mission, 1873. MS.).

Church record at the Shoshone reservation, Wyoming, of baptism of eleven Indians, among whom were four great-grandchildren of Sacajawea, descendants of Bazil and Baptiste. Entered under the date of August 19, 1873, baptismal records, number 1, page 12. Similar entries are found in the records from the archives of St. John's Episcopal cathedral, Denver, book 1, page 477, entered by Bishop John F. Spalding.

REES, John E. Idaho chronology, nomenclature, bibliography (Chicago, 1918).

—— Pictographic vocabulary (Original MS., in possession of the author).

Consists of drawings and manuscript, especially prepared.

—— Shoshone contribution to the Lewis and Clark expedition (Original MS., in possession of the author).

Chief Camahwaite, Tobe, and Sacajawea contributed greatly to the success of the expedition.

RICHMAN, Irving B. Ioway to Iowa: in Iowa state historical society Proceedings, 1931.

Shows growth of names, particularly those of Indian tribes.

RIVINGTON, Tom. Original letters and manuscript, March, 1930, in possession of the author.

Personal knowledge of Sacajawea and her travels.

ROBERTS, E. N. Original letters and typed interviews, 1929, in possession of the author.

Relate the belief of the Shoshone Indians about, and their fear of, the death of a gopher.

ROBERTS, Rev. John. Original letters and transcripts of records, in possession of the author.

Roberts, missionary of the Protestant Episcopal church to the Indians, provided the author with the following transcripts: certified copy, from the burial records of the Shoshone and Arapaho Indian mission, Shoshone agency, of the death of Sacajawea, April 9, 1884, recorded by Rev. Roberts on that date in the parish register, number 1, page 114; certified copy, from the baptismal records of the Shoshone and Arapaho Indian mission, Shoshone agency, of the baptism of four of Sacajawea's great-grandchildren, August 19, 1873, recorded by Rt. Rev. John F. Spalding on that date in the mission records, number 1, page 12.

ROBINSON, Doane. Brief history of South Dakota (New York, 1919).

> Public school text of the history of the Lewis and Clark expedition in South Dakota.

ROYCE, Charles C. Indian land cessions: in bureau of American ethnology *Eighteenth annual report* (Washington, 1899).

RUXTON, George F. Life in the far west (New York, 1849).

> Early days of the fur-trappers and interpreters, with frequent mention of Baptiste.

SABIN, Henry. Making of Iowa (Chicago, 1900).

> A popular history of the Lewis and Clark expedition up the Missouri.

SAGE, Rufus B. Rocky mountain life, during an expedition of three years (Boston, 1860).

[——] Scenes in the Rocky mountains, by a New Englander (Philadelphia, 1846).

SALMON RIVER MISSION. Original historical manuscript, in archives of Church of Jesus Christ of the Latter Day Saints, Salt Lake city.

> Gives information concerning Bazil's progress in agriculture under the supervision of the Mormons.

SCHULTZ, James W. Bird-woman, the guide of Lewis and Clark (Boston, 1918).

> Purely historical fiction.

SCOTT, Laura Tolman. Manuscripts, letters, map of Sacajawea and the Beaverhead valley, Montana.

SETON, E. Thompson. Sign talk (New York, 1918).

> A universal signal code, including gestures used by Cheyenne Indians, with additional signs used by other tribes.

SEYMOUR, F. W. Story of the red man (New York, 1929).

> A popular history of the Indian from the arrival of Columbus to the period of reservation tribal relations. Mrs. Seymour, the first woman to be appointed a member of the board of Indian commissioners, pays tribute to Sacajawea and points out her value to the expedition of Lewis and Clark.

SHOSHONE INDIAN TESTIMONY. Original typed interviews, in possession of the author.

> Obtained direct from Andrew Bazil, Enga Peahrora, Susan Perry, James McAdam, Barbara Meyers, Quantan Quay, Dick Washakie, Heb-chee-chee, Edmo La Clair, and Grandma Herford by the author with the help of Dr. C. A. Eastman, Jim Faris, and Judge Ute during 1915, 1926, 1929, 1931.

SMET, P. J. de, S. J. Life, letters, and travels, 1801-1873, edited by H. M. Chittenden and A. T. Richardson (New York, 1905), 4 vols.

   Particularly valuable for the material relative to author's meeting and conversation with Prince Paul on the Platte river, September 23, 1851.

SMITH, E. Willard. Journal while with the fur-traders Vasquez and Sublette in the Rocky mountain region, 1839-1840: in Oregon historical society *Quarterly*, vol. xiv, number 3.

   Contains account of Jean Baptiste Charbonneau, who was beaver hunting with the party on the South Platte river, Laramie plains, Little Snake, Green, and Bear rivers.

SMITH, Joseph F. Original letters, September, 1929, in possession of the author.

   Smith, historian of the Church of Jesus Christ of the Latter Day Saints at Salt Lake city, furnished information about Bazil's relation to the Mormons and the instruction given him in the art of agriculture.

SNYDER, R. M. Jr. An old book reveals an unsung hero in earliest Kansas history: in *Kansas City Star*, July 14, 1929.

   Tells of Jean Baptiste.

—— Original letters, in possession of the author.

   Relate to the Prince Paul publications.

STANDAGE, Henry. March of the Mormon battalion, edited by F. A. Golder (New York, 1928).

   Taken from the journal of Henry Standage.

STUART, Granville. Montana as it is (Original MS., in Wyoming university library, 1865).

—— Raid on the Indian village, 1862 (Original MS., in possession of the author, 1917).

   Two-page original manuscript, telling of the raid in which Chugean or Bazil received a leg wound disabling him for active service in war, though he remained a sub-chief under Chief Washakie.

TAYLOR, Gov. Alfred Alexander. Manuscript and letter. Great treaty, July 3, 1868.

[THERMOPOLIS, WYOMING] BIG HORN RIVER PILOT, July 23, 1902, vol. vi, number 25, pages 3-4.

   Contains material about Sacajawea. Newspaper published by E. T. Payton at the Washakie hot springs where the chief, his people, and Sacajawea used the curative waters.

THOBURN, J. B. Oklahoma, a history of the state and its people (New York, 1930).

THWAITES, R. G., editor. Early western travels, 1748-1846 (The Arthur H. Clark Company, 1904-1906), 32 vols.

A valuable series of annotated reprints of some of the best and rarest contemporary volumes of travel descriptive of the middle and far west during the period of early American settlement.

TRUE, Rodney H. Some neglected botanical results of the Lewis and Clark expedition: in American philosophical society *Proceedings,* vol. lxvii, number 1, 1928.

UNITED STATES GEOGRAPHIC BOARD *Decisions,* October 1, 1930, November 5, 1930.

UNITED STATES HOUSE OF REPRESENTATIVES. Secretary of interior report of commissioner of Indian affairs on Shoshone Indian agency [Wyoming], 54 congress, 1 session, document 5, August 16, 1895; 54 congress, 2 session, document 5, August 20, 1896; 54 congress, 2 session, document 5, August 30, 1896; 55 congress, 2 session, document 5, August 25, 1897.

Reports on the results of agriculture carried on by the Shoshone Indians.

VESTAL, Stanley (pseudonym). See *Campbell, W. S.*

VICTOR, F. F. River of the west; life and adventure in the Rocky mountains and Oregon (Hartford, 1870).

Tales of Indian fights, fur-trading and trapping, as told by those who participated. Baptiste or "Cabeneau" is mentioned as being busy at the mouth of the Platte in 1831. This son of Sacajawea, in historical records bears many names as well as variations of his father's name, *i.e.,* Charboneau, Charboneaux, Charbonard, Charbenau.

WADSWORTH, H. E. Manuscripts for author informative on Sacajawea.

WHEELER, O. D. Trail of Lewis and Clark, 1804-1904 (New York, 1904), 2 vols.

Retraces the trail, visits old camping sites of the expedition, photographs important topographical regions. In addition, biographical sketches of those who accompanied Lewis and Clark make this publication varied and entertaining.

WILSON, Col. Richard H. Original letters, dated August, 1929, in possession of the author.

These record the agricultural efforts of the Shoshones on the reservation.

WILSON and Chowning. Spotted or tick fever of the Rocky mountains: in *Journal of Infectious Diseases,* vol. i.

Associates the gopher with tick fever. The Shoshone Indians were afraid of the gopher, believing that he brought death with him.

WISE, Jennings C. Red man in the new world (Washington, 1931).

The social, legal, and political history of the Indian.

WISLIZENUS, F. A. Journey to the Rocky mountains, 1839 (Missouri historical society, 1912).

Trip to the Wind river country where the Shoshones hunted and ultimately made their reservation home.

WYETH, Capt. N. J. Correspondence and journals, 1831-1836, edited by F. G. Young: in Oregon historical society *Sources of the history of Oregon,* vol. i, parts 3-6.

WYOMING STATE JOURNAL, December 3, 1930.

Article and editorial on the naming of Mount Sacajawea and its topographical location in the Wind river range in Wyoming, edited by L. L. Newton.

Index

A CATALOG OF SELECTED
DOVER BOOKS
IN ALL FIELDS OF INTEREST

A CATALOG OF SELECTED DOVER
BOOKS IN ALL FIELDS OF INTEREST

CONCERNING THE SPIRITUAL IN ART, Wassily Kandinsky. Pioneering work by father of abstract art. Thoughts on color theory, nature of art. Analysis of earlier masters. 12 illustrations. 80pp. of text. 5⅜ x 8½.   23411-8

ANIMALS: 1,419 Copyright-Free Illustrations of Mammals, Birds, Fish, Insects, etc., Jim Harter (ed.). Clear wood engravings present, in extremely lifelike poses, over 1,000 species of animals. One of the most extensive pictorial sourcebooks of its kind. Captions. Index. 284pp. 9 x 12.   23766-4

CELTIC ART: The Methods of Construction, George Bain. Simple geometric techniques for making Celtic interlacements, spirals, Kells-type initials, animals, humans, etc. Over 500 illustrations. 160pp. 9 x 12. (Available in U.S. only.)   22923-8

AN ATLAS OF ANATOMY FOR ARTISTS, Fritz Schider. Most thorough reference work on art anatomy in the world. Hundreds of illustrations, including selections from works by Vesalius, Leonardo, Goya, Ingres, Michelangelo, others. 593 illustrations. 192pp. 7⅛ x 10¼.   20241-0

CELTIC HAND STROKE-BY-STROKE (Irish Half-Uncial from "The Book of Kells"): An Arthur Baker Calligraphy Manual, Arthur Baker. Complete guide to creating each letter of the alphabet in distinctive Celtic manner. Covers hand position, strokes, pens, inks, paper, more. Illustrated. 48pp. 8¼ x 11.   24336-2

EASY ORIGAMI, John Montroll. Charming collection of 32 projects (hat, cup, pelican, piano, swan, many more) specially designed for the novice origami hobbyist. Clearly illustrated easy-to-follow instructions insure that even beginning papercrafters will achieve successful results. 48pp. 8¼ x 11.   27298-2

THE COMPLETE BOOK OF BIRDHOUSE CONSTRUCTION FOR WOODWORKERS, Scott D. Campbell. Detailed instructions, illustrations, tables. Also data on bird habitat and instinct patterns. Bibliography. 3 tables. 63 illustrations in 15 figures. 48pp. 5¼ x 8½.   24407-5

BLOOMINGDALE'S ILLUSTRATED 1886 CATALOG: Fashions, Dry Goods and Housewares, Bloomingdale Brothers. Famed merchants' extremely rare catalog depicting about 1,700 products: clothing, housewares, firearms, dry goods, jewelry, more. Invaluable for dating, identifying vintage items. Also, copyright-free graphics for artists, designers. Co-published with Henry Ford Museum & Greenfield Village. 160pp. 8¼ x 11.   25780-0

HISTORIC COSTUME IN PICTURES, Braun & Schneider. Over 1,450 costumed figures in clearly detailed engravings–from dawn of civilization to end of 19th century. Captions. Many folk costumes. 256pp. 8⅜ x 11¾.   23150-X

STICKLEY CRAFTSMAN FURNITURE CATALOGS, Gustav Stickley and L. & J. G. Stickley. Beautiful, functional furniture in two authentic catalogs from 1910. 594 illustrations, including 277 photos, show settles, rockers, armchairs, reclining chairs, bookcases, desks, tables. 183pp. 6½ x 9¼. 23838-5

AMERICAN LOCOMOTIVES IN HISTORIC PHOTOGRAPHS: 1858 to 1949, Ron Ziel (ed.). A rare collection of 126 meticulously detailed official photographs, called "builder portraits," of American locomotives that majestically chronicle the rise of steam locomotive power in America. Introduction. Detailed captions. xi+ 129pp. 9 x 12. 27393-8

AMERICA'S LIGHTHOUSES: An Illustrated History, Francis Ross Holland, Jr. Delightfully written, profusely illustrated fact-filled survey of over 200 American light-houses since 1716. History, anecdotes, technological advances, more. 240pp. 8 x 10¾. 25576-X

TOWARDS A NEW ARCHITECTURE, Le Corbusier. Pioneering manifesto by founder of "International School." Technical and aesthetic theories, views of industry, economics, relation of form to function, "mass-production split" and much more. Profusely illustrated. 320pp. 6⅛ x 9¼. (Available in U.S. only.) 25023-7

HOW THE OTHER HALF LIVES, Jacob Riis. Famous journalistic record, exposing poverty and degradation of New York slums around 1900, by major social reformer. 100 striking and influential photographs. 233pp. 10 x 7⅞. 22012-5

FRUIT KEY AND TWIG KEY TO TREES AND SHRUBS, William M. Harlow. One of the handiest and most widely used identification aids. Fruit key covers 120 deciduous and evergreen species; twig key 160 deciduous species. Easily used. Over 300 photographs. 126pp. 5⅜ x 8½. 20511-8

COMMON BIRD SONGS, Dr. Donald J. Borror. Songs of 60 most common U.S. birds: robins, sparrows, cardinals, bluejays, finches, more–arranged in order of increasing complexity. Up to 9 variations of songs of each species.
Cassette and manual 99911-4

ORCHIDS AS HOUSE PLANTS, Rebecca Tyson Northen. Grow cattleyas and many other kinds of orchids–in a window, in a case, or under artificial light. 63 illustrations. 148pp. 5⅜ x 8½. 23261-1

MONSTER MAZES, Dave Phillips. Masterful mazes at four levels of difficulty. Avoid deadly perils and evil creatures to find magical treasures. Solutions for all 32 exciting illustrated puzzles. 48pp. 8¼ x 11. 26005-4

MOZART'S DON GIOVANNI (DOVER OPERA LIBRETTO SERIES), Wolfgang Amadeus Mozart. Introduced and translated by Ellen H. Bleiler. Standard Italian libretto, with complete English translation. Convenient and thoroughly portable–an ideal companion for reading along with a recording or the performance itself. Introduction. List of characters. Plot summary. 121pp. 5¼ x 8½. 24944-1

TECHNICAL MANUAL AND DICTIONARY OF CLASSICAL BALLET, Gail Grant. Defines, explains, comments on steps, movements, poses and concepts. 15-page pictorial section. Basic book for student, viewer. 127pp. 5⅜ x 8½. 21843-0

THE CLARINET AND CLARINET PLAYING, David Pino. Lively, comprehensive work features suggestions about technique, musicianship, and musical interpretation, as well as guidelines for teaching, making your own reeds, and preparing for public performance. Includes an intriguing look at clarinet history. "A godsend," *The Clarinet,* Journal of the International Clarinet Society. Appendixes. 7 illus. 320pp. 5⅜ x 8½. 40270-3

HOLLYWOOD GLAMOR PORTRAITS, John Kobal (ed.). 145 photos from 1926-49. Harlow, Gable, Bogart, Bacall; 94 stars in all. Full background on photographers, technical aspects. 160pp. 8⅜ x 11¼. 23352-9

THE ANNOTATED CASEY AT THE BAT: A Collection of Ballads about the Mighty Casey/Third, Revised Edition, Martin Gardner (ed.). Amusing sequels and parodies of one of America's best-loved poems: Casey's Revenge, Why Casey Whiffed, Casey's Sister at the Bat, others. 256pp. 5⅜ x 8½. 28598-7

THE RAVEN AND OTHER FAVORITE POEMS, Edgar Allan Poe. Over 40 of the author's most memorable poems: "The Bells," "Ulalume," "Israfel," "To Helen," "The Conqueror Worm," "Eldorado," "Annabel Lee," many more. Alphabetic lists of titles and first lines. 64pp. 5³⁄₁₆ x 8¼. 26685-0

PERSONAL MEMOIRS OF U. S. GRANT, Ulysses Simpson Grant. Intelligent, deeply moving firsthand account of Civil War campaigns, considered by many the finest military memoirs ever written. Includes letters, historic photographs, maps and more. 528pp. 6⅛ x 9¼. 28587-1

ANCIENT EGYPTIAN MATERIALS AND INDUSTRIES, A. Lucas and J. Harris. Fascinating, comprehensive, thoroughly documented text describes this ancient civilization's vast resources and the processes that incorporated them in daily life, including the use of animal products, building materials, cosmetics, perfumes and incense, fibers, glazed ware, glass and its manufacture, materials used in the mummification process, and much more. 544pp. 6⅛ x 9¼. (Available in U.S. only.) 40446-3

RUSSIAN STORIES/RUSSKIE RASSKAZY: A Dual-Language Book, edited by Gleb Struve. Twelve tales by such masters as Chekhov, Tolstoy, Dostoevsky, Pushkin, others. Excellent word-for-word English translations on facing pages, plus teaching and study aids, Russian/English vocabulary, biographical/critical introductions, more. 416pp. 5⅜ x 8½. 26244-8

PHILADELPHIA THEN AND NOW: 60 Sites Photographed in the Past and Present, Kenneth Finkel and Susan Oyama. Rare photographs of City Hall, Logan Square, Independence Hall, Betsy Ross House, other landmarks juxtaposed with contemporary views. Captures changing face of historic city. Introduction. Captions. 128pp. 8¼ x 11. 25790-8

AIA ARCHITECTURAL GUIDE TO NASSAU AND SUFFOLK COUNTIES, LONG ISLAND, The American Institute of Architects, Long Island Chapter, and the Society for the Preservation of Long Island Antiquities. Comprehensive, well-researched and generously illustrated volume brings to life over three centuries of Long Island's great architectural heritage. More than 240 photographs with authoritative, extensively detailed captions. 176pp. 8¼ x 11. 26946-9

NORTH AMERICAN INDIAN LIFE: Customs and Traditions of 23 Tribes, Elsie Clews Parsons (ed.). 27 fictionalized essays by noted anthropologists examine religion, customs, government, additional facets of life among the Winnebago, Crow, Zuni, Eskimo, other tribes. 480pp. 6⅛ x 9¼. 27377-6

FRANK LLOYD WRIGHT'S DANA HOUSE, Donald Hoffmann. Pictorial essay of residential masterpiece with over 160 interior and exterior photos, plans, elevations, sketches and studies. 128pp. 9¼ x 10¾. 29120-0

THE MALE AND FEMALE FIGURE IN MOTION: 60 Classic Photographic Sequences, Eadweard Muybridge. 60 true-action photographs of men and women walking, running, climbing, bending, turning, etc., reproduced from rare 19th-century masterpiece. vi + 121pp. 9 x 12. 24745-7

1001 QUESTIONS ANSWERED ABOUT THE SEASHORE, N. J. Berrill and Jacquelyn Berrill. Queries answered about dolphins, sea snails, sponges, starfish, fishes, shore birds, many others. Covers appearance, breeding, growth, feeding, much more. 305pp. 5¼ x 8¼. 23366-9

ATTRACTING BIRDS TO YOUR YARD, William J. Weber. Easy-to-follow guide offers advice on how to attract the greatest diversity of birds: birdhouses, feeders, water and waterers, much more. 96pp. 5³⁄₁₆ x 8¼. 28927-3

MEDICINAL AND OTHER USES OF NORTH AMERICAN PLANTS: A Historical Survey with Special Reference to the Eastern Indian Tribes, Charlotte Erichsen-Brown. Chronological historical citations document 500 years of usage of plants, trees, shrubs native to eastern Canada, northeastern U.S. Also complete identifying information. 343 illustrations. 544pp. 6½ x 9¼. 25951-X

STORYBOOK MAZES, Dave Phillips. 23 stories and mazes on two-page spreads: Wizard of Oz, Treasure Island, Robin Hood, etc. Solutions. 64pp. 8¼ x 11. 23628-5

AMERICAN NEGRO SONGS: 230 Folk Songs and Spirituals, Religious and Secular, John W. Work. This authoritative study traces the African influences of songs sung and played by black Americans at work, in church, and as entertainment. The author discusses the lyric significance of such songs as "Swing Low, Sweet Chariot," "John Henry," and others and offers the words and music for 230 songs. Bibliography. Index of Song Titles. 272pp. 6½ x 9¼. 40271-1

MOVIE-STAR PORTRAITS OF THE FORTIES, John Kobal (ed.). 163 glamor, studio photos of 106 stars of the 1940s: Rita Hayworth, Ava Gardner, Marlon Brando, Clark Gable, many more. 176pp. 8⅜ x 11¼. 23546-7

BENCHLEY LOST AND FOUND, Robert Benchley. Finest humor from early 30s, about pet peeves, child psychologists, post office and others. Mostly unavailable elsewhere. 73 illustrations by Peter Arno and others. 183pp. 5⅜ x 8½. 22410-4

YEKL and THE IMPORTED BRIDEGROOM AND OTHER STORIES OF YIDDISH NEW YORK, Abraham Cahan. Film Hester Street based on *Yekl* (1896). Novel, other stories among first about Jewish immigrants on N.Y.'s East Side. 240pp. 5⅜ x 8½. 22427-9

SELECTED POEMS, Walt Whitman. Generous sampling from *Leaves of Grass*. Twenty-four poems include "I Hear America Singing," "Song of the Open Road," "I Sing the Body Electric," "When Lilacs Last in the Dooryard Bloom'd," "O Captain! My Captain!"–all reprinted from an authoritative edition. Lists of titles and first lines. 128pp. 5³⁄₁₆ x 8¼. 26878-0

THE BEST TALES OF HOFFMANN, E. T. A. Hoffmann. 10 of Hoffmann's most important stories: "Nutcracker and the King of Mice," "The Golden Flowerpot," etc. 458pp. 5⅜ x 8½.   21793-0

FROM FETISH TO GOD IN ANCIENT EGYPT, E. A. Wallis Budge. Rich detailed survey of Egyptian conception of "God" and gods, magic, cult of animals, Osiris, more. Also, superb English translations of hymns and legends. 240 illustrations. 545pp. 5⅜ x 8½.   25803-3

FRENCH STORIES/CONTES FRANÇAIS: A Dual-Language Book, Wallace Fowlie. Ten stories by French masters, Voltaire to Camus: "Micromegas" by Voltaire; "The Atheist's Mass" by Balzac; "Minuet" by de Maupassant; "The Guest" by Camus, six more. Excellent English translations on facing pages. Also French-English vocabulary list, exercises, more. 352pp. 5⅜ x 8½.   26443-2

CHICAGO AT THE TURN OF THE CENTURY IN PHOTOGRAPHS: 122 Historic Views from the Collections of the Chicago Historical Society, Larry A. Viskochil. Rare large-format prints offer detailed views of City Hall, State Street, the Loop, Hull House, Union Station, many other landmarks, circa 1904-1913. Introduction. Captions. Maps. 144pp. 9⅜ x 12¼.   24656-6

OLD BROOKLYN IN EARLY PHOTOGRAPHS, 1865-1929, William Lee Younger. Luna Park, Gravesend race track, construction of Grand Army Plaza, moving of Hotel Brighton, etc. 157 previously unpublished photographs. 165pp. 8⅞ x 11¾.
                                                                        23587-4

THE MYTHS OF THE NORTH AMERICAN INDIANS, Lewis Spence. Rich anthology of the myths and legends of the Algonquins, Iroquois, Pawnees and Sioux, prefaced by an extensive historical and ethnological commentary. 36 illustrations. 480pp. 5⅜ x 8½.   25967-6

AN ENCYCLOPEDIA OF BATTLES: Accounts of Over 1,560 Battles from 1479 B.C. to the Present, David Eggenberger. Essential details of every major battle in recorded history from the first battle of Megiddo in 1479 B.C. to Grenada in 1984. List of Battle Maps. New Appendix covering the years 1967-1984. Index. 99 illustrations. 544pp. 6½ x 9¼.   24913-1

SAILING ALONE AROUND THE WORLD, Captain Joshua Slocum. First man to sail around the world, alone, in small boat. One of great feats of seamanship told in delightful manner. 67 illustrations. 294pp. 5⅜ x 8½.   20326-3

ANARCHISM AND OTHER ESSAYS, Emma Goldman. Powerful, penetrating, prophetic essays on direct action, role of minorities, prison reform, puritan hypocrisy, violence, etc. 271pp. 5⅜ x 8½.   22484-8

MYTHS OF THE HINDUS AND BUDDHISTS, Ananda K. Coomaraswamy and Sister Nivedita. Great stories of the epics; deeds of Krishna, Shiva, taken from puranas, Vedas, folk tales; etc. 32 illustrations. 400pp. 5⅜ x 8½.   21759-0

THE TRAUMA OF BIRTH, Otto Rank. Rank's controversial thesis that anxiety neurosis is caused by profound psychological trauma which occurs at birth. 256pp. 5⅜ x 8½.   27974-X

A THEOLOGICO-POLITICAL TREATISE, Benedict Spinoza. Also contains unfinished Political Treatise. Great classic on religious liberty, theory of government on common consent. R. Elwes translation. Total of 421pp. 5⅜ x 8½.   20249-6

MY BONDAGE AND MY FREEDOM, Frederick Douglass. Born a slave, Douglass became outspoken force in antislavery movement. The best of Douglass' autobiographies. Graphic description of slave life. 464pp. 5⅜ x 8½. 22457-0

FOLLOWING THE EQUATOR: A Journey Around the World, Mark Twain. Fascinating humorous account of 1897 voyage to Hawaii, Australia, India, New Zealand, etc. Ironic, bemused reports on peoples, customs, climate, flora and fauna, politics, much more. 197 illustrations. 720pp. 5⅜ x 8½. 26113-1

THE PEOPLE CALLED SHAKERS, Edward D. Andrews. Definitive study of Shakers: origins, beliefs, practices, dances, social organization, furniture and crafts, etc. 33 illustrations. 351pp. 5⅜ x 8½. 21081-2

THE MYTHS OF GREECE AND ROME, H. A. Guerber. A classic of mythology, generously illustrated, long prized for its simple, graphic, accurate retelling of the principal myths of Greece and Rome, and for its commentary on their origins and significance. With 64 illustrations by Michelangelo, Raphael, Titian, Rubens, Canova, Bernini and others. 480pp. 5⅜ x 8½. 27584-1

PSYCHOLOGY OF MUSIC, Carl E. Seashore. Classic work discusses music as a medium from psychological viewpoint. Clear treatment of physical acoustics, auditory apparatus, sound perception, development of musical skills, nature of musical feeling, host of other topics. 88 figures. 408pp. 5⅜ x 8½. 21851-1

THE PHILOSOPHY OF HISTORY, Georg W. Hegel. Great classic of Western thought develops concept that history is not chance but rational process, the evolution of freedom. 457pp. 5⅜ x 8½. 20112-0

THE BOOK OF TEA, Kakuzo Okakura. Minor classic of the Orient: entertaining, charming explanation, interpretation of traditional Japanese culture in terms of tea ceremony. 94pp. 5⅜ x 8½. 20070-1

LIFE IN ANCIENT EGYPT, Adolf Erman. Fullest, most thorough, detailed older account with much not in more recent books, domestic life, religion, magic, medicine, commerce, much more. Many illustrations reproduce tomb paintings, carvings, hieroglyphs, etc. 597pp. 5⅜ x 8½. 22632-8

SUNDIALS, Their Theory and Construction, Albert Waugh. Far and away the best, most thorough coverage of ideas, mathematics concerned, types, construction, adjusting anywhere. Simple, nontechnical treatment allows even children to build several of these dials. Over 100 illustrations. 230pp. 5⅜ x 8½. 22947-5

THEORETICAL HYDRODYNAMICS, L. M. Milne-Thomson. Classic exposition of the mathematical theory of fluid motion, applicable to both hydrodynamics and aerodynamics. Over 600 exercises. 768pp. 6⅛ x 9¼. 68970-0

SONGS OF EXPERIENCE: Facsimile Reproduction with 26 Plates in Full Color, William Blake. 26 full-color plates from a rare 1826 edition. Includes "The Tyger," "London," "Holy Thursday," and other poems. Printed text of poems. 48pp. 5¼ x 7.
24636-1

OLD-TIME VIGNETTES IN FULL COLOR, Carol Belanger Grafton (ed.). Over 390 charming, often sentimental illustrations, selected from archives of Victorian graphics–pretty women posing, children playing, food, flowers, kittens and puppies, smiling cherubs, birds and butterflies, much more. All copyright-free. 48pp. 9¼ x 12¼.
27269-9

PERSPECTIVE FOR ARTISTS, Rex Vicat Cole. Depth, perspective of sky and sea, shadows, much more, not usually covered. 391 diagrams, 81 reproductions of drawings and paintings. 279pp. 5⅜ x 8½. 22487-2

DRAWING THE LIVING FIGURE, Joseph Sheppard. Innovative approach to artistic anatomy focuses on specifics of surface anatomy, rather than muscles and bones. Over 170 drawings of live models in front, back and side views, and in widely varying poses. Accompanying diagrams. 177 illustrations. Introduction. Index. 144pp. 8⅜ x11¼. 26723-7

GOTHIC AND OLD ENGLISH ALPHABETS: 100 Complete Fonts, Dan X. Solo. Add power, elegance to posters, signs, other graphics with 100 stunning copyright-free alphabets: Blackstone, Dolbey, Germania, 97 more–including many lower-case, numerals, punctuation marks. 104pp. 8⅛ x 11. 24695-7

HOW TO DO BEADWORK, Mary White. Fundamental book on craft from simple projects to five-bead chains and woven works. 106 illustrations. 142pp. 5⅜ x 8. 20697-1

THE BOOK OF WOOD CARVING, Charles Marshall Sayers. Finest book for beginners discusses fundamentals and offers 34 designs. "Absolutely first rate . . . well thought out and well executed."–E. J. Tangerman. 118pp. 7¾ x 10⅝. 23654-4

ILLUSTRATED CATALOG OF CIVIL WAR MILITARY GOODS: Union Army Weapons, Insignia, Uniform Accessories, and Other Equipment, Schuyler, Hartley, and Graham. Rare, profusely illustrated 1846 catalog includes Union Army uniform and dress regulations, arms and ammunition, coats, insignia, flags, swords, rifles, etc. 226 illustrations. 160pp. 9 x 12. 24939-5

WOMEN'S FASHIONS OF THE EARLY 1900s: An Unabridged Republication of "New York Fashions, 1909," National Cloak & Suit Co. Rare catalog of mail-order fashions documents women's and children's clothing styles shortly after the turn of the century. Captions offer full descriptions, prices. Invaluable resource for fashion, costume historians. Approximately 725 illustrations. 128pp. 8⅜ x 11¼. 27276-1

THE 1912 AND 1915 GUSTAV STICKLEY FURNITURE CATALOGS, Gustav Stickley. With over 200 detailed illustrations and descriptions, these two catalogs are essential reading and reference materials and identification guides for Stickley furniture. Captions cite materials, dimensions and prices. 112pp. 6½ x 9¼. 26676-1

EARLY AMERICAN LOCOMOTIVES, John H. White, Jr. Finest locomotive engravings from early 19th century: historical (1804–74), main-line (after 1870), special, foreign, etc. 147 plates. 142pp. 11⅜ x 8¼. 22772-3

THE TALL SHIPS OF TODAY IN PHOTOGRAPHS, Frank O. Braynard. Lavishly illustrated tribute to nearly 100 majestic contemporary sailing vessels: Amerigo Vespucci, Clearwater, Constitution, Eagle, Mayflower, Sea Cloud, Victory, many more. Authoritative captions provide statistics, background on each ship. 190 black-and-white photographs and illustrations. Introduction. 128pp. 8⅞ x 11¾. 27163-3

LITTLE BOOK OF EARLY AMERICAN CRAFTS AND TRADES, Peter Stockham (ed.). 1807 children's book explains crafts and trades: baker, hatter, cooper, potter, and many others. 23 copperplate illustrations. 140pp. 4⅝ x 6. 23336-7

VICTORIAN FASHIONS AND COSTUMES FROM HARPER'S BAZAR, 1867–1898, Stella Blum (ed.). Day costumes, evening wear, sports clothes, shoes, hats, other accessories in over 1,000 detailed engravings. 320pp. 9⅜ x 12¼. 22990-4

GUSTAV STICKLEY, THE CRAFTSMAN, Mary Ann Smith. Superb study surveys broad scope of Stickley's achievement, especially in architecture. Design philosophy, rise and fall of the Craftsman empire, descriptions and floor plans for many Craftsman houses, more. 86 black-and-white halftones. 31 line illustrations. Introduction 208pp. 6½ x 9¼. 27210-9

THE LONG ISLAND RAIL ROAD IN EARLY PHOTOGRAPHS, Ron Ziel. Over 220 rare photos, informative text document origin (1844) and development of rail service on Long Island. Vintage views of early trains, locomotives, stations, passengers, crews, much more. Captions. 8⅞ x 11¾. 26301-0

VOYAGE OF THE LIBERDADE, Joshua Slocum. Great 19th-century mariner's thrilling, first-hand account of the wreck of his ship off South America, the 35-foot boat he built from the wreckage, and its remarkable voyage home. 128pp. 5⅜ x 8½. 40022-0

TEN BOOKS ON ARCHITECTURE, Vitruvius. The most important book ever written on architecture. Early Roman aesthetics, technology, classical orders, site selection, all other aspects. Morgan translation. 331pp. 5⅜ x 8½. 20645-9

THE HUMAN FIGURE IN MOTION, Eadweard Muybridge. More than 4,500 stopped-action photos, in action series, showing undraped men, women, children jumping, lying down, throwing, sitting, wrestling, carrying, etc. 390pp. 7⅞ x 10⅝. 20204-6 Clothbd.

TREES OF THE EASTERN AND CENTRAL UNITED STATES AND CANADA, William M. Harlow. Best one-volume guide to 140 trees. Full descriptions, woodlore, range, etc. Over 600 illustrations. Handy size. 288pp. 4½ x 6⅜. 20395-6

SONGS OF WESTERN BIRDS, Dr. Donald J. Borror. Complete song and call repertoire of 60 western species, including flycatchers, juncoes, cactus wrens, many more–includes fully illustrated booklet. Cassette and manual 99913-0

GROWING AND USING HERBS AND SPICES, Milo Miloradovich. Versatile handbook provides all the information needed for cultivation and use of all the herbs and spices available in North America. 4 illustrations. Index. Glossary. 236pp. 5⅜ x 8½. 25058-X

BIG BOOK OF MAZES AND LABYRINTHS, Walter Shepherd. 50 mazes and labyrinths in all–classical, solid, ripple, and more–in one great volume. Perfect inexpensive puzzler for clever youngsters. Full solutions. 112pp. 8⅛ x 11. 22951-3

PIANO TUNING, J. Cree Fischer. Clearest, best book for beginner, amateur. Simple repairs, raising dropped notes, tuning by easy method of flattened fifths. No previous skills needed. 4 illustrations. 201pp. 5⅜ x 8½.   23267-0

HINTS TO SINGERS, Lillian Nordica. Selecting the right teacher, developing confidence, overcoming stage fright, and many other important skills receive thoughtful discussion in this indispensible guide, written by a world-famous diva of four decades' experience. 96pp. 5⅜ x 8½.   40094-8

THE COMPLETE NONSENSE OF EDWARD LEAR, Edward Lear. All nonsense limericks, zany alphabets, Owl and Pussycat, songs, nonsense botany, etc., illustrated by Lear. Total of 320pp. 5⅜ x 8½. (Available in U.S. only.)   20167-8

VICTORIAN PARLOUR POETRY: An Annotated Anthology, Michael R. Turner. 117 gems by Longfellow, Tennyson, Browning, many lesser-known poets. "The Village Blacksmith," "Curfew Must Not Ring Tonight," "Only a Baby Small," dozens more, often difficult to find elsewhere. Index of poets, titles, first lines. xxiii + 325pp. 5⅜ x 8¼.   27044-0

DUBLINERS, James Joyce. Fifteen stories offer vivid, tightly focused observations of the lives of Dublin's poorer classes. At least one, "The Dead," is considered a masterpiece. Reprinted complete and unabridged from standard edition. 160pp. 5³⁄₁₆ x 8¼.   26870-5

GREAT WEIRD TALES: 14 Stories by Lovecraft, Blackwood, Machen and Others, S. T. Joshi (ed.). 14 spellbinding tales, including "The Sin Eater," by Fiona McLeod, "The Eye Above the Mantel," by Frank Belknap Long, as well as renowned works by R. H. Barlow, Lord Dunsany, Arthur Machen, W. C. Morrow and eight other masters of the genre. 256pp. 5⅜ x 8½. (Available in U.S. only.)   40436-6

THE BOOK OF THE SACRED MAGIC OF ABRAMELIN THE MAGE, translated by S. MacGregor Mathers. Medieval manuscript of ceremonial magic. Basic document in Aleister Crowley, Golden Dawn groups. 268pp. 5⅜ x 8½.   23211-5

NEW RUSSIAN-ENGLISH AND ENGLISH-RUSSIAN DICTIONARY, M. A. O'Brien. This is a remarkably handy Russian dictionary, containing a surprising amount of information, including over 70,000 entries. 366pp. 4½ x 6⅛.   20208-9

HISTORIC HOMES OF THE AMERICAN PRESIDENTS, Second, Revised Edition, Irvin Haas. A traveler's guide to American Presidential homes, most open to the public, depicting and describing homes occupied by every American President from George Washington to George Bush. With visiting hours, admission charges, travel routes. 175 photographs. Index. 160pp. 8¼ x 11.   26751-2

NEW YORK IN THE FORTIES, Andreas Feininger. 162 brilliant photographs by the well-known photographer, formerly with *Life* magazine. Commuters, shoppers, Times Square at night, much else from city at its peak. Captions by John von Hartz. 181pp. 9¼ x 10¾.   23585-8

INDIAN SIGN LANGUAGE, William Tomkins. Over 525 signs developed by Sioux and other tribes. Written instructions and diagrams. Also 290 pictographs. 111pp. 6⅛ x 9¼.   22029-X

ANATOMY: A Complete Guide for Artists, Joseph Sheppard. A master of figure drawing shows artists how to render human anatomy convincingly. Over 460 illustrations. 224pp. 8⅜ x 11¼. 27279-6

MEDIEVAL CALLIGRAPHY: Its History and Technique, Marc Drogin. Spirited history, comprehensive instruction manual covers 13 styles (ca. 4th century through 15th). Excellent photographs; directions for duplicating medieval techniques with modern tools. 224pp. 8⅜ x 11¼. 26142-5

DRIED FLOWERS: How to Prepare Them, Sarah Whitlock and Martha Rankin. Complete instructions on how to use silica gel, meal and borax, perlite aggregate, sand and borax, glycerine and water to create attractive permanent flower arrangements. 12 illustrations. 32pp. 5⅜ x 8½. 21802-3

EASY-TO-MAKE BIRD FEEDERS FOR WOODWORKERS, Scott D. Campbell. Detailed, simple-to-use guide for designing, constructing, caring for and using feeders. Text, illustrations for 12 classic and contemporary designs. 96pp. 5⅜ x 8½. 25847-5

SCOTTISH WONDER TALES FROM MYTH AND LEGEND, Donald A. Mackenzie. 16 lively tales tell of giants rumbling down mountainsides, of a magic wand that turns stone pillars into warriors, of gods and goddesses, evil hags, powerful forces and more. 240pp. 5⅜ x 8½. 29677-6

THE HISTORY OF UNDERCLOTHES, C. Willett Cunnington and Phyllis Cunnington. Fascinating, well-documented survey covering six centuries of English undergarments, enhanced with over 100 illustrations: 12th-century laced-up bodice, footed long drawers (1795), 19th-century bustles, 19th-century corsets for men, Victorian "bust improvers," much more. 272pp. 5⅝ x 8¼. 27124-2

ARTS AND CRAFTS FURNITURE: The Complete Brooks Catalog of 1912, Brooks Manufacturing Co. Photos and detailed descriptions of more than 150 now very collectible furniture designs from the Arts and Crafts movement depict davenports, settees, buffets, desks, tables, chairs, bedsteads, dressers and more, all built of solid, quarter-sawed oak. Invaluable for students and enthusiasts of antiques, Americana and the decorative arts. 80pp. 6½ x 9¼. 27471-3

WILBUR AND ORVILLE: A Biography of the Wright Brothers, Fred Howard. Definitive, crisply written study tells the full story of the brothers' lives and work. A vividly written biography, unparalleled in scope and color, that also captures the spirit of an extraordinary era. 560pp. 6⅛ x 9¼. 40297-5

THE ARTS OF THE SAILOR: Knotting, Splicing and Ropework, Hervey Garrett Smith. Indispensable shipboard reference covers tools, basic knots and useful hitches; handsewing and canvas work, more. Over 100 illustrations. Delightful reading for sea lovers. 256pp. 5⅜ x 8½. 26440-8

FRANK LLOYD WRIGHT'S FALLINGWATER: The House and Its History, Second, Revised Edition, Donald Hoffmann. A total revision–both in text and illustrations–of the standard document on Fallingwater, the boldest, most personal architectural statement of Wright's mature years, updated with valuable new material from the recently opened Frank Lloyd Wright Archives. "Fascinating"–*The New York Times*. 116 illustrations. 128pp. 9¼ x 10¾. 27430-6

PHOTOGRAPHIC SKETCHBOOK OF THE CIVIL WAR, Alexander Gardner. 100 photos taken on field during the Civil War. Famous shots of Manassas Harper's Ferry, Lincoln, Richmond, slave pens, etc. 244pp. 10⅝ x 8¼. 22731-6

FIVE ACRES AND INDEPENDENCE, Maurice G. Kains. Great back-to-the-land classic explains basics of self-sufficient farming. The one book to get. 95 illustrations. 397pp. 5⅜ x 8½. 20974-1

SONGS OF EASTERN BIRDS, Dr. Donald J. Borror. Songs and calls of 60 species most common to eastern U.S.: warblers, woodpeckers, flycatchers, thrushes, larks, many more in high-quality recording. Cassette and manual 99912-2

A MODERN HERBAL, Margaret Grieve. Much the fullest, most exact, most useful compilation of herbal material. Gigantic alphabetical encyclopedia, from aconite to zedoary, gives botanical information, medical properties, folklore, economic uses, much else. Indispensable to serious reader. 161 illustrations. 888pp. 6½ x 9¼. 2-vol. set. (Available in U.S. only.) Vol. I: 22798-7
Vol. II: 22799-5

HIDDEN TREASURE MAZE BOOK, Dave Phillips. Solve 34 challenging mazes accompanied by heroic tales of adventure. Evil dragons, people-eating plants, blood-thirsty giants, many more dangerous adversaries lurk at every twist and turn. 34 mazes, stories, solutions. 48pp. 8¼ x 11. 24566-7

LETTERS OF W. A. MOZART, Wolfgang A. Mozart. Remarkable letters show bawdy wit, humor, imagination, musical insights, contemporary musical world; includes some letters from Leopold Mozart. 276pp. 5⅜ x 8½. 22859-2

BASIC PRINCIPLES OF CLASSICAL BALLET, Agrippina Vaganova. Great Russian theoretician, teacher explains methods for teaching classical ballet. 118 illustrations. 175pp. 5⅜ x 8½. 22036-2

THE JUMPING FROG, Mark Twain. Revenge edition. The original story of The Celebrated Jumping Frog of Calaveras County, a hapless French translation, and Twain's hilarious "retranslation" from the French. 12 illustrations. 66pp. 5⅜ x 8½. 22686-7

BEST REMEMBERED POEMS, Martin Gardner (ed.). The 126 poems in this superb collection of 19th- and 20th-century British and American verse range from Shelley's "To a Skylark" to the impassioned "Renascence" of Edna St. Vincent Millay and to Edward Lear's whimsical "The Owl and the Pussycat." 224pp. 5⅜ x 8½. 27165-X

COMPLETE SONNETS, William Shakespeare. Over 150 exquisite poems deal with love, friendship, the tyranny of time, beauty's evanescence, death and other themes in language of remarkable power, precision and beauty. Glossary of archaic terms. 80pp. 5$\frac{3}{16}$ x 8¼. 26686-9

THE BATTLES THAT CHANGED HISTORY, Fletcher Pratt. Eminent historian profiles 16 crucial conflicts, ancient to modern, that changed the course of civilization. 352pp. 5⅜ x 8½. 41129-X

THE WIT AND HUMOR OF OSCAR WILDE, Alvin Redman (ed.). More than 1,000 ripostes, paradoxes, wisecracks: Work is the curse of the drinking classes; I can resist everything except temptation; etc. 258pp. 5⅜ x 8½. 20602-5

SHAKESPEARE LEXICON AND QUOTATION DICTIONARY, Alexander Schmidt. Full definitions, locations, shades of meaning in every word in plays and poems. More than 50,000 exact quotations. 1,485pp. 6½ x 9¼. 2-vol. set.
Vol. 1: 22726-X
Vol. 2: 22727-8

SELECTED POEMS, Emily Dickinson. Over 100 best-known, best-loved poems by one of America's foremost poets, reprinted from authoritative early editions. No comparable edition at this price. Index of first lines. 64pp. 5³⁄₁₆ x 8¼. 26466-1

THE INSIDIOUS DR. FU-MANCHU, Sax Rohmer. The first of the popular mystery series introduces a pair of English detectives to their archnemesis, the diabolical Dr. Fu-Manchu. Flavorful atmosphere, fast-paced action, and colorful characters enliven this classic of the genre. 208pp. 5³⁄₁₆ x 8¼. 29898-1

THE MALLEUS MALEFICARUM OF KRAMER AND SPRENGER, translated by Montague Summers. Full text of most important witchhunter's "bible," used by both Catholics and Protestants. 278pp. 6⅝ x 10. 22802-9

SPANISH STORIES/CUENTOS ESPAÑOLES: A Dual-Language Book, Angel Flores (ed.). Unique format offers 13 great stories in Spanish by Cervantes, Borges, others. Faithful English translations on facing pages. 352pp. 5⅜ x 8½. 25399-6

GARDEN CITY, LONG ISLAND, IN EARLY PHOTOGRAPHS, 1869–1919, Mildred H. Smith. Handsome treasury of 118 vintage pictures, accompanied by carefully researched captions, document the Garden City Hotel fire (1899), the Vanderbilt Cup Race (1908), the first airmail flight departing from the Nassau Boulevard Aerodrome (1911), and much more. 96pp. 8⅞ x 11¾. 40669-5

OLD QUEENS, N.Y., IN EARLY PHOTOGRAPHS, Vincent F. Seyfried and William Asadorian. Over 160 rare photographs of Maspeth, Jamaica, Jackson Heights, and other areas. Vintage views of DeWitt Clinton mansion, 1939 World's Fair and more. Captions. 192pp. 8⅞ x 11. 26358-4

CAPTURED BY THE INDIANS: 15 Firsthand Accounts, 1750-1870, Frederick Drimmer. Astounding true historical accounts of grisly torture, bloody conflicts, relentless pursuits, miraculous escapes and more, by people who lived to tell the tale. 384pp. 5⅜ x 8½. 24901-8

THE WORLD'S GREAT SPEECHES (Fourth Enlarged Edition), Lewis Copeland, Lawrence W. Lamm, and Stephen J. McKenna. Nearly 300 speeches provide public speakers with a wealth of updated quotes and inspiration–from Pericles' funeral oration and William Jennings Bryan's "Cross of Gold Speech" to Malcolm X's powerful words on the Black Revolution and Earl of Spenser's tribute to his sister, Diana, Princess of Wales. 944pp. 5⅜ x 8⅜. 40903-1

THE BOOK OF THE SWORD, Sir Richard F. Burton. Great Victorian scholar/adventurer's eloquent, erudite history of the "queen of weapons"–from prehistory to early Roman Empire. Evolution and development of early swords, variations (sabre, broadsword, cutlass, scimitar, etc.), much more. 336pp. 6⅛ x 9¼. 25434-8

AUTOBIOGRAPHY: The Story of My Experiments with Truth, Mohandas K. Gandhi. Boyhood, legal studies, purification, the growth of the Satyagraha (nonviolent protest) movement. Critical, inspiring work of the man responsible for the freedom of India. 480pp. 5⅜ x 8½. (Available in U.S. only.) 24593-4

CELTIC MYTHS AND LEGENDS, T. W. Rolleston. Masterful retelling of Irish and Welsh stories and tales. Cuchulain, King Arthur, Deirdre, the Grail, many more. First paperback edition. 58 full-page illustrations. 512pp. 5⅜ x 8½. 26507-2

THE PRINCIPLES OF PSYCHOLOGY, William James. Famous long course complete, unabridged. Stream of thought, time perception, memory, experimental methods; great work decades ahead of its time. 94 figures. 1,391pp. 5⅜ x 8½. 2-vol. set. Vol. I: 20381-6 Vol. II: 20382-4

THE WORLD AS WILL AND REPRESENTATION, Arthur Schopenhauer. Definitive English translation of Schopenhauer's life work, correcting more than 1,000 errors, omissions in earlier translations. Translated by E. F. J. Payne. Total of 1,269pp. 5⅜ x 8½. 2-vol. set. Vol. 1: 21761-2 Vol. 2: 21762-0

MAGIC AND MYSTERY IN TIBET, Madame Alexandra David-Neel. Experiences among lamas, magicians, sages, sorcerers, Bonpa wizards. A true psychic discovery. 32 illustrations. 321pp. 5⅜ x 8½. (Available in U.S. only.) 22682-4

THE EGYPTIAN BOOK OF THE DEAD, E. A. Wallis Budge. Complete reproduction of Ani's papyrus, finest ever found. Full hieroglyphic text, interlinear transliteration, word-for-word translation, smooth translation. 533pp. 6½ x 9¼. 21866-X

MATHEMATICS FOR THE NONMATHEMATICIAN, Morris Kline. Detailed, college-level treatment of mathematics in cultural and historical context, with numerous exercises. Recommended Reading Lists. Tables. Numerous figures. 641pp. 5⅜ x 8½. 24823-2

PROBABILISTIC METHODS IN THE THEORY OF STRUCTURES, Isaac Elishakoff. Well-written introduction covers the elements of the theory of probability from two or more random variables, the reliability of such multivariable structures, the theory of random function, Monte Carlo methods of treating problems incapable of exact solution, and more. Examples. 502pp. 5⅜ x 8½. 40691-1

THE RIME OF THE ANCIENT MARINER, Gustave Doré, S. T. Coleridge. Doré's finest work; 34 plates capture moods, subtleties of poem. Flawless full-size reproductions printed on facing pages with authoritative text of poem. "Beautiful. Simply beautiful."–*Publisher's Weekly*. 77pp. 9¼ x 12. 22305-1

NORTH AMERICAN INDIAN DESIGNS FOR ARTISTS AND CRAFTSPEOPLE, Eva Wilson. Over 360 authentic copyright-free designs adapted from Navajo blankets, Hopi pottery, Sioux buffalo hides, more. Geometrics, symbolic figures, plant and animal motifs, etc. 128pp. 8⅜ x 11. (Not for sale in the United Kingdom.) 25341-4

SCULPTURE: Principles and Practice, Louis Slobodkin. Step-by-step approach to clay, plaster, metals, stone; classical and modern. 253 drawings, photos. 255pp. 8⅛ x 11. 22960-2

THE INFLUENCE OF SEA POWER UPON HISTORY, 1660–1783, A. T. Mahan. Influential classic of naval history and tactics still used as text in war colleges. First paperback edition. 4 maps. 24 battle plans. 640pp. 5⅜ x 8½. 25509-3

CATALOG OF DOVER BOOKS

THE STORY OF THE TITANIC AS TOLD BY ITS SURVIVORS, Jack Winocour (ed.). What it was really like. Panic, despair, shocking inefficiency, and a little heroism. More thrilling than any fictional account. 26 illustrations. 320pp. 5⅜ x 8½. 20610-6

FAIRY AND FOLK TALES OF THE IRISH PEASANTRY, William Butler Yeats (ed.). Treasury of 64 tales from the twilight world of Celtic myth and legend: "The Soul Cages," "The Kildare Pooka," "King O'Toole and his Goose," many more. Introduction and Notes by W. B. Yeats. 352pp. 5⅜ x 8½. 26941-8

BUDDHIST MAHAYANA TEXTS, E. B. Cowell and others (eds.). Superb, accurate translations of basic documents in Mahayana Buddhism, highly important in history of religions. The Buddha-karita of Asvaghosha, Larger Sukhavativyuha, more. 448pp. 5⅜ x 8½. 25552-2

ONE TWO THREE . . . INFINITY: Facts and Speculations of Science, George Gamow. Great physicist's fascinating, readable overview of contemporary science: number theory, relativity, fourth dimension, entropy, genes, atomic structure, much more. 128 illustrations. Index. 352pp. 5⅜ x 8½. 25664-2

EXPERIMENTATION AND MEASUREMENT, W. J. Youden. Introductory manual explains laws of measurement in simple terms and offers tips for achieving accuracy and minimizing errors. Mathematics of measurement, use of instruments, experimenting with machines. 1994 edition. Foreword. Preface. Introduction. Epilogue. Selected Readings. Glossary. Index. Tables and figures. 128pp. 5⅜ x 8½. 40451-X

DALÍ ON MODERN ART: The Cuckolds of Antiquated Modern Art, Salvador Dalí. Influential painter skewers modern art and its practitioners. Outrageous evaluations of Picasso, Cézanne, Turner, more. 15 renderings of paintings discussed. 44 calligraphic decorations by Dalí. 96pp. 5⅜ x 8½. (Available in U.S. only.) 29220-7

ANTIQUE PLAYING CARDS: A Pictorial History, Henry René D'Allemagne. Over 900 elaborate, decorative images from rare playing cards (14th–20th centuries): Bacchus, death, dancing dogs, hunting scenes, royal coats of arms, players cheating, much more. 96pp. 9¼ x 12¼. 29265-7

MAKING FURNITURE MASTERPIECES: 30 Projects with Measured Drawings, Franklin H. Gottshall. Step-by-step instructions, illustrations for constructing handsome, useful pieces, among them a Sheraton desk, Chippendale chair, Spanish desk, Queen Anne table and a William and Mary dressing mirror. 224pp. 8⅛ x 11¼. 29338-6

THE FOSSIL BOOK: A Record of Prehistoric Life, Patricia V. Rich et al. Profusely illustrated definitive guide covers everything from single-celled organisms and dinosaurs to birds and mammals and the interplay between climate and man. Over 1,500 illustrations. 760pp. 7½ x 10⅛. 29371-8

Paperbound unless otherwise indicated. Available at your book dealer, online at **www.doverpublications.com**, or by writing to Dept. GI, Dover Publications, Inc., 31 East 2nd Street, Mineola, NY 11501. For current price information or for free catalogues (please indicate field of interest), write to Dover Publications or log on to **www.doverpublications.com** and see every Dover book in print. Dover publishes more than 500 books each year on science, elementary and advanced mathematics, biology, music, art, literary history, social sciences, and other areas.